W9-CBW-891

pg 54 -55

BRITISH POLITICS
AND THE AMERICAN REVOLUTION

BRITISH POLITICS
AND THE
AMERICAN REVOLUTION

———

CHARLES R. RITCHESON

———

UNIVERSITY OF OKLAHOMA PRESS

NORMAN

ST. BONAVENTURE LIBRARY
ST. BONAVENTURE, N.Y.

DA
510
.R5

Library of Congress Catalog Card Number: 54–5933

Copyright 1954 by the University of Oklahoma Press
Publishing Division of the University
Composed and printed at Norman, Oklahoma, U.S.A.
by the University of Oklahoma Press
First Edition

399973

APR 9 '92

FOR MY PARENTS

PREFACE

THE EIGHTEENTH-CENTURY conflict between the North
American Colonies and Great Britain was a clash of rights.
Neither side possessed a monopoly on love of parliamentary
institutions or civil liberties. Both firmly grounded their arguments in a common political heritage. Britain was committed
to the principle of parliamentary supremacy as the only safeguard against absolute monarchy. Americans asserted they were
not to be taxed for revenue except by their own representative
assemblies. The failure to reconcile these two positions would
mean the destruction of the first British Empire.

The task facing British politicians at the close of the Seven
Years' War was an unprecedented one. The antiquated colonial
system had not worked well. The Colonies had behaved badly.
Jealous and squabbling, they had repeatedly ignored or only
partially fulfilled urgent requisitions from the mother country
for troops and money. They had persisted in trading with the
enemy's West Indian islands even during a struggle which
had as its stake their very existence. With the end of the war,
the mother country had to cope with the additional problem
of absorbing the great new conquests into the Empire, of co-
ordinating them with the older colonies, and of protecting
them both. Pontiac's revolt in 1763 had underscored the need
for military occupation of the back country. Surely, British

reasoning ran, the colonists could not expect the mother country to assume the whole financial burden of imperial defense. Britain already labored under an unparalleled debt, much of it contracted to finance a war fought largely in the colonists' behalf. The Americans could not object to bearing a fraction of the cost of their own protection. But imperial defense was a sphere of action outside the competence of individual colonial assemblies. It would therefore have to be undertaken by Parliament. Since the requisition system had proved inadequate and altogether unsatisfactory, a new method of defraying the increased expenditures would have to be found. That Parliament possessed no authority to devise a new imperial system and to finance it as they saw fit appeared to be a position so patently absurd that it needed no serious refutation. Such logic buttressed Grenville's classic concept of empire: a supreme center and subordinate parts. This concept of empire did not belong to that statesman alone, however. It was that of the great majority of the British political nation.

As the controversy developed, colonial leaders, justifying their resistance with British precedents, denied the validity of revenue laws passed by Parliament. When no lasting abatement of efforts to derive a revenue from them was forthcoming, Americans proceeded to a complete denial of Parliament's supremacy. Franklin, Jefferson, and John Adams proclaimed that the Colonies were bound to Britain only through the person of the King. American petitions appealed to George III for relief from parliamentary measures and for deliverance from evil ministers who had "interposed" themselves between his Majesty and his loyal subjects in the Colonies. This "federal" idea, had it been implemented, would have saved the empire; but it could not be made to work in the eighteenth-century political framework. In Britain, the American argument seemed outlandish and even pernicious. It implied a limiting of the supreme power of Parliament and an enlargement of the scope of royal activity. Neither Parliament nor the King would allow it.

The monumental work of Sir Lewis B. Namier has gone far to dispel the clouds of misunderstanding gathered about the figure of that unfortunate, neurotic, but thoroughly whiggish monarch George III. Habitually mistaking obstinacy for perseverance and honest differences of opinion for "faction," he had no lust for absolute power. He possessed no wish to enslave the colonists. Venerating the British Constitution as the most perfect revelation of a mode of government, he aimed to "purify" politics. He desired to regain what he considered to be his rightful place in British politics: as active executive of the state, the source of all power and honor. Seeking to tyrannize over nobody, he went to fantastic lengths to keep himself free of chains. To extirpate "party," to allow no group of selfish, grasping men—those who disagreed with him—to "give him the law," to preside in a firm and harmonious union with Parliament over a united nation was his plan. And it is a fact of considerable irony that the King managed to attain a position at the center of politics by expelling the Old Whigs, whose frequent and sporadic incursions upon the royal powers under the first two Georges had created a false dawn of the modern British party system. Taking the means of patronage, which Walpole and the Pelhams had monopolized for half a century, into his own hands, the King made himself the heir of the Old Whigs.

For ten years, George III, aided by his Friends and, not a little, by the misguided zeal of Chatham in 1766, fought his battle. Fleeing from the Old Whigs to Grenville, he was forced to return to those he had dismissed. On he went to Chatham and to Grafton. These years of chaos were brought to an end only with the formation of the North Ministry. But an empire was lost. By committing himself to the role of an active agent in domestic politics, the King was unable to rise above that scene, as Americans asked, to serve as a symbol of imperial union.

The American problem was the first fully developed issue in British politics since the lingering death of Jacobitism. Its impact was twofold. As American radicalism grew, it combined with a domestic radicalism, the outward manifestation of which was the scapegrace John Wilkes. The result was a powerful conservative reaction. Centered about the King and dedicated to upholding the Whig doctrine of parliamentary supremacy, this conservatism became the seedbed of a new Tory party which would reach full development in the next century.

Secondly, the American problem produced in Britain an amazing development in imperial thinking—in the very concept of empire. As the struggle over rights reached revolutionary proportions, the British government retreated from Grenville's ideal of a mercantilistic empire of supreme center and subordinate parts. The first indication of such a withdrawal was not the repeal of the Stamp Act. It was North's Conciliatory Proposition. The next faltering step came with the Howe Peace Commission. Finally—too late and all lost—the Carlisle Commission, formed under the unrelieved pressure of Burgoyne's surrender and the fear of French intervention, represented the acceptance in elemental form of the idea of a federal empire or commonwealth of nations.

When embattled Americans rejected the terms held out by Carlisle and his colleagues, reaction in Britain against any devolution of authority within the empire was great. Indeed, after the Peace of 1783, the reaction extended to questioning the worth of an empire at all. There followed a strong resurgence of mercantilism. Then came the wars with revolutionary France; and the conservatism aroused by the American war increased tenfold. In the new century, however, Britain would crush the French menace. The Industrial Revolution would free her of the fear of an empire of manufacturing competitors. She would possess her modern party system; and her monarch, removed from the center of domestic politics, would become a symbol wherein all members of the empire might find union on terms of equality. Her American experience had pointed out the only way in which Britain, as a free nation, could build and keep an empire of free men.

SHOULD I attempt to pay tribute to, or even to name the many friends and colleagues who have given their assistance and encouragement to me while writing this book, the list would be long indeed. I must mention Professor Samuel Eliot Morison of Harvard. He remains for the author—as he must for all his former students—a constant encouragement and inspiration. Professor Keith G. Feiling of All Souls College, Oxford (retired), and Mr. Alfred B. Emden, principal of St. Edmund Hall, Oxford (retired), have ever given freely of their friendly counsel and great learning.

To my friend and colleague Professor Donnell M. Owings goes my deep appreciation for his unstinting devotion to, and excellent performance of, a tedious task: the reading of the manuscript. To Mr. and Mrs. Charles R. Spackman, of Portland, Oregon, go profound thanks for aiding and abetting my work.

I am indebted to the Trustees of the British Museum and to the officials of the Public Record Office for permission to make use of the extensive manuscript sources listed in the bibliography. I must also make acknowledgment to the Right Honorable the Earl Fitzwilliam and the trustees of the Fitzwilliam settled estates for my use of the papers of the Marquis of Rockingham and Edmund Burke on deposit at the Public Library, Sheffield. For the use of the papers of the fourth Earl of Sandwich, I owe a special debt of gratitude to the Viscount Hinchingbrooke, M.P., whose gracious hospitality and illuminating conversation aided me immeasurably.

Finally, it would be no exaggeration to say that without

the constant and unfailing aid and encouragement of my wife, this book would not now be in the reader's hands.

CHARLES R. RITCHESON

Kenyon College
January 5, 1954

CONTENTS

Illustrations

BRITISH POLITICS
AND THE AMERICAN REVOLUTION

CHAPTER ONE

THE AMERICAN PROBLEM
AND THE
GRENVILLE MINISTRY

GREAT BRITAIN emerged from the Seven Years' War possessing the most extensive empire since the days of Rome. The great subcontinent of India had been torn from France, and French and Spanish commercial competition practically destroyed. The greatest conquest, however, was that of Canada and the Mississippi Valley, whereby Great Britain established her unquestioned supremacy on the North American continent. The vast hinterland beyond the older seaboard colonies promised untold riches in raw materials, an indefinitely expanding empire, and unlimited markets for British trade. This territory the British government had chosen to retain in preference to the conquests in the West Indies, the French Sugar Islands, Guadeloupe, and Martinique. By doing so, Great Britain committed herself to a policy of westward expansion and of exploitation of the interior of North America; to fail to do so would be to fail to justify the retention of Canada and the Mississippi Valley.

The home government was now faced with a problem of staggering proportions. How were the new conquests, with a large body of alien people, the French Canadians, to be assimilated? How co-ordinated with the older Atlantic seaboard colonies into a coherent imperial system? This question involved a yet more fundamental one. What was the proper and

3

constitutional relationship between the mother country and her Colonies?

The internal political development of the Colonies had been such that an amazing degree of self-government had been achieved by 1763. Usually this had been at the expense of the royal prerogative. As early as the middle of the eighteenth century, the usurpation of royal power by the colonial assemblies and their undermining of the system of colonial government by royal instructions had begun to cause serious alarm in London. The expulsion of France from the North American continent had now cleared the way for a reckoning between Great Britain and her Colonies. British politicians, among them the Earl of Halifax and Francis Bernard, generally thought that the moment had come for a readjustment of the imperial relationship. A reorientation of the Colonies about the mother country, they felt, should now be undertaken.[1]

A second cause of British dissatisfaction with the old colonial system was also in evidence. The mercantile theory had produced a body of Laws of Trade and Navigation designed to secure to Great Britain a monopoly of colonial trade. In practice, however, habitual and flagrant violations by the colonists had seriously undermined these palladia of mercantilism.[2] Even during the war colonial fortunes had been made by trade with the enemy's West Indian islands.

There was yet a third consideration which emphasized the need to reform the old colonial system as it had existed prior to 1763. When the home government had desired aid in troops

[1] E. Channing and A. C. Coolidge (eds.), *Barrington-Bernard Correspondence*, 42–45, 53, Francis Bernard to Lord Barrington, December 15, 1761; May 1, 1762.

[2] Additional Manuscripts, British Museum (hereafter Add. MSS) 38335, f. 217. Charles Jenkinson computed that 250,000 families were then living in North America. Theoretically, they would consume 6 pounds of tea annually. In 1763, however, only 182,000 pounds came from England, from January 1 to November 17, leaving a total of 1,318,000 pounds imported illegally.

4

or money from the Colonies in order to prosecute the struggle against a common enemy, a letter from the secretary of state setting forth the amount of the aid "requisitioned" and the purpose for which it was to be used would be sent to the colonial governors. Such "requisitions" would then be presented to the assemblies, who were expected to take action upon them. This system of imperial finance had been shown to be thoroughly unsatisfactory and inadequate during the Seven Years' War. Each colony had feared it would contribute more than its rightful share to the common defense. As a consequence, urgent requisitions had often gone unanswered, or only token aid been given. In the end, the elder Pitt, the great director of the war with France, was able to cajole the Colonies into giving effective assistance only by promising to reimburse them for a major portion of their expenditures.

Under these conditions, how was an imperial structure, including both new conquests and the established colonies, to be created? What was to be the relation of the various parts of the empire to the mother country? How was the British trade monopoly to be preserved? The need for a general imperial reorganization was obvious, but how was it to be financed?

These issues, which troubled the imperial relationship, also figured in the British domestic political scene. Indeed, the American problem from 1763 until the colonies were hopelessly lost to the empire was strongly conditioned by political developments inside Great Britain. In turn, that problem reacted upon domestic politics, bringing a change in imperial thinking, a modification of the mercantile view of empire, and the development of something approaching the "federal" view. Moreover, this American problem helped prepare the ground for the growth of the modern British party system.

The death of King George II and the succession of his grandson George III, in October, 1760, marked a watershed in British political history. The advent of the young King, determined to take his rightful place as the active chief executive of the kingdom, spelled the end of the half-century of Whig political domination. Sir Lewis B. Namier has brilliantly portrayed George III's capture of the Old Whig "system" of patronage which had allowed that party to monopolize the political stage under the first two Georges.[3] By doing so, George III thrust himself into the center of British politics. Furthermore, he threw into sharp perspective the degree to which the assumption and the facts of the Old Whig dominance in the latter years of his grandfather's reign had outrun the constitutional balance of power established in the last years of the seventeenth and early years of the eighteenth century.

From his accession, George III's battle was against "party" or "faction," against groups of men who sought to "give him the law." During the first decade of his reign, he fled from one combination of men to another, but he could find no sanctuary from "faction." In the end, the young King was forced to create and lead his own political group, his "Friends" whom he viewed as the proper answer to "party." In reality, the "Friends," in combination with certain splinter groups of the Old Whig party, represent the origin of the modern British party system. The King's position as a party leader with the free exercise of the royal powers was naturally stronger than that of any would-be competitor.[4] Men such as Pitt, the Duke of Bedford, the Duke of Newcastle, or Grenville could be charged with factious conduct, but the King was a center in whom both the ambitious and the patriotic might find a common head.

The opportunity to crush "faction" seemed at hand when the young King succeeded to the throne. Pitt, the great genius of the war, had lost the support of the Tory country gentlemen.

[3] L. B. Namier, *England in the Age of the American Revolution;* and *The Structure of Politics at the Accession of George III.*

[4] Add. MSS 38200, f. 121; printed in N. S. Jucker, *Jenkinson Papers,* 90, Tom Ramsden, Latin secretary to the King and political agent of Sir James Lowther, to Charles Jenkinson, November 20, 1762.

They had sustained him throughout the war, but growing tired of the expense and satisfied with the victory already achieved, they had declared for peace. By the end of 1762, the Tories, leaving the dead to bury the dead and forgetting their fathers' hatred of "Hanoverian rats," were counted as supporters of the King's and Bute's administration.[5] The first great royal victory, then, was the dismissal of Pitt, that "blackest of hearts" who had refused to work with the King's friend the Scottish Earl of Bute. Pitt's wartime ally, the Duke of Newcastle, leader of the Old Whigs and ever eager to grasp and hold power, congratulated himself for the moment on having divorced his fate from Pitt's.

Having betrayed Pitt, however, Newcastle now engineered his own fall. The furious onslaught against the Old Whigs, led by the King's agent *pro tempore*, Henry Fox, proved that the King regarded them, not Pitt, as the real enemy. Every office holder, great or humble, who owed preferment to Old Whig patronage was summarily turned out of place, and Old Whig power was broken forever. For half a century, the Old Whigs had preached that opposition to the "present system" was factious and disloyal. They had now to hear their own words from other mouths. Furthermore, the Duke of Newcastle, by refusing to resign with Pitt, had created an almost insurpassable gulf between Pitt's friends and his own. In addition, he had lost valuable men, for instance, Lord Barrington, who chose to follow Newcastle's earlier example and remain in office rather than join an unlucrative opposition. While apologizing "with the greatest heartbreaking" to erstwhile patrons, many found it expedient "to join in with the stream."[6]

[5] Add. MSS 38458, f. 23, Shute Barrington to Jenkinson, December 16, 1762. Barrington told his friend of the election of Sir William Bagot, a Tory, for Oxford University: "As I conclude that he will continue to act with the tories whose principles he adopted early, I congratulate you on having gained an additional vote; which tho' not necessary will render future victories more complete."

[6] Hinchingbrooke Papers; extracts quoted in Namier, *The Structure of Politics*, II, 354–55, Earl of Sandwich to the Duke of Cumberland, November 10, 1762.

7

George III's Friends soon became as real a political factor as the Old Whigs themselves or as the groups centered around the Duke of Bedford and George Grenville.

The Grenville Ministry which took office in April, 1763, was a legacy of that pompous and vague idealist the Earl of Bute. It was formed under Bute's tutelage and was designed to achieve two purposes. First, it was to allow him, hidden behind a ministry with which ostensibly he was unconnected, to continue his intimate relationship with the King. The immense personal unpopularity which had come to him as a result of his brief ministry dictated such a move. Secondly, the Grenville Ministry was designed to protect the King from the Old Whigs who had held George II in "captivity." Bute chose George Grenville to be his successor as first lord of the Treasury, and was content to see his own friends in small, lucrative offices outside the cabinet. The Scot had hoped to place his young protégé, the Earl of Shelburne, as secretary of state for the Southern Department, but Grenville flatly refused to acquiesce in turning out his own brother-in-law, the Earl of Egremont. Shelburne, deprived of his chance to act as Bute's check on Grenville, was accordingly made first lord of trade.

Bute's plan to garner support from all groups who would give it led to offers to the friends of the Duke of Bedford. The Duke, on bad terms with Egremont as a result of a squabble during the negotiation of the peace, refused office himself but gave his blessing to his friends. Lord Gower consequently became the new chamberlain; the Duke of Marlborough took the privy seal and Lord Sandwich the Admiralty. Further in keeping with the policy of flouting "party" groups, offers were held out to Sir George Savile, later to become a trusted lieutenant in the Rockingham Whig group, and to the Old Tory Prowse. Lord Henley, soon to become Lord Northington, continued as lord chancellor, and was thus the only real King's Friend in the cabinet.

The choice of the new ministry was manifestly an effort

to stamp out "party," but in seeking to do so, Bute and the King had laid the groundwork for the emergence of a new party system. The Old Whigs and Pitt had been condemned to wander in the wilderness; they were soon to overcome their reluctance to oppose the King's ministers.

With these colleagues and under these conditions, George Grenville began an administration which was to make America a problem of the first magnitude in British politics. It is much to Grenville's credit that he saw the importance of this problem and undertook to solve it. He alone among British statesmen, before the outbreak of the American Revolution, offered a comprehensive plan which demonstrated true imperial statesmanship and a deep understanding of the British Constitution. That old attitudes and doctrines could no longer be applied successfully to the American Colonies had to be established by the events of the next decade.

Even before he came to power, certain suggestions and basic decisions had been brought forward which preconditioned Grenville's American policy. Soon after the Peace of Paris, Governor Dinwiddie of Virginia had written to his friend and first lord of the Treasury, Lord Bute.[7] The Governor assumed that Canada and the West would be retained and that rapid settlement of that area would follow. To secure the new conquests, Dinwiddie recommended the creation of a military government along the frontier, with the Colonies bearing the expense of a three-year military occupation of the territory. The cost, he estimated, would be thirty thousand pounds sterling per annum. This sum should be raised in the Colonies by a "Stamp Duty on all Bonds, obligations, and other Instruments of Writing . . . similar to that Duty in Great Britain." He predicted that the Colonies would cheerfully acquiesce in such a plan since the revenue was to be devoted to the cost of their own defense. The Governor's paper included, indeed, all the elements of Grenville's later plan. The Indians were to be

[7] Add. MSS 38308, ff. 297–301.

secured in their land titles and pacified, the Indian trade regulated by the imperial authority, western expansion allowed in an orderly fashion, and a military force established to insure the execution of the plan and to protect the Colonies from Indian attack or foreign invasion.[8]

A more important guide for Grenville in the formation of his American policy was the Board of Trade Report of November 11, 1761, the Mohawk Valley Report.[9] It had been approved by the Privy Council, and instructions based on it had been issued to royal governors. Originally drawn up by Egremont and approved by Halifax, both of whom were now in Grenville's cabinet, the report became a basis for Grenville's plan.

The report sharply criticized indiscriminate granting of Indian lands, a practice to which many colonial governors had become addicted as a means of accumulating personal fortunes. Great discontent among the savages had thus been caused. The practice was an open violation of the compacts with them wherein Great Britain had guaranteed their hunting grounds and wherein "they had yielded to Us the Dominion but not the property of those Lands." It was therefore deemed highly expedient to order colonial governors to stop white settlement on Indian lands; and any idea of establishing new colonies before the rights of the Indians had been clarified was "a measure

---

[8] The urgency for supplying the new conquests with military protection as a method of integrating them with the rest of the empire is stated by C. E. Carter, "The Significance of the Military Office in America, 1763–1775," *American Historical Review*, Vol. XXVIII (April, 1923), 475–88. See also Add. MSS 38335, ff. 1–5, "Hints respecting our acquisitions in America." The author was undoubtedly William Knox. See Knox, *Extra Official State Papers*, 28–29. Both Knox and Dinwiddie argued powerfully for wholesale reforms of the established colonial system.

[9] W. L. Grant and J. Munro (eds.), *Acts of the Privy Council (Colonial), George III*, I, 494–501. See also C. E. Carter, "British Policy toward the American Indians in the South," *English Historical Review*, Vol. XXXIII (January, 1918), 37–56; "Observations of Superintendent John Stuart and Governor James Grant of East Florida on the Proposed Plan of 1764," *American Historical Review*, Vol. XX (July, 1915), 815–31.

of the most dangerous tendency." The report is not to be construed as a perpetual prohibition of westward expansion but as a temporary suspension until the conclusion of the war. At that time, the whole question of Indian-white relations, including a reform of the Indian trade, could be canvassed.[10]

Yet another decision of far reaching consequence had been made before Grenville's rise to power. During the Bute Administration, steps had been taken to maintain ten thousand British troops in the American West, and it had been generally understood that the American Colonies would shoulder at least a part of the expense. When the army estimates, including the force for America, had been moved in the House of Commons in March, 1763, they had passed with even Pitt's blessing, his only complaint being that the estimates did not provide Britain with a greater military establishment.

Accepting these decisions, Grenville now determined to create an imperial system embracing the new acquisitions and the older colonies alike. From his first assumption of office, he was preoccupied with absorbing the new conquests into the empire, settling a satisfactory financial basis for so doing, and, indirectly, creating better order among the older colonies by pulling them more firmly into the imperial orbit of the British Constitution.

In essence, the Grenville plan was to create an orderly administration for the new conquests, financed in part by the older colonies. These would receive protection from the imperial military occupation of the West, and would therefore be paying—or helping to pay—for services rendered. Probably Grenville was already beginning to question the constitutionality

[10] See Grant and Munro, *Acts of the Privy Council*, I, 502–506, wherein the Privy Council annulled three acts of the North Carolina Assembly which attempted to impose the tenure of judges during good behavior. The governor was sharply reprimanded: if governors continued to disobey their instructions, "the Dependence of those Colonies upon the Authority of the Crown and the Just Government of the Mother Country already too much relaxed, will stand upon a very precarious foot."

of the requisition system which provided a source of funds for the Crown independent of the control of Parliament. At any rate, the irksome and ineffective requisitions would be abandoned, and an American revenue derived by redrawing the Acts of Trade and Navigation in such a way that they would cease being merely safeguards to the British trade monopoly but would also produce a revenue. Grenville's plan was therefore more conservative than the suggestions of Bernard, the governor of Massachusetts, who was calling for a wholesale revamping of the colonial governments. Violent changes in the existing apparatus of government would be avoided. At the same time, the Colonies would be drawn gradually into a well-ordered, mercantilistic empire.

Grenville's plan was firmly based upon the spirit of the British Constitution. The colonial view that the assembly was a miniature Parliament within its own borders, with all the rights and privileges possessed by its prototype, had not as yet been formally enunciated by American political leaders. When it was, it came as a distinct shock, not only to Grenville, but to the overwhelming majority of British statesmen and politicians. To these latter, colonial assemblies were constituted by the Crown's special grace and favor, and possessed no authority except that exercised under the supreme power of Parliament. In the time ahead, both American and British politicians were to seek to justify their stands by historical appeals to the Glorious Revolution. Time after time, colonial assemblies, in dispute with their governors and the ministry, were to appeal to the principle put forward in 1688: the supremacy of the legislative body over an encroaching executive. Eventually, Parliament was to intervene in colonial affairs, and American radicals were to be forced to drive their argument on to the final assertion of the integrity of their legislatures against all encroachments, even Parliament's. As a last resort, they were to appeal to the royal prerogative for protection against Parliament. This colonial position would be, however, in British eyes indefensible. It would be the Colonies who denied the fundamentals of the Glorious Revolution and sought to re-establish the royal power after it had been finally defeated in Great Britain. The conflict between Great Britain and her Colonies was a tragedy in the classic sense; it was a conflict of rights. These were arguments of the future. As Grenville methodically began to formulate his plan to create an imperial system, he had no suspicion of the turbulent stage upon which Anglo-American relations were about to embark.

To the Secretary of State for the Southern Department, Lord Egremont, and to the President of the Board of Trade, Lord Shelburne, fell the task of formulating the ministry's western policy. In May, 1763, Egremont, on account of his senior position, took the lead by requesting of Shelburne a complete report. Shelburne immediately fell to work collecting all available information. Meantime, in June, he sent to his chief an interim report based on the Mohawk Valley Report.[11] It called for assuring to the Indians their hunting grounds, and for subsequent creation of new colonies in the west after a boundary line had been run and land been procured by imperial purchase. Until then, only the newly won lands of Nova Scotia and the Floridas should be formed into new governments.

In mid-July, Egremont informed Shelburne that his report had been approved and ordered the Board of Trade to prepare papers for the creation of these new colonies. He also suggested that the Indian lands be put under the province of Quebec for purposes of the administration of justice. Shelburne countered with a recommendation that the commander-in-chief of the military forces in that territory be given a royal commission for that end, but no agreement was reached.

Implementation of the new policy was prevented by a series of unfortunate incidents. In May, 1763, Pontiac struck

---

[11] See R. A. Humphreys, "Lord Shelburne and the Proclamation of 1763," *English Historical Review*, Vol. XLIX (April, 1934), 241–64.

and for a time carried all before him. What had been so long feared had happened. The Indians had found a leader with great organizing powers and the spark of military genius. At this crucial moment, when a firm and decisive settlement of the western question was urgently necessary, Egremont died, leaving to Halifax the burden of both Departments of State. Finally, on September 3, Shelburne, outraged by what he considered to be royal bad faith in an abortive negotiation to bring his new hero, Pitt, into office, resigned as president of the Board of Trade. He was succeeded by a hanger-on of the Court, the Earl of Hillsborough. Thus, at this delicate conjuncture, the direction of American affairs underwent a complete change.

Under great pressure himself, Halifax ordered Hillsborough to draft a proclamation promulgating the policy already settled by Egremont and Shelburne.[12] Using Shelburne's plan of such a proclamation, the new President of the Board of Trade soon drew up his own. Shelburne had intended to provide for the creation of three new governments, Nova Scotia and the two Floridas. As inducements to prospective settlers, English law and the speedy calling of an elective assembly were promised. Having embodied these provisions, Hillsborough then added a recital of the boundaries of the province of Quebec, thereby including this province in the provisions for the civil government of the three new colonies. The Alleghenies were selected as the temporary boundary line between the Colonies and the lands reserved to the Indians. Trade with the Indians was to be free, but traders were to obtain licenses from a governor and to bind themselves to abide by imperial regulations. Egremont and Shelburne had never settled their difference over the administration of justice in the Indian reservations; Hillsborough now completely overlooked the point, and no provision was made at all. Time was pressing, however, and the King signed and dated the document October 7, 1763. It was not, indeed, until mid-year 1764 that the Board of Trade

[12] *Ibid.* Corrects C. W. Alvord, *The Mississippi Valley.*

was able to present a comprehensive plan for the imperial control of Indian affairs.[13]

The rebellion of Pontiac was to have an important indirect result. It not only underlined the need for a new system of Indian regulations, but it again demonstrated the hopeless inadequacy of a scheme of imperial finance based upon requisitions. When hostilities commenced, General Amherst, commander-in-chief in America, called upon the Colonies for aid, telling them that since it was primarily a colonial struggle, no reimbursement for their expenditures was to be expected. Had any doubts remained in the minds of the British politicians concerning the efficacy of requisitions, they were now removed. Only four colonies, New York, Virginia, Connecticut, and New Jersey, made even a gesture of compliance. The others, most of them relatively safe from attack, refused to send any aid whatsoever. In this conflict, as in the Seven Years' War, it fell largely to the lot of the mother country to protect the Colonies.

Grenville, having left the "western" aspect of his problem to Egremont, Shelburne, and the Board of Trade, had immersed himself in another facet of it. The Seven Years' War had seen Great Britain's public debt doubled to about £130,-000,000, with an annual interest of over £4,000,000. Grenville knew that an imperial system which included the management of Indian affairs, the erection of new colonies, the purchase of land from the Indians, and the military protection of the new acquisitions demanded new sources of revenue. The British public, however, was taxed already to the breaking point, the

[13] The Board of Trade informed Superintendent Johnson in August, 1763, that a plan for the imperial management of Indian affairs was under consideration and asked for his suggestions. He accordingly sent the deputy agent, George Croghan, to England, and it was not until the following July that the report outlining the new plan was made. There was to be an independent imperial department of Indian affairs, and the new plan would cost about twenty thousand pounds a year. Indian trade and prices were to be strictly regulated. Only the Crown would acquire land from the Indians. The cost was the great disadvantage which prevented the immediate execution of the plan, and the ministry decided to wait until the American revenue was settled.

indicative land tax standing at four shillings in the pound. It would be unfair, Grenville believed, to ask subjects in Great Britain to undertake to pay from their own pockets the cost of maintaining an army whose primary function was to protect the North American colonists. And when the British exchequer was being defrauded of thousands of pounds a year through the illicit trade of those same colonists! Before the war, the army in America and the West Indies had not cost above £100,000 per annum. Now, however, with ten thousand troops to be maintained in North America, and thirty-four hundred in the West Indies, the cost had soared to £320,000. To defray at least a part of this cost, Grenville resolved to tax Americans for revenue, for he believed it just that they should contribute to the cost of their own defense.

It soon became evident what direction Grenville's plan was taking. Always thorough, he now began a period of intensive research utilizing the services of his undersecretaries, particularly those of Charles Jenkinson. He also conferred frequently with Richard Jackson, the colonial agent who served as solicitor to the Board of Trade.

Jenkinson wrote on May 21, 1763, at the command of the Lords of the Treasury, to the Commissioners of the Customs in London, asking them to investigate why the revenue arising from duties imposed on America and the West Indies by the Acts of Trade had fallen so far below what might reasonably be expected. A month later, the commissioners reported.[14]

They declared that the most obvious cause of the deficiency was the fraudulent evasion of the Laws of Trade, particularly that of 25 Charles II. This had imposed duties, upon export from colony to colony, on white sugar, brown and white muscovado, tobacco, indigo, ginger, fustic, dyewoods, and certain other articles. The amount collected under the act for the past thirty years came to only £35,216 7s. 9d. This low sum proved habitual fraud by ships supposedly clearing out for Great Brit-

[14] Add. MSS 38335, ff. 144-47.

ain, but in reality proceeding to other colonial ports. The situation was, however, beyond the remedy of customs officers, and the only solution would be the imposition of further checks and restraints by Parliament.

The commissioners also took note of the Molasses Act (6 George II), which heavily taxed several articles of foreign produce when imported into the Colonies: rum and spirits at 9*d*. per gallon; molasses and syrups at 6*d*. per gallon; and sugar at 5/- per hundredweight. To enforce these duties more officers had been appointed, but during the past thirty years, the act had produced only £21,652 10*s*. 11¼*d*., a sum insufficient to pay even the cost of collection. The commissioners then reiterated a principle which they had laid down in a report of May, 1759: if these high duties were continued, smuggling and illicit trade would persist and could not be prevented because of the long and sinuous coastline of North America. They then proceeded to outline their plan. All American customs officers were to be required to reside constantly in America. This, in conjunction with a wartime Act of Parliament giving commanders of royal ships in American waters additional powers in dealing with vessels suspected of engaging in illegal trade, would go far to suppress smuggling. Those fees and perquisites which tended to entice customs officers into collusion should be replaced by poundages based upon the amount of revenue collected.

The Lords of the Treasury accepted this report and took the only steps which they felt authorized to take without direct parliamentary action. They ordered the commissioners to write at once to all officers absent from their posts and to direct them to return by August 31 on pain of dismissal. They were also to prepare instructions for all officers in America and the West Indies, calling on them for the strictest attention to duty and requiring regular and constant correspondence with the home government. To change established fees into a poundage and to embody the other points in the commissioners' plan would require an Act of Parliament, but in the meantime, the Lords of the Treasury asked the commissioners to recommend new checks and restraints.[15]

Secretary of State Egremont was also asked to write to the colonial governors conveying His Majesty's command that all support and assistance be given to officers of the revenue. He accordingly dispatched a circular letter referring to smuggling as an "iniquitous practice [which] has been carried to a great height in America." In it he called on the governors to see that the Laws of Trade were vigorously enforced. Illicit trade, he declared, had led "to the diminution and impoverishment of the public revenue, at a time when this Nation is labouring under a heavy Debt, incurred the last War for the protection of America."[16] Here then is the first official indication that the ministry had ceased to regard the Laws of Trade and Navigation as merely commercial regulations, and now intended them to become, in addition, a source of revenue.

Grenville fell to work immediately to tighten the system of trade laws, cut expenses, and produce his revenue. By October, it was decided to amend the Molasses Act in line with the report of the Commissioners of the Customs. At the same time, the commander-in-chief in America and the governors were forbidden to incur debts, the money for which had not previously been appropriated by Parliament or approved by the Treasury Board.

Charles Jenkinson, to whom fell the task of redrafting the Molasses Act, began laborious researches lasting well into 1764. Long hours were spent studying the Laws of Trade and Navigation; questionnaires were dispatched to the colonial governors to get information on colonial commerce. He requested of William Wood, secretary of the London Board of Customs, lists of all enumerated articles since 1710; and of John Free-

---

[15] *Ibid.*, ff. 154–56, Treasury minutes, July 22, 29, 1763.

[16] Chatham Papers, Public Record Office, 96, copy. In footnote references to the Chatham Papers the Arabic numeral refers to the bundle number in this collection. See Bibliography.

Courtesy Library of Congress

GEORGE III

mantle in the London Customs House, he asked a statement of the net produce for the past fifteen years of the duties of the chief Laws of Trade. Significantly enough, Jenkinson also asked for a statement of the amounts arising from the stamp tax in Great Britain. Moreover, in his search for sources of revenue, he did not neglect to consider the colonial postal system. It could have been a clever move since the American post existed already under imperial supervision, but the report of Anthony Todd of the London Post Office was discouraging.[17]

One result of Jenkinson's research was the Revenue Act of 1764, presented to the Committee of Supply in March, 1764. This act lowered the duty on molasses to three pence per gallon. Thus made more practical, the Molasses Act became perpetual. New duties were laid on foreign sugar, indigo, coffee, wines, silk, calicoes, cambric, and French lawns. It was thought that these would produce twenty-five thousand pounds a year, while the repeal of certain drawbacks was to save an additional twenty thousand pounds annually. Parliament's purpose was clearly stated in the act, it being considered just and necessary to raise a revenue from America for "defending, protecting, and securing the same."

Grenville by no means considered forty-five thousand pounds a year to be an adequate American contribution to the cost of her own defense. Part of the deficit was to be made up by extending the Mutiny Act to America. The colonists would then have to provide barracks for the troops and certain items of supply. Even so, a new and hitherto untapped source of funds was necessary.

[17] Add. MSS 38202, f. 23; printed in Jucker, *Jenkinson Papers*, 254, William Wood to Jenkinson, January 10, 1764. On the basis of Wood's report, Jenkinson calculated a revenue of £75,000 per annum on tea alone, should it be subjected to a tax of 1/- per pound. Colonial importations of foreign sugar (estimated at fifteen thousand hogsheads) when taxed at 2/6*d*. the hundredweight would yield £16,875 a year. Likewise, nine million gallons of molasses, the estimated annual importation, would, when taxed at a rate of 2*d*. per gallon, give £75,000 a year, all in all a total estimated revenue of £166,875. See Add. MSS 38335, ff. 223–24; ff. 66, 78, Anthony Todd to Jenkinson, January 28, February 2, 1764.

When the Revenue Act of 1764 had been presented to Parliament, Grenville had also stated that an extension of the Stamp Act to America might become necessary.[18] As early as 1722, an American stamp act had been suggested, and, periodically, the proposal had been renewed. In use in England since William III, it had been found to be an easy and self-executing device and one that did not require a large addition to the personnel of the customs. It had been suggested to Lord Halifax in 1757 by Henry McCulloh, and to Lord Bute by Governor Dinwiddie some years later. The idea of a stamp act for America was thus not a Grenville invention, but Grenville determined very early in his administration to investigate the practicability of its application to the American Colonies.

The Stamp Act of 1765 had its origin in a draft bill and a paper on the subject submitted to Jenkinson for Grenville's consideration by Henry McCulloh, formerly a political dependent of the Duke of Newcastle and an inveterate speculator in American land grants.[19] McCulloh, old and unemployed in 1763, was not unacquainted with the American Colonies. He had made three trips there and had twice held places in the colonial customs services, experience which gave some support to his pose as an expert in American affairs. While Jenkinson was deeply engaged upon his research into the problem of increasing the American revenue, McCulloh's second plan for an American stamp act arrived. This attempt to bring himself to the notice of government was unsolicited but opportune. Particularly attractive to both Jenkinson and Grenville must have been McCulloh's estimate that a stamp act would produce a revenue of £60,000 to £120,000 annually.[20] McCulloh soon

[18] Wm. Cobbett and J. Wright (eds.), *Parliamentary History*, XV, 1426. In his search for a revenue, Grenville did not overlook the West Indies. The 4½ per cent export duty was extended to the Ceded Islands, Granada, the Grenadines, Tobago, St. Vincent, and Dominica.

[19] For detailed information concerning McCulloh's land speculations, see Charles G. Sellers, Jr., "Private Profits and British Colonial Policy," *William and Mary Quarterly*, Third Series, Vol. VIII (1951), 535–51.

[20] W. J. Smith (ed.), *Grenville Papers*, II, 273–74.

found the principle of his bill approved and himself employed as a government consultant charged with the task of redrafting his proposed act more in accordance with the ideas of the ministry.

In autumn, 1763, he was given a colleague and a competitor for the dubious honor of writing the law which was to stir up such bitterness in the North American Colonies. The name of the second consultant has not come to light, but that he played an important role in the preparation of the American Stamp Act is clear.[21] In early September, Jenkinson ordered the two men to consult together "on a Plan for a general Stamp Law throughout America and the West Indies."[22] Work on a stamp act for the Colonies therefore proceeded simultaneously with Jenkinson's labors on the Molasses Act.

It was deemed expedient that McCulloh and his colleague work separately, only occasionally meeting for conferences. In October, Thomas Whately, Jenkinson's fellow secretary to the Treasury, replaced him as the immediate superior of the two consultants. Jenkinson's own work, no doubt, had become so heavy that it was felt wise to divide the labor on the American revenue. Soon McCulloh and his colleague were in disagreement on the nature of the act. McCulloh was the more optimistic, believing that an eventual revenue of £500,000 an-

[21] For detailed information concerning McCulloh's connection with the Stamp Act, see my "The Preparation of the Stamp Act," *William and Mary Quarterly*, Third Series, Vol. X (1953), 543–59. In this same article, I identified McCulloh's anonymous colleague as John Tabor Kempe, attorney-general of the province of New York. It has subsequently been established, however, that Kempe was not in England during the period of the preparation of the act, and therefore could not have been the second consultant. Kempe did, however, transmit to the home government an extensive list of legal documents, forms, etc., representing his suggestions of proper objects of taxation under the projected Stamp Act. See Add. MSS 36226, ff. 361–72. For the problem of the identification of the author of this document, see the article to which reference has been made.

[22] Add. MSS 35911, ff. 17–37, a bill for services rendered presented to the Treasury by the anonymous consultant and extending from September 8, 1763 to January, 1765.

nually could be derived from America.[23] The great point of difference, however, was in their plans for the disposal of the revenue to be raised. McCulloh favored application of such funds not only to the cost of colonial defense and presents to the Indians but also to the creation of a colonial civil list.[24]

No copy of the draft act written by McCulloh's anonymous colleague has been discovered, but both his and that of Mc-Culloh were considered by Grenville and the Treasury Board on November 19, 1763. McCulloh then had the mortification of seeing his own bill rejected as the basis for further work while that of his brother consultant was accepted. Apparently the latter's plan was more moderate than McCulloh's, and was, consequently, more in accord with Grenville's own views, namely, that the new revenue should be applied solely to the cost of colonial defense. The tremendous constitutional implications inherent in establishing a colonial civil list were thus avoided.

After the important meeting of the nineteenth, McCulloh's successful rival, conferring often with officials in the London Stamp Office, fell to work redrawing the bill, a task which engaged him for several months. Just as he was about to bring his bill to completion, however, he was informed, on March 10, 1764, that the Stamp Act would not be introduced during that session of Parliament. His work was accordingly halted.

The day before this surprising message was received, Grenville had presented his budget to the House of Commons. In his speech, he referred to the heavy cost of the recent war and to the reasonable expectation that America contribute to her own defense. The speech came as a surprise to many supporters of the ministry. During the winter, persistent and well-founded

[23] Add. MSS 36226, ff. 356–60, minutes of a conference with McCulloh, October 12, 1763.

[24] Add. MSS 35910, ff. 136–59, "A State of the several articles proposed by M. McCullo to be Stamp'd and Duties thereon." See also Add. MSS 35910, ff. 204–205, McCulloh's preamble to the Appropriation Clause.

rumors had suggested that a stamp act was in preparation and would be introduced with the budget. Now, however, Grenville contented himself with introducing the resolutions upon which the new version of the Molasses Act, the Revenue Act of 1764, was to be based. In addition, he merely announced that a stamp act for America might become necessary at some future date.

Underlying Grenville's hesitation to proceed with the Stamp Act must have been a conviction that the ministry possessed inadequate information concerning the application of a stamp act in America and a desire to wait until that lack could be remedied. Furthermore, in Grenville's own thinking, as well as in his talks with men conversant with American affairs— Richard Jackson; William Allen, chief justice of Pennsylvania, then visiting in London; John Huske, originally from New Hampshire but now a merchant in London and a Member of Parliament; and others—the great question of the constitutionality of a colonial stamp act must have arisen. Grenville well knew that the act was an innovation. It was therefore of the greatest moment that Grenville, strict constitutionalist that he was, put himself in an unimpeachable position. Before him was the British pattern: taxes imposed by the consent of the governed expressed through their representatives, the members of the House of Commons. Grenville must have hoped to extend a variation of that pattern to America. He postponed the Stamp Act, not only to receive more information from the Colonies, but also to give America an opportunity to express her consent through the various colonial legislatures.[25] A prece-

[25] Add. MSS 38202, f. 23, William Wood to Jenkinson, January 10, 1764, referred to above. Wood suggested a year's postponement of "every-[th]ing which may have been thought of respecting the Plantations" except continuing the Molasses Act, since "I conceive you want Information of several things from the Plantations, especially an 'Acc[oun]t what Duties are payable by an Act of Assembly.' " See further Royal Historical Manuscripts Commission Report (hereafter RHMCR.), *Knox Papers, Various Collections,* Governor Lyttelton to William Knox, July 22, 1764, 88–89. See also Huntington Library, Stowe Collection, Letterbook, "Copies of Letters that passed

dent of prior consultation with the Colonies in matters of imperial taxation would thus be established. It was not inconceivable that, in time, such a precedent could become as potent as that whereby the House of Commons in England had come to possess the power of the purse.

Unfortunately, Grenville allowed his position to become ambiguous. In his budget speech, he had stated that if the Colonists could suggest satisfactory alternatives to the Stamp Act, he would be glad to hear them.[26] The colonial agents immediately fastened upon this statement, and Grenville must have been chagrined, since it is clear that he had no expectation or desire that the Colonists would tax themselves for the imperial government. Certainly, they had never demonstrated in the past the spirit of co-operation necessary to carry through any common plan. When the colonial agents met with Grenville on May 17 and asked what propositions from the Colonies might be acceptable, Grenville, carefully refraining from repudiating his "offer," strongly stated his opinion that the Colonies would never co-operate in a scheme of self-taxation and recommended, as the most equitable and practicable means of a colonial contribution to the cost of their own defense, a stamp act passed with colonial consent.[27] His situation had indeed be-

---

between Mr. Whately, Secretary to the Treasury, and Mr. Temple, Surveyor General of the Customs in North America," Whately to Temple, June 8, 1764: "I shall be glad to hear what are the Sentiments of the Americans upon the New Taxes and what they think of a Stamp Duty, which was thought of but postponed to next Winter out of Regard to the Colonies to give them time to Consider of it. To Us it appears the most eligible of any, as being equal, extensive, not burthensome, likely to yield a considerable Revenue, and collected without a great number of officials." For an example of the home government's attempts to gain more information upon which to base the Stamp Act, see the Stowe Collection, Whately to Temple, August 14, 1764; and Add. MSS 36226, ff. 361–72. See also E. S. Morgan, "The Postponement of the Stamp Act," *William and Mary Quarterly*, Third Series, Vol. VII (1950), 353–92. Morgan's criticism of Grenville and his colleagues is unduly harsh.

[26] Cobbett and Wright, *Parliamentary History*, XV, 1426.

[27] Only two reports of the conference survive. One, written by Jasper Mauduit, agent for Massachusetts, and dated May 26, 1764, is printed in

come very awkward. What he must have seen initially as a highly satisfactory means of eliminating a constitutional anomaly—Parliament had no control over funds raised by requisitions—and of cultivating the goodwill of the Colonies by consulting with them had become a boomerang, laying him open to colonial charges of bad faith.

One result of this conference with the agents was to demonstrate to Grenville that his hope for an expression of colonial consent to the Stamp Act was a forlorn one. He stood pledged to the House, however, on the issue of an American revenue. There was no question of abandoning the plan. If the Colonies would not express their consent, then they would have to bow to an omnipotent Parliament. The question of the right of Parliament to tax the Colonies did not exist for Grenville. The Glorious Revolution had established the supremacy of Parliament; that Parliament itself, the guardian of the people's rights and the protector of the empire, might be thought tyrannical was a patent absurdity which needed no serious refutation.

Disappointed in his hope that the Stamp Act would be passed with American consent, Grenville took stock of his constitutional position. Long conversations with confidential friends such as Charles Jenkinson and Lord Mansfield, the eminent jurist, now followed. Indeed, his re-evaluation of the situation continued until July. Jenkinson then found it necessary to remind his chief that the summer was wearing on and that the time had come when definite steps for the introduction of the act had to be taken. Otherwise the ministry might have to bear the charge of neglect when Parliament reassembled in the autumn. On several occasions, Jenkinson forwarded memoranda to Grenville, wherein he argued powerfully in

Massachusetts Archives, XXII, 375. The other, by Charles Garth, agent for South Carolina, and dated June 5, is printed in the *English Historical Review*, Vol. LIV (1939), 646–48. Both are used extensively by Morgan, "Postponement of the Stamp Act," *William and Mary Quarterly*, Third Series, Vol. VII (1950), 353–92.

ST. BONAVENTURE LIBRARY
ST. BONAVENTURE, N.Y.

behalf of the expediency and justice of a stamp act and urged Grenville to order the drafting of a final bill.[28] Mansfield added his opinion that Parliament possessed the right to tax the Colonies. Moreover, any colony of a corporate or proprietary nature which claimed exemption from parliamentary taxation would have to base its contention upon the letters patent which had given it existence. Exemption for the royal colonies could be derived only from governors' commissions and instructions.[29]

It is when such arguments are compared with the American position that the essential conflict between Colonies and mother country comes to light. The views expressed by Mansfield and Jenkinson were legal and constitutionally unquestionable, but they failed to take into account the political evolution of the Colonies, a development not bound by statute books or formal parchments. There was love and affection for the mother country in the Colonies, but the sense of unity with Great Britain had already disappeared. British politicians presumed too much on a feeling which did not exist, refusing to recognize the unmistakable signs of a nascent American nationalism. The Colonies had already developed politically to the point where they considered self-government a right. They insisted upon investing their assemblies with the same sovereignty, within their individual borders, which the prototypic British Parliament possessed within the home islands. And they were determined to defend their stand upon the same grounds which British political thinkers had adduced in support of the Glorious Revolution.

It was not until shortly before the meeting of Parliament

---

[28] Add. MSS 38339, *passim*, and especially ff. 131–35, a paper of great value in demonstrating the wide gulf which had already developed between British and American views of the imperial relationship. It is summarized in C. R. Ritcheson, "Preparation of the Stamp Act," *William and Mary Quarterly*, Third Series, Vol. X, (1953), 543–59.

[29] Smith, *Grenville Papers*, II, 476–78, Mansfield to Grenville, December 24, 1764.

in autumn, 1764, that work on drafting the Stamp Act was resumed. Already grumblings had been heard from America. To the agents' notification of Grenville's plan, the Colonies returned answers differing in tone but agreeing in content. The Massachusetts Assembly warned that the goodwill and quiet of the Colonies would be endangered by a stamp act. Indeed, so far were they from taxing themselves for imperial purposes that they directed their agent to obtain a repeal of the Revenue Act of 1764. Their hint at united colonial action was unmistakable: "Measures will be taken, that you may be joined by all the other agents."[30] Grenville, sure of his constitutional position, was unperturbed.

Two months later, on December 6, 1764, Thomas Whately, using the sustained labors of his underlings as a basis, reported to a full meeting of the Treasury Board.[31] By-passing in one sentence the entire American argument, he declared that "a Stamp Act in the Colonies difers from those in England, only in the Rates with which the several Subjects of this Duty are to be charged, and in the mode of distributing the Stamps." Fully accepting the principle that stamp tax receipts should be applied solely to the cost of colonial defense, he further made a recommendation which was to be adopted in modified form in the final act. He proposed a graduated stamp duty on land grants in the Colonies, ranging from 6d. per 100 acres to 1/6d. for every grant of 320 acres. Certainly, the purpose of the tax was not to eliminate the westward movement. Whately admitted that the tax "does give some small check to the Settling of uncleared lands, which is directly contrary to the first Principles of Colonization," but, being a small duty, it would not

[30] Add. MSS 38202, f. 342, June 14, 1764, extracts.

[31] Add. MSS, 35910, ff. 310–23, copy. The administration of the act, Whately outlined as follows: The London Commissioners of the stamp duty would act as the administrative agency and would supply all stamps. Each colonial capital would have a head distributor who would possess authority to prosecute. Salaries would be a poundage of the amount collected. To insure smooth operation of the act, four traveling inspectors would be assigned to the Colonies.

hamper those who wanted grants of a reasonable size for the legitimate purpose of establishing new homes in the west. At the same time, it would give "some check" to the extravagant grants to speculators.

Whately's report was quickly approved by the Treasury Board, and during the remainder of the month, the final and formal act was drafted. Meantime, American reaction to the Revenue Act of 1764, while not violent, was annoying to the home government. There were colonial petitions asserting that Americans should not be taxed for revenue save by their own assemblies. This strengthened a growing conviction among British politicians that America's "absurdities" demanded firm action: The imperial Parliament should demonstrate in the most positive manner its right and authority to tax the Colonies.[32] In England, then, even before the Stamp Act had become law, a sentiment for "authoritarianism" had begun to form, and with it, the crisis which was to demonstrate how fragile were the ties binding mother country and Colonies.

As the time for parliamentary action approached, the colonial agents called upon Grenville once more in an attempt to "ward off the intended blow."[33] Again, Grenville asserted the absolute necessity of American financial aid to the mother country and his belief that this could best be accomplished by a stamp act. When the agents suggested that the old requisition system be employed, Grenville, to underscore the impracticability of that method, asked the agents if they could agree upon the proportions which each colony would pay. In conclusion, he vigorously denied any intention of undermining the power of the colonial assemblies: it was simply that the au-

[32] RHMCR. *Weston Papers*, 82, Edward Sedgwick to Edward Weston, February 14 and 28, 1765.

[33] Reports of the conference were written by Charles Garth and Jared Ingersoll. For that of the former, see *English Historical Review*, Vol. LIV (1939), 649. That of the latter is printed in the *Collections of the Connecticut Historical Society*, XVIII, 324–25. Both are used extensively by Morgan, "Postponement of the Stamp Act," *William and Mary Quarterly*, Third Series, Vol. X (1953).

thority of those assemblies did not reach to matters of common imperial defense.

On March 22, 1765, the Stamp Act passed the House of Commons without noticeable opposition. Pitt was ill, and the Newcastle Whigs did not oppose. The bill, scheduled to take effect on November 1, soon became law. By mid-April, Jenkinson was able to report to Grenville that he had devised a plan "for remitting the American Revenue" between the receiver general of the customs and those contracting to send the pay of the troops to North America. It would therefore be unnecessary to send American specie out of the Colonies. Henry McCulloh, too, was helping to put the final touches to the new plan by assisting the Board of Commissioners of the Stamp Office in London to proportion the stamps and to fix a security for them.[34]

In England, the framers of the act congratulated themselves on America's quiet reception of it. Early in May, Benjamin Hallowell, customs officer in Boston, had written an optimistic letter, and Jenkinson gleefully passed it on to Grenville, adding that it "shews that our Firmness here has got the better of the Obstinacy of the Colonies and that all there will end well." Grenville, however, cautiously sent word that he himself was not so certain that there would be no difficulty "in that part of America."[35] He was wise to wait. On May 29, the Virginia House of Burgesses in its famous Resolves expressed the American position of unconditional opposition to the Stamp Act which rode so roughshod over their doctrine of internal and external taxation.

When judged in the light of subsequent events, Grenville's decision to tax America "internally" was fatal. At the time, however, the equity and justice of it was generally conceded

[34] Add. MSS 38204, f. 166, John Brettely, secretary to the Board of the Stamp Commissioners, to Jenkinson, March 26, 1765.

[35] Add. MSS 38305, f. 11, June 19, 1765; printed in Jucker, *Jenkinson Papers*, 364–65. Add. MSS 38204, f. 285, Charles Lloyd, Grenville's secretary, to Jenkinson.

in England. Grenville had faced the tremendous problem of creating an orderly empire. The North American Colonies he proposed to tax to help provide for their own defense. Westward expansion under imperial supervision was to be allowed, the Indian rights being carefully and amicably extinguished beforehand. Nor was Canada neglected. A plan had been drawn which included Roman Catholic toleration. But by June, it was obvious that Grenville was falling. The Lord Chancellor, Northington, now intriguing against his former colleagues, curtly told Lord Sandwich, who had sent him the plan, that he could not "think this Plan for an established Roman Catholic Church in the Province of Quebec either approvable or practicable."[36]

Grenville's answer to the imperial problem had been comprehensive and in keeping with the British Constitution of his time. His attempt to find an American revenue, however, raised the question of the right of parliamentary taxation of the Colonies, a question which was increasingly to supplant the problem which Grenville had tried to solve.

The taxation of America for revenue represents one terminal of a process of change in British imperial thinking. Under the pressure of American resistance and revolution, British politicians eventually receded from the static and ultimately disastrous position of a proprietary empire consisting of a supreme center and subordinate parts. The belief in the unquestioned authority of Parliament to legislate for, and to tax, the Colonies was to give way, in the course of only thirteen years, to an offer of what amounted to "home rule" or "dominion status" for them. The true impact of the American problem on British politics must therefore be sought in this line of development.

Meantime, on the domestic political scene, the beginnings of coherent lines of "party" were in evidence. New groupings

[36] Hinchingbrooke Papers, Lord Northington to Lord Sandwich, June 9, 1765.

were emerging from the splinters of the Old Whig party. The alliance of Grenville, Bedford, the King, and their friends was becoming the seedbed of a new Tory party, although it was not to come to fruition for many decades.

The consolidation of the alliance was to be a hectic process. Bute had brought Grenville to power to be used as a tool in helping the King set himself at the head of the Old Whig system of patronage, although the King would have it that he was merely trying to resume those powers which the Old Whigs had snatched from the first two Georges. Both Bute and the King soon learned, however, that the tedious, boring lecturer was as much a Whig as Newcastle ever had been. He himself demanded the monopoly of patronage, stating that otherwise it would be impossible to control the House of Commons. By July, then, the King and Bute were attempting to displace Grenville. They were to fail disastrously.

When Egremont died in August, 1763, a ministerial re-shuffle became necessary. The King and Bute seized this opportunity to make overtures to Pitt, and were answered with demands that the Grenville Ministry be completely overturned, that Pitt and the Newcastle Whigs—with whom he was temporarily in alliance—be given carte blanche, and that those responsible for the Peace of 1763 be absolutely proscribed. This last demand was especially unfortunate for the Opposition, since it threw the Duke of Bedford wholeheartedly into the arms of the ministry. He himself became lord president of the Council, while his friend Sandwich was promoted to the vacant secretaryship of state. Grenville, offended by Bute's and the King's intrigue, refused to continue in office unless the Scot should be removed from the King's presence. Hatred of Bute and all irresponsible advisers was in the future to furnish a strong ground for union between Bedford and Grenville.

In the reshuffle, the King's Friends received more offices. Lord Egmont took the Admiralty; Hillsborough became first lord of trade; and a few others were given minor places. The struggle for control of patronage now became a three-sided one between the King, Grenville, and Bedford. Quarrels became so warm that serious trouble appeared inevitable. A dramatic event was to force them into union.

On April 19, 1763, the King closed the spring session of Parliament with a speech in praise of the Treaty of Paris. Four days later, John Wilkes, a Member of Parliament, published his *North Briton*, No. 45, charging the ministers with putting a lying speech into the King's mouth, castigating the general inadequacy of the terms of peace, and condemning the promotion to high office of Scots and Jacobites. He ended his tirade with a declaration of the responsibility of the King to the people. It was a daring insult to the King and his ministers, and they, thinking it would be a popular point, decided to punish Wilkes. Lord Halifax immediately issued a general warrant under which forty-nine persons, Wilkes among them, were arrested. The affair from the ministerial side became a series of blunders, and Wilkes, cleverly utilizing all the engines of propaganda, quickly turned the contest into an attack of the prerogative of the Crown upon the privileges of Parliament.

The ministers' persecution of Wilkes culminated in his expulsion from the House of Commons in January, 1764, both Houses having pusillanimously voted that parliamentary privilege did not extend to writing or publishing seditious libels. The culprit had fled to France, but this did not prevent the Court of King's Bench declaring him to be an outlaw.

The significance of the Wilkes affair was that the harshness of the ministry served to make this reprobate the darling of the London mob, provided the Opposition with a promising issue, and set the ministry in opposition to the people. Much as the case embarrassed Grenville and his colleagues, however, it acted as a unifying factor within the cabinet. Petty squabbles over patronage ceased, or at least moderated, and the ministry, firmly supported by the King, turned a united front to the public and to the Opposition from whom they expected a formidable attack. A deeper meaning is to be attached to the Wilkes affair. Causing tumult and unrest on the domestic scene, it was to join with events in America to produce in British political circles a new conservatism. The King had come to loathe Grenville and Bedford, but eventually he was to find in a union of their friends with his own the safest harbor in the gathering storm.

Among the Opposition, Pitt had forgiven Newcastle's desertion of 1761 when their forces had joined to attack the budget in March, 1763. From the first, however, both Newcastle Whigs and Pitt saw the weakness of the alliance. A number of points were rankling with Pitt. The Newcastle Whigs' desire to diminish the military establishment, and their intimacy with the Duke of Cumberland, Pitt's old enemy, disturbed the Great Commoner. Further, as a result of Pontiac's rebellion, Pitt was turning his mind increasingly to America and was determined—if he came to power—to effect "the settlement of our colonies upon a proper foot with regard to themselves and their mother country."[37] He was uncertain and doubtful of Old Whig co-operation on this score. Several Old Whigs, particularly the younger group, were also dubious about the long duration of the alliance. Rockingham, for instance, reported himself as "flustered" when Pitt requested his presence in London to advise concerning the negotiations with the King in August.[38]

In such a state, the Wilkes affair should have been a godsend to the Opposition, affording an opportunity to unite firmly among themselves and with the public in support of parliamentary privilege and against general warrants. Unfortunately, it was not to be so; the Wilkes affair put a strain upon the Pitt-Newcastle alliance from which it never fully

[37] Quoted by Basil Williams, *The Life of William Pitt*, II, 160.
[38] RHMCR. *Savile-Foljambe Papers*, 144–45, Rockingham to Sir George Savile, August 28, 1763.

recovered. Initial unanimity was prevented since the Old Whig Charles Yorke, who preferred to hold his office rather than resign with his colleagues, still acted as attorney general. He had been consulted by Halifax before the general warrant had been issued, and had given a favorable opinion on its legality. This position Yorke now refused to abandon, although great pressure from Newcastle was to bring him soon to resign his post.

At the bottom of the friction between Pitt and Newcastle's group was the question of leadership, the Old Whigs feeling keenly Pitt's attempts to dictate to them. Failure to co-ordinate measures in the autumn session of 1763, when Pitt flew to the attack on the ministry's handling of the Wilkes affair, nearly led to the breakdown of the alliance then and there. In the succeeding session, Pitt was able to lead a united Opposition in an assault against general warrants, at one point cutting government majorities to ten and fourteen, but this was the highwater mark. His health failing under the great strain, Pitt retired to a sickbed. Some Old Whigs, notably Charles Townshend and Charles Yorke, promptly began to put out feelers to the government. Furthermore, during Pitt's absence, Grenville violently attacked his conduct and finance of the war. None rose to defend him. Pitt never forgave Newcastle for this second desertion, and the same session which saw a united Opposition almost overturning the ministry saw Pitt declare himself unconnected. In the future, the Old Whigs were to seek Pitt's advice and leadership in vain. Old Newcastle could only moan, "Let them say what they will, Mr. Grenville, I say, will have *champ libre*."[39]

At the beginning of the New Year, however, both Grenville and Bedford found their positions extremely irksome. They feared the revival of the struggle over general warrants; the Attorney and Solicitor Generals had raised a minor crisis

[39] Earl of Albemarle (ed.), *Rockingham Memoirs*, I, 181–82, Newcastle to Rockingham, March 26, 1765.

Courtesy New York Public Library

GEORGE GRENVILLE

by allowing the order extending the 4½ per cent export duty to the Ceded Islands to pass under the Great Seal, and then raising doubts concerning the legality of the action.[40] Furthermore, Grenville was suspicious of his colleagues; and he was well aware of the King's cold dislike for him.

A new pitfall lay ahead. In February and March, 1765, the King suffered his first attack of insanity. Upon his recovery, he made known his desire that a Bill of Regency be prepared to insure the orderly carrying-on of government in case of another attack. Grenville, Halifax, and Sandwich, who took the lead in drawing the bill, were temperamentally incapable of exercising the great tact necessary in such a task. The King, already determined to rid himself of the ministers at the earliest possible moment, was hypercritical and took no pains to conceal his hostility. In May, therefore, after an apparently gratuitous insult to the King's mother who was excluded from the list of possible regents, George III authorized his uncle, Cumberland, to begin negotiations with Pitt.

Difficult months lay ahead for the young sovereign. Grenville's group—for he had accumulated one during his years in office, men such as William Knox, Thomas Whately, Lord Buckinghamshire, and Soame Jenyns—stood firmly united with the Bedfords. They had found their union in the Wilkes affair; it was confirmed by the weight of the royal displeasure. When Pitt refused to come into office, the King had no choice but to recall the old ministry upon their own terms. The humiliation for George III was too great to be borne, and although Grenville and Bedford had returned to office, there was no return of the royal confidence. The King was even more hostile toward the ministry than before. On June 12, the Duke of Bedford, having strongly remonstrated with the King, left London. Two days later, Grenville, too, retired to the country, and the King, rightly or wrongly, considered the ministry in

[40] Add. MSS 38191, ff. 81–82; printed in Jucker, *Jenkinson Papers*, 319–20, Grenville to Jenkinson, August 19, 1764.

a state of resignation. Once more he turned to Pitt, but it was only a gesture. Already he was writing of "those worthy Men, Ld. Rockingham, the Dukes of Grafton, Newcastle, and others," men who possessed "principles and therefore cannot approve of seeing the Crown dictated to by low men." Already he was hoping that they would "join amicably the few persons that have zealously stood by Me, and that the World will see that this Country is not at that low Ebb that no Administration can be formed without the Greenville family."[41]

On Wednesday, July 10, Grenville had his last audience of the King. Declaring that the new ministry would be "a total subversion of every act of the former," he warned the King that he was prepared to defend his measures in Parliament, especially since none of them had been undertaken without the King's approbation. Particularly was this true of "the regulations concerning the colonies." In that last interview, Grenville, with characteristic bluntness, advised George III "as he valued his own safety" not to allow anyone "to separate or draw the line between his British and American dominions" since the Colonies were "the richest jewel of his Crown." Should anyone try "to defeat the regulations laid down for the Colonies, by a slackness in the execution," Grenville would consider him "a criminal and the betrayer of his country."[42]

Grenville and his allies knew the chief point upon which their administration was to be arraigned. His last speech to the King indicated that for Grenville, America had become the touchstone of politics. There was no hesitation among the outgoing ministers concerning opposition as there had been with Newcastle. Halifax, Sandwich, and Grenville conferred at once, and their sentiment was stated by Sandwich when he declared to the Bedfordite Richard Rigby that the country "must

[41] Sir John Fortescue (ed.), *Correspondence of George III*, I, No. 88, the King to Cumberland.
[42] Smith, *Grenville Papers*, III, 215–16.

be governed by Combinations of People," a maxim of conduct out of office as well as in.[43]

Colonial reaction to the Stamp Act was forming. There had already been ominous indications. The American problem was about to enter British politics, dividing party from party, making old political divisions deeper, and cutting new ones just as deep.

[43] Hinchingbrooke Papers, Sandwich to Rigby, October 28, 1763.

CHAPTER TWO

THE YEAR OF THE
OLD WHIGS

THE American problem had assumed acute form during the ministry of George Grenville, whose vision of empire first brought that problem to a head. From his concept of a "supreme centre and subordinate parts," a retreat was now forced upon the government. The Old Whigs, who succeeded Grenville, were to seek to bring quiet by appeasing British merchant interests—interests which coincided for the moment with the colonial position. Their temporary success would not, however, represent a reversal of Grenville's basic maxim. Indeed, with the Declaratory Act, they were to give it official sanction in a very positive manner.

William Pitt refused to come to the aid of the King in his struggle to be free of his Grenville-Bedford captors. Fighting hard to maintain his independence, George III now turned unwillingly to the Old Whigs for deliverance: In July, 1765, the young, amiable, but ungifted Marquis of Rockingham led into office the inheritors of the Pelham "present system." Meanwhile the Old Whig group was in a process of transformation. Younger men who lacked experience in the art of government were assuming the lead, and old Newcastle found himself relegated to the position of a respected nuisance.

Both in point of number and of abilities the ministry was weak. Rockingham took the Treasury. The fickle and unsteady General Conway undertook to lead the House of Commons as secretary of state for the Northern Department. William

Dowdeswell, formerly of Tory connections but long since a mainstay of the Old Whigs, became chancellor of the exchequer. The great "Revolution families" were well represented, and Newcastle took office for the last time in his long career as lord privy seal. Lacking number and talent themselves, the Old Whigs were obliged to fill some vacancies with the King's Friends. Egmont took the Admiralty; Barrington became secretary at war. Moreover, Rockingham and his associates represented the King's necessity, not his wish, and it was generally supposed that their administration would be short lived. Sir Grey Cooper, for instance, refused to engage as secretary of the Treasury until he had secured a pension to commence when he should lose his place. And yet despite such gloom the Old Whigs were pleased because they had held together in the wilderness and had taken office as a party.

From the beginning it was evident that Pitt's attitude toward the new ministry would be decisive. A powerful Opposition was to be faced; and not much trust could be placed in the King's Friends. Outside support was thus imperative. Newcastle observed that "the world is running mad again about Mr. Pitt,"[1] and so the Old Whigs now made every effort to court his favor. Indeed, they had come into office with no set policy save that which Pitt would dictate. At a meeting on July 6, ministerial leaders decided "as far as It shall appear proper, and practicable To follow Mr. Pitt's plan" put forward in his recent interviews with the King.[2] The new administration in its construction was to be made "as palatable to Mr. Pitt, and as agreeable, as possible, to His Notions and Ideas." Since Pitt had intended the Duke of Grafton to serve

[1] Wentworth-Woodhouse, Rockingham Papers, Newcastle to Rockingham, July 12, 1765.
[2] Pitt's program included the formation of alliances with Prussia and Russia to contain the House of Bourbon; a parliamentary declaration against general warrants; a restitution of those removed from office because of their votes in Parliament, especially military officers; and a demonstration that Bute had no influence with the new administration by a removal of his chief friends from their places.

with him as secretary of state, this young and untalented noble-man was to be given that office and instructed "To keep up His Correspondence with Mr. Pitt." He was to make certain that Pitt knew the ministry was executing his own proposals. Never before had men come into office with so weak a plan. So eager was Newcastle to gain Pitt's support that, aware of the latter's personal hostility toward him, he offered to resign all claim to office, truly a great sacrifice for one who loved so much the pomp, the circumstance, and power of office.[3]

As a further gesture toward the Great Commoner, his friend Charles Pratt, the judge who had won his admiration by an uncompromising stand against general warrants, was made a peer and, as Lord Camden, called to the cabinet. A second Pitt supporter, Thomas Nuthall, became solicitor to the Treasury. Advances were made to other Pittites, particu-larly to Isaac Barré and Shelburne, but they held aloof, letting it be known that they would regulate their conduct by the measures of the ministry.

Formation of the new government lasted through July. It was not until August 7 that the new Lord Camden could report to Pitt that the ministry was "at last upon its legs." But he wondered who would "steal fire from Heaven" and give it animation.[4] Nursing a hope that Pitt would be their Prome-theus, and sustained by fear of Grenville, the Old Whigs waited for events to fix their course in Parliament.

By August, Anglo-American relations had reached a criti-cal stage. In that month, the Virginia Resolves, an "alarm Bell to the disaffected," were widely known in England. Seri-ous rioting had broken out, especially in Boston, when the names of the stamp distributors had been published. It was also learned that Massachusetts had invited her sister colonies to a general congress to consider the state of affairs arising from the mother country's attempt to enforce the Stamp Act.

[3] Wentworth-Woodhouse, Rockingham Papers, minutes of July 6, 1765; and also Newcastle to Albemarle, July 3, 1765.

It was with something like satisfaction that the Old Whigs viewed the storm now rising in America. Ever fearful of Grenville and the Opposition, they believed that these disorders would wholly discredit Grenville, and give color to their picture of him as a willful disrupter of the empire. "I don't imagine," wrote Rockingham to a Yorkshire friend, "Mr. G. Greenville's popularity is very high in your neighbourhood. The difficulties he has thrown upon trade by very inconsiderate regulations must affect any opinion in his favour among the mercantile gentlemen, and the notable confusion which he has raised in America, tho' it lays difficulties upon the present administration, yet so far it serves them, as it shows that he had neither prudence or foresight."[5] Under pressure, then, of convulsions in the Colonies, faced with an increasingly anti-American Opposition—which they longed to discredit—and still courting the favor of Pitt, Rockingham's administration now turned its attention perforce to colonial affairs.

Certainly, the Old Whigs could not be called "pro-American" at the outset. In September, they decided that the Virginia Resolves and the proceedings of the Massachusetts Assembly were "of too high a Nature" for the Privy Council and determined to lay the papers before Parliament itself. The action of Virginia they condemned as an "absolute Disavowal of the Right of the Parliament of Great Britain to impose Taxes upon the Colonies and a daring attack upon the Constitution of this Country." Such words might well have come from Grenville himself. In October, after Governor Bernard's report on the Boston riots, the Privy Council commanded that the governors, the Admiralty, and the secretary at war take all measures to maintain the honor and safety of the government. As it was admitted that the civil power might be inadequate, each governor was told he could apply to the com-

---

[4] Smith, *The Grenville Papers*, III, 77.
[5] RHMCR. *Lindley Wood Papers, Various Collections*, 183, to Lord Irwin.

manders-in-chief in America for military aid.[6] Thus there
might have been a clash of arms; and the Revolution might
have begun much earlier than it did.

Parliament would not meet until December. Meanwhile,
the disorders in America grew more violent. Stamp distributors were intimidated and forced to resign; the stamps were
impounded and destroyed. Radical organizations, the "Sons
of Liberty," began to form throughout the Colonies. They
had considerable success in inducing colonial merchants to give
up British imports.[7] The absence of stamped paper rendered
legal proceedings technically void, and many courts now closed.
This in turn distressed British creditors who could no longer
sue for the recovery of debts. In October, the Stamp Act Congress met at New York. However, the moderate tone of their
resolutions and petitions proved that the radicals were not yet
in command. Protesting their affection for the King and ac-
knowledging "all due subordination" to Parliament, the Congress argued that the colonists possessed all the rights and
exemptions of Englishmen: they could not be taxed but
through their own assemblies. Great Britain's monopoly of
her trade, it was asserted, was America's sufficient contribution
to the expense of empire. Not yet, then, had the Colonies been
driven to refuge in the laws of nature, although that doctrine
had already had classic statement in America.[8] Still willing to
submit to external taxes for the regulation of trade, they based
their denial of Britain's right to tax them for revenue upon
the British Constitution.

[6] Grant and Munro, *Acts of the Privy Council*, IV, 729-33.

[7] During the year of disturbance, American imports fell from £3,000,000
to half that amount. See E. Channing, *History of the United States*, III, 65,
footnote. See also RHMCR. *Bathurst Papers*, 146-47, William Crawle to
Lord Huntington, January 16, 1766, wherein Crawle quotes Lord Dartmouth as declaring in a House of Lords debate that "not less than 50,000
men in this kingdom were at this time ripe for rebellion for want of work,
from the uneasy situation in the colonies."

[8] See James Otis, "The Rights of the British Colonies," and Daniel Du-
laney, "Considerations," printed in extract in S. E. Morison, *Sources and
Documents*, 4-9, and 24-32.

Despite these relatively mild words, the violence in America seemed to indicate impending revolution. The moderate John Dickinson wrote to Pitt from Philadelphia, warning him that the disorders were not to be taken lightly. The Revenue Act of 1764 had been "extremely disgusting and afflicting; though a high Veneration for the august Authority" which had imposed it had induced the Americans to accept it. The Stamp Act, however, had united them in a will to defend their invaded liberty. American dependence could be maintained only while affection for the mother country was unimpaired. The colonists would never regard the superintending of trade as a grievance; but the Stamp Act, an internal tax, must be repealed at once if their love were to continue.[9]

Governor Bernard, reporting from Boston, moaned that the home administration had failed to heed his advice of a year ago: wholesale reforms in the colonial governments were urgent and should have been made before "the Business of Finances." His warning was ominous. Defining the essence of the growing conflict, he stated, "In Britain the American Governments are considered as Corporations empowered to make by-Laws, existing only during the Pleasure of Parliament. . . . In America they claim . . . to be perfect States, not otherwise dependent upon Great Britain than by having the same King." The question was no longer "whether there shall be a Stamp Act or not; but whether America shall or shall not be Subject to the Legislature of Great Britain."[10] Colonial theorists were moving rapidly toward what can only be termed a "federal" concept of the imperial relation, wherein colonies were bound to Great Britain through the symbol of the Crown alone. Such a solution was, however, to remain in the realm of the impossible until the modern British party system had developed.

[9] Chatham Papers, 97, Dickinson to Pitt, December 21, 1765.
[10] Channing and Coolidge, *Barrington-Bernard Correspondence*, 93–102, Governor Bernard to Lord Barrington, November 23, 1765. For a confirmation of Bernard's assertion of the developing American view of the imperial relationship, see Jared Sparks (ed.), *Franklin's Works*, IV, 206–10.

Only then could a "commonwealth of nations" emerge, because the person of the sovereign had been removed from the center of domestic politics and had become a symbol in whom self-governing commonwealths could find their union. Just as British demands for an American revenue cut across the lines of internal political development in the Colonies, so did American assertions that they owed allegiance to the King and not to Parliament violate the sacred settlement of 1688.

In Great Britain it was generally perceived that a crisis in Anglo-American relations was at hand—and this at a time when the ministry was singularly weak and confused. Fearing hasty and ill-considered action, the King believed it to be "the most serious matter that ever came before Parliament."[11] The Grenville-Bedford group, convinced that the Old Whigs intended to repeal the Stamp Act, were intent on frustrating any such concession to "rebels." Even moderate Members to whom America had hitherto been but a name were alarmed at events and distrustful of Old Whig ability to cope with them. A new member of the government itself, the notorious Lord George Sackville—whose sins at Minden had been washed clean by the new King—was writing of America, "The Spirit that rages there is beyond conception. God only knows how it will end, for as yet I have heard no human reasoning that promises a happy issue to it."[12]

With America in flames, the weak Rockingham Ministry had now to face a domestic crisis which threatened its existence. As the opening of Parliament—in December—drew near, the Old Whigs, aware that Pitt's attitude could make or break them, were driven to measures of near desperation to gain his support. The Great Commoner was at Bath, however, and lashing out bitterly at Newcastle, he refused every overture. He was now increasingly loath to associate himself with any

[11] Albemarle, *Rockingham Memoirs*, I, 256–57, the King to General Conway, December 5, 1765.
[12] RHMCR. *Stopford-Sackville Papers*, I, 103, letter of December 23, 1765.

political group. It was not alone his animosity and suspicion of Newcastle. He had begun to recur to an earlier day when Walpole and the Pelhams had called down hell-fire upon "faction," and when Bolingbroke, taking them at their word, had called for a coalition of all persuasions in a truly national government around a "Patriot King." Already then, in 1765, Pitt, the supreme egotist, confident in his own great power, had begun to see himself the unifier of the nation, the extirpator of "faction." His persistent refusal to work with the Rockingham Ministry foreshadowed the "mosaic ministry" of 1766. In this attitude he was to find a solitary point of union with the King; but he was to make two cardinal errors when finally he was called upon to do what he had advocated. He was to underestimate the deep, dividing power of those principles which had entered politics since the accession of George III. Secondly, in his attempt to heal the divisions caused by Wilkes and America, he was to overestimate his own strength, political and physical. The turbulent sea from which, in years to come, the modern British party system would emerge was not so early to subside even at Pitt's command.

Pitt's aloofness shook the hopes of the Old Whigs, but it also disappointed the Opposition, who had hoped to draw him into alliance. They, too, failed to understand the growing importance of the American issue, which was solidifying the right wing of politics.[13] This process was soon to bring Pitt's brother-in-law and Grenville's brother, Lord Temple, into the conservative camp; but it was to drive Pitt to the left, separating him from them forever.

Grenville knew the course he must pursue at the opening of Parliament, and he exhorted Bedford to mobilize their friends for the event. Their working alliance intact, and believing that the ministry would push for a repeal of the Stamp

[13] Hinchingbrooke Papers, Sandwich to Augustus Hervey, August 11, 1765. See also Lord John Russell (ed.), *Bedford Correspondence*, III, 315–17, Sandwich to Bedford, August 26, 1765.

Act, Grenville and Bedford resolved to stun them by an early and violent onslaught. They had, however, misjudged the administration. The Old Whigs, preoccupied with gaining urgently needed support in Parliament, had actually reached no decision at all about the American crisis.

The question of their outside support grew ever more acute. Pitt had spurned their advances. Even unattached Members such as Lord North, half-brother of Dartmouth, president of the Board of Trade, would have naught of them. Furthermore, Paymaster Charles Townshend, miffed because he had not been made leader of the Commons, persistently declined to use his talents for their effective support. True, Sackville had accepted the office of vice treasurer of Ireland, a minor post. While he himself was pathetically pleased at "once more belonging to Court," even Newcastle was "very Doubtful" about the wisdom of his appointment. It would serve, he feared, further to alienate Pitt whose contempt for Sackville's behavior at the Battle of Minden was unabated. Furthermore, the King's Friends were ominously reserved.

In his necessity, Rockingham turned to the merchants of the country for that support which Pitt had refused him. Since the close of the Seven Years' War, there had been a steady increase in the political strength of those merchants with interests in the American and West Indian trade. In 1761, fifty or fifty-one merchants held seats in the Commons. At least ten of these had active American connections. About twenty-one or twenty-two, the "Jamaica cousinhood," had West Indian interests.[14] All were naturally concerned in questions relating to colonial trade. As long as the Laws of Trade and Navigation were enforced, all were eager to preserve friendly relations with the Colonies. Actually, they had more influence than the fifty-odd votes they commanded, for commercial considerations tempted Members from all larger urban constitu-

[14] Namier, *The Structure of Politics*, I, 61; *England in the Age of the American Revolution*, 277.

encies to vote with them.[15] What tended to dissipate this strength was that the aims of the American and the West In- Indian groups often diverged. Indeed, they sometimes came into violent conflict, as in the controversy over retention of Canada or the French Sugar Islands during negotiation of the Peace of Paris. Now, however, Rockingham found them united. Merchants trading to North America desired peaceable rela- tions in order to restore trade and collect their debts. The West Indian group, fearing the effect of colonial nonimportation— and nonexportation of essential victual supplies—were equally desirous of placating the Americans.

The discontented merchants represented, then, Rocking- ham's best hope of survival. Parliament had ever shown itself solicitous for their welfare, and would now be apt to heed their complaints. By courting such support, however, the Old Whigs showed themselves determined to avoid the deep constitution- al issues of the American problem. Fundamentally, they were to demonstrate that regarding Parliament's right to tax the Colonies, no great difference separated them from Grenville. Far more were they divided from Pitt, who was soon to deny the competence of Parliament to lay internal taxes.

As early as mid-November, the Lords of the Treasury had received memorials from mercantile and manufacturing cen- ters throughout the kingdom: Bristol, Manchester, Liverpool, Lancaster, and many others. Rockingham and his colleagues were told that "the Export Trade of these Kingdoms has lately suffered a great and sudden Diminution and Stagnation." The American combinations against British trade were increasing their distress, and they begged for relief.[16]

To capitalize better on the distress of the merchants, Rock- ingham now began a series of conferences with their leaders in London. Prominent among them were Barlow Trecothick, William Beckford of Fonthill, and Stephen and Rose Fuller,

[15] Namier, *The Structure of Politics*, II, 80.
[16] Chatham Papers, 83. Treasury minutes.

47

all Members of Parliament possessing large interests in the American and West Indian trade. Rockingham's immediate object was to organize their discontent so that it might be brought more forcibly to bear upon Parliament as a whole. In so doing, he was to demonstrate a technique which the Old Whigs were to perfect in 1780, when a flood of petitions would threaten to engulf the North Ministry.

A committee of twenty-eight London merchants was quickly organized to agitate among their colleagues throughout the country. Leaving nothing to chance, Rockingham and Trecothick drafted an appeal from the committee addressed to merchants in all major ports and manufacturing towns. An open bid for their support, the letter declared, "The present State of the British Trade to North America, and the prospect of encreasing Embarrassments which threaten the Loss of our depending prosperity there as well as to annihilate the Trade itself have occasioned a general meeting to be called of the Merchants of this City concerned in that Branch of Business." Because the merchants of other cities must be suffering also, the London group asked their concurrence and assistance "in Support of a regular application to Parliament, or otherwise by a petition from your Body and all the Interest you can make with your Members [of Parliament] in your Neighbourhood. . . . We desire to unite with you in a measure so essential to the best Interests of Great Britain . . . it being our Opinion, that conclusive Arguments for granting every Ease or Advantage the North Americans can with propriety desire, may be fairly deduced from that principle only."[17] Rockingham thus made it clear that measures undertaken for the relief of British trade should not be viewed as concessions to the Americans.

Response to Rockingham's and Trecothick's letter was not

[17] Wentworth-Woodhouse, Rockingham Papers, December 6, 1765. Only Burke's endorsement calling the letter "the principal Instrument in the happy repeal of the Stamp Act" is printed in Albemarle, *Rockingham Memoirs*, I, 319.

long in coming, and revealed a genuine concern among commercial circles. Sir William Meredith, formerly a Tory, but baptized anew under the Old Whigs, wrote exultingly to a newcomer on the political stage, Edmund Burke: "I am just come from Manchester and am happy to tell you that Mr. Pitt was never more popular than Lord Rockingham and the present administration. T'is the same at Liverpool and all over this country."[18] The appeal to the merchants, however, had come too late to have any considerable effect before the opening of Parliament, but events were to play into the hands of the administration.

Although the ministry had formed no definite American policy before Parliament opened on December 17, the King in the speech from the throne referred to recent "matters of importance" in the Colonies. These, he said, demanded the serious attention of Parliament. New advices were expected daily, and of these Parliament would be at once informed. Battle lines were promptly drawn. Scarcely allowing the ministers to move their loyal address, Grenville lunged to the attack, indignant at so mild a reference to the "outrages" in America. For him, he declared, the colonial actions were rebellion, and he moved an amendment to the address calling them such. No serious test of strength was at hand, however. Grenville had given up his premeeting plan to stun the ministry by an initial defeat. Success would have depended upon the support of at least a large portion of the King's Friends. Many of them were to be with Grenville in the crucial vote on the repeal of the Stamp Act, but now, at the outset of the session, they refused to oppose the King's government. Grenville consequently withdrew his motion. It was significant, however, that two members of the government, Charles Townshend and Lord George Sackville, while speaking against Grenville's motion, had declared strongly in favor of the execution of the Stamp Act. The ministers could take some comfort from the uncom-

18 Wentworth-Woodhouse, Burke Papers, December 11, 1765.

promising stand which Pitt's friend George Cooke had taken against Grenville. Furthermore, Shelburne, in the House of Lords, had led the defense of the government, strongly combating the application of the term "rebels" to the Americans, and falling in with Rockingham's plan to consider the Stamp Act "in a commercial view."[19]

This pre-Christmas meeting of Parliament, though short, was important. The ministry had come through it unscathed, but the Opposition had shown "a great deal of factious ability." Bedford and Grenville had been aided by Temple, who had joined with them "on the principle of strongly asserting the rights of the English parliament over America."[20] Indeed, many Members had concluded that America would not be content to question the right of the mother country to lay internal taxes. She would also deny the supreme authority of Parliament in other spheres. Thus early arose a conviction that America aimed at independence. This was in turn to lead to measures which finally would drive the Americans themselves to embrace it.[21]

Reassured of Pitt's attitude, somewhat easier about the King's Friends, and awaiting the petitions of the merchants, Rockingham and his brother ministers set about the formation of a concrete American policy. Indeed, Newcastle and Sir George Savile had been urging such action since October. But it was only now that Rockingham called together the Old Whig leaders, Newcastle excepted, to discuss American measures. Conway, Dartmouth, Charles Yorke, Dowdeswell, Rock-

[19] Cobbett and Wright, *Parliamentary History*, XVI, 83–90, speech and debate.

[20] Chatham Papers, 2, Shelburne to Pitt, December 21, 1765; printed in W. S. Taylor and J. H. Pringle (eds.), *Chatham Correspondence*, II, 354–55. Shelburne feared that Parliament was becoming increasingly anti-American, and that America would not be quieted even by a repeal unless it was "accompanied with some circumstances of a firm Conduct, and some system immediately following such a concession."

[21] See RHMCR. *Weston Papers*, 399, Edward Sedgwick to Edward Weston, December 24, 1765, for an expression of this "all or nothing" attitude.

Courtesy New York Public Library

MARQUIS OF ROCKINGHAM

ingham, and Egmont, the moderate King's Friend, met in the evening of December 27.

Yorke at once revealed himself a firm opponent of any concession to the Colonies. His family was traditionally Old Whig. His father, the first Lord Hardwicke, had been a mainstay in the Pelham "present system." Furthermore, to a man, they hated Pitt and feared his domination of their group. Imbued with the family traits of pride, ambition, hauteur, a legalistic mind, and a love of "firm" measures, Charles Yorke was determined to allow no "undignified" concessions. He now sought to seize control by bringing forward his own proposals. Probably, he favored an amendment to the Stamp Act, but his immediate concern was to "sell" Old Whig leaders a declaratory act which would affirm the unbounded power of Parliament. It should also, he said, be accompanied by addresses from both Houses assuring the King of their support of British sovereignty "to the Utmost Instant." The meeting now disintegrated into a wrangle between Yorke on the one hand and Conway and Egmont on the other. Consequently, no decision was reached. Yorke attributed the failure to a fear of offending Pitt and sarcastically wrote to Rockingham of his vexation with "the disjointed state of things for I know not what Reason, and with what expectation of a *Messiah*."[22]

Rockingham's first attempt to bring his cabinet to a decision on the Stamp Act had thus failed. Although he had accepted in principle Yorke's proposal of a declaratory act, the young Marquis seemed curiously unwilling to proceed further. Several days after the unsuccessful meeting, he was writing vaguely that "dignity must go hand in hand with Temper and Management"—which implied at least a partial retreat from the Stamp Act. Old Newcastle, understandably annoyed at being left out of the conclave, strongly urged on Rockingham

---

[22] Wentworth-Woodhouse, Rockingham Papers, Charles Yorke to Rockingham, December 30, 1765. See also Add. MSS 32973, ff. 3, 11, 25, referred to by D. A. Winstanley, *Personal and Party Government*, 256.

a positive course of action and lashed out at "the Idea of *Authority and Relief* going Hand in Hand." Far better, he believed, "to be Deficient in That which is only a Declaration in words, Than in the Other, in which depends the most material Interests of this Country, viz., The Recovery of our Trade and Commerce."[23] The old man was for outright repeal, but still Rockingham hesitated to commit himself until Pitt had given him his cue. To go against the Great Commoner's desires, Rockingham felt, would be fatal.

Pitt had coldly rebuffed all Old Whig attempts both to bring him into the ministry and to discover his American sentiments. Concerning the latter, a great part of Pitt's reticence arose from the fact that he himself had not reached a firm conclusion. To Shelburne's report on the parliamentary debates of December, Pitt had replied that those who argued for upholding the legislative and executive authority over America were in a strong position. The Grenville Ministry had been guilty of "preposterous and infatuated errors of policy" which force alone could make good. He had not yet, then, concluded that the Stamp Act, as such, was a violation of constitutional principles, although he would soon do so. It can be no coincidence that he was, at the time, in close and friendly communication with several proponents of the American view, particularly with Stephen Sayre, the radical American and future sheriff of London. Such correspondents supplied Pitt with information which must have influenced his thinking considerably.[24] In the meantime, Rockingham had no choice but to wait impatiently for the reconvening of Parliament when Pitt was expected to appear in London.

Parliament sat on January 14, 1766. It was soon apparent that the ministry had gained no new strength. Indeed, the

[23] Wentworth-Woodhouse, Rockingham Papers, Newcastle to Rockingham, January, 1766.

[24] Taylor and Pringle, *Chatham Correspondence*, II, 358–61, Pitt to Shelburne, December, 1765. See Chatham Papers, 55, for Pitt's correspondence with Sayre. Sayre to Pitt, January 27, 1766, is of special interest.

unrest of Grafton and Conway, increasingly eager to call Pitt to the leadership of the government, had served to weaken them. So dubious was their strength that the King would allow himself to hope only that they would last "till the arduous business of the American Colonys is over, then I can stand upon my own feet."[25] Their weakness was to be of little moment. They were to be dwarfed by a battle of giants. Pitt faced Grenville; both championed contradictory and mutually exclusive theories of empire. The ministry was hardly more than an onlooker.

The first attack came from Grenville's friend Robert Nugent, one day to rise upon the wealth of his successive wives to be Lord Clare. The honor and dignity of Parliament, he urged, required an execution of the Stamp Act "except the right was acknowledged, and the repeal solicited as a favour," for "a peppercorn in acknowledgment of the right [is] of more value, than millions without."

Pitt then rose and, in one of his greatest speeches, charged that every step of the Grenville Ministry in its American policy had been wrong. The difference between external and internal taxes was clear, and Britain had no right to levy those of the latter kind. The mother country was indeed sovereign and possessed supreme authority over America "in every circumstance of government and legislation whatsoever," but taxation was no part of the legislative power. It was a free gift of the people through their repesentatives. The House of Commons was in no way representative of the Colonies. So while Great Britain could bind the colonists' trade, she could not tax them for revenue. The great man had spoken. The ministers had their long awaited cue, and Conway hastened to espouse Pitt's thesis.

The rejoinder was to come from another quarter, and it was an able one. Grenville took the floor and, denying any distinction between internal and external taxes, asserted that

[25] Fortescue, *Correspondence of George III*, I, No. 186.

the power to tax was most assuredly a part of that supreme sovereignty of Parliament which Pitt admitted. Great Britain gave America protection; in return, the Colonies owed obedience. Pressing his attack home to Pitt, he charged that the tumults in America stemmed directly from "factions in this House."

Technically out of order, Pitt spoke a second time. In glowing phrases, he praised American resistance to the Stamp Act. The Americans were the champions of constitutional liberty. By submitting to the British trade monopoly, the colonists paid their share of the imperial expense. They may perhaps have acted imprudently, but "they have been wronged. They have been driven to madness by injustice." Concluding, he called for the Stamp Act to be repealed "absolutely, totally, and immediately," because it was "founded on an erroneous principle." At the same time, "let the sovereign authority of this country over the colonies be asserted in as strong terms as can be devised, and be made to extend to every point of legislation whatsoever. That we may bind their trade, confine their manufactures, and exercise every power whatsoever, except that of taking their money out of their pockets without their Consent."[26]

America had found her advocate. Although his victory was to be a transient one, Pitt's viewpoint contained the germ of a new imperial concept: the paradox of subordinate political units each possessing a sphere of autonomy which the supreme power of Parliament could not invade. With his unreasoning, instinctive genius, Pitt had risen above Grenville's legalistic constitutionalism. He was decades ahead of his time, and did not himself understand what he demanded. A necessary prerequisite to a "federalized" empire would be the development of the modern British party system and of a figurehead king in whom the components of the empire might find a common head.

[26] Cobbett and Wright, *Parliamentary History*, XVI, 103–108, debate.

Grenville had had his vision, too. He had proposed to create an empire within the framework of the eighteenth-century British Constitution. He had, however, gone at it tactlessly and ruthlessly, and he had failed to see that his attempt came too late, cutting across the whole political development of the Colonies. Yet Grenville's view of empire, with its supreme center and subordinate parts, solidly based on British political development, was finally to prevail in the rising domestic controversy. It was only natural that it should. It was just as natural that America should thereby be lost.

Pitt had asserted that he would be content with nothing less than a repeal of the Stamp Act. Secretary of State Conway, by his public agreement with Pitt, had committed the ministry to such a measure. Even so, all was not harmony within the ranks of the Old Whigs. Lord George Sackville, accepting Grenville's doctrine of the identity of internal and external taxation, had expressed admiration for his speech in Parliament. The Yorke family was openly adverse to repeal. Attorney General Charles Yorke would not accept the idea until a near-desperate Rockingham had assured him that a strong declaratory act would go with it, and that it would not seem a concession to the Colonies. Rather, Rockingham told him, the Stamp Act would be repealed because of "its own demerits and Inconveniences *felt here*."[27]

Still Yorke was dissatisfied. When the Old Whig leaders met on the night of January 20, Conway presented his draft of resolutions upon which the declaratory act was to be based. Asserting the supreme authority of Parliament over the Colonies in all cases whatsoever, they went on to condemn the tumults in America. These were destructive of the just dependency of the Colonies upon the mother country. All governors were, therefore, to punish the authors of such riots and to insure the compensation of the victims. Yorke objected to the

[27] Add. MSS 35430, ff. 31–32, Rockingham to Yorke, quoted in part by Winstanley, *Personal and Party Government*, 262, n. 2.

mildness of the measures proposed in General Conway's resolves. Moreover, when they were sent to him for approval, he
inserted specific references to Parliament's right to tax the Colonies. Rockingham, eager to avoid this constitutional quagmire,
crossed out Yorke's harsh changes which were personally ob-
jectionable to him, and would be very goading to Pitt.[28]

Thus, the ministry at length agreed to a declaratory act
and to repeal, but Rockingham had yet to face his greatest
problem: how was he to achieve a parliamentary majority? He
was assured of the support of Pitt's friends and of the merchant representation. But against him was the violent opposition of Grenville, Bedford, Temple, and their associates, whose
strength in the Commons may conservatively be estimated at
seventy-five votes.[29] They were alike contemptuous of the ministry, "our little masters," and of "those wretched merchants
who living upon expedients . . . would adopt the same miserable plan for the Publick."[30] Moreover, most of the King's
Friends were doubtful. Many were openly hostile to a repeal,
while the King himself seemed strangely supine. In addition,
Bute and his Scottish friends—with a maximum of forty-five
seats in Commons—were beginning to reach an understanding
with the leaders of the Opposition. The situation was thus extremely volatile. The idea of an amendment to the act, rather
than a repeal, was gaining popularity among the Opposition,
among unattached Members, and even among the ministry itself, where the Yorke family called loudly for such a solution.
Nor were Pitt and his followers improving the temper of the
House.

[28] Add. MSS 35430, ff. 37–38, Rockingham to Yorke, January 25, 1766;
printed in Albemarle, Rockingham Memoirs, I, 287–88.
[29] Namier, England in the Age of the American Revolution, 247, estimates the Grenville-Bedford strength at not more than fifty in 1767; but
the higher number for 1765, although a rough estimate, is justified, due to
the tendency of group "fringes" to leave an unprofitable Opposition as favorable opportunities arose.
[30] RHMCR. Lothian Papers, 258, Lord Buckinghamshire to Robert
Nugent, October, 1765.

On January 27, Pitt's friend George Cooke presented the petition of the Stamp Act Congress to the House of Commons. His action was much against the wishes of the ministry who feared it would merely inflame the situation. King's Friends joined Grenville in denouncing the Congress as a "dangerous federal union." And Pitt, whose tactlessness and violence now reached new heights, seized the opportunity to deliver his "second dissertation upon Government," as Sackville sneeringly called it. Demanding that the petition be received, Pitt declared that the Stamp Act had broken the original compact of government and that the Americans now had every right to resist. The conservative reaction was immediate. High words passed between Pitt and King's Friend Sir Fletcher Norton who called the Great Commoner a "trumpet of rebellion." Lord Hardwicke later declared that Pitt deserved the Tower; and he heatedly called for sending more troops to America to protect government from riot. Obviously, Pitt had merely angered those already against the repeal and alarmed moderates who had not yet decided.

Furthermore, Benjamin Franklin did nothing to calm the growing fear of American intentions. While examining the American papers in late January, the Commons called him in as agent for Pennsylvania. He readily admitted Britain's right to regulate colonial trade, but he resolutely denied any right to lay internal taxes—not even if the revenue were applied to the protection of the colonists. Concurring in Pitt's earlier argument, he declared that America paid her share of the common expense by submitting to the British trade monopoly. Besides there was not the least occasion for a British force in America. The colonists were "perfectly able to defend themselves." Franklin's final warning was unmistakable. Should Britain insist upon disregarding the difference between internal and external taxes, the colonists themselves might be driven to that position. Then, however, America's conclusion would be just opposite that of Britain's: she would refuse to pay *any* taxes levied by the home government.[31]

In such an atmosphere, panic began to stir among Rockingham and his friends. The King, preferring an amendment to the Stamp Act, refused to commit his Friends to a repeal despite Rockingham's remonstrances. Indeed, there was grave cause for concern. On a Scottish election petition presented against the wishes of the ministry on January 31, the government was saved by a margin of only nine votes. Joined against them in the division were Bute's friends, the Grenville group, the Bedfordites, and several placemen, including Lords Sackville and Strange. There were rumors that the King's Friends were planning to desert the ministry because it was pledged to a repeal, that Pitt was being called, and that the government was falling.

To Rockingham's anguished appeals for the support of the Friends, the King returned platitudes but not promises. Among the Old Whigs, however, there was a hardening core of wounded pride and a determination to take the plunge, come what might. On February 3, therefore, Conway moved the resolution embodying the Declaratory Act. Pitt, with Barré and Beckford, fought the motion tooth and nail, contending that Britain had no right to lay internal taxes on America. It was a forlorn stand, both Opposition and ministry vying with each other in answering Pitt's position. It is noteworthy that during this debate, a new Member of Parliament and an adherent of the ministry made his maiden speech, an argument for the supremacy of Parliament in all cases whatsoever. This man was Edmund Burke.

The House's acceptance of the Declaratory Act was, however, no test of strength for the ministry. (The conservative Opposition would scarcely combat so emphatic a statement of Parliament's right to tax the Colonies.) Indeed, the position of the government was gradually worsening. In the House of

[31] Sparks, *Franklin's Works*, IV, 161-200.

Lords, in debate on the Declaratory resolutions, the Old Whigs found themselves in a minority on two minor divisions, Bute's, Bedford's, and Grenville's followers having united against them with several of the King's Friends. These were relatively unimportant setbacks, but they showed Rockingham that his position had now become so precarious that immediate and effective royal support had become an absolute necessity. It was of ominous import that American affairs had pushed Bute into a union with his old enemies Bedford and Temple. The Scot must have been provided with ironic amusement in a scene which saw both Opposition and ministry competing in pouring out compliments upon the same man whom, a short time ago, they had so bitterly reviled as a "secret influence" and "minister behind the curtain."

In the Stamp Act crisis, it is possible to gauge the success of the King's project, adopted at the commencement of his reign, to recover what he considered his constitutional function as the center of British politics. In this highly critical period, it was generally believed that the King and his Friends had become the decisive factor. Courted by both sides, they were able to give victory to whomever they chose to support. The King desired an amendment of the Stamp Act rather than a repeal. Such a course, he believed, would be "more consistent with the honour of this Country and all the Americans would with any degree of Justice hope for."[32] For the ministry, however, amendment was impossible: they had declared publicly for repeal. Had the King so wished, he could have easily overturned the ministry by simply remaining silent. His Friends, following their own inclination, would have gone overwhelmingly against a repeal, and the ministry would have fallen. George III saw clearly, however, that the failure of the Old Whigs would restore the hated Grenville and Bedford to power. Understanding, therefore, that the issue had become either total

[32] Fortescue, *Correspondence of George III*, I, No. 247, memorandum by the King, February 10, 1766.

repeal or total enforcement, George acceded, in a limited manner, to Rockingham's demands for royal support. The minister was allowed to say that the King preferred repeal of the act to its enforcement. This statement, however equivocal, helped combat a belief that George was being forced to accept the repeal by his ministers.

Even with the King's lukewarm support—George had refused to crack the whip over his Friends by threatening a general dismissal from place of all those who went against the repeal—Rockingham very nearly resigned. The implication in the King's statement that he favored amendment was immediately seized upon by the Opposition. Seeking to open communication with the King through Bedford, they offered their services "in any possible way." George's reply, a cold rebuff, goes far to dispel the Old Whig legend that he intrigued against them and the repeal: "I do not think it constitutional for the Crown personally to interfere in Measures which it has thought proper to refer to the advice of Parliament."[33] It was evident, therefore, that the Opposition would not have royal support or that of the majority of the Friends in their fight against the ministry.

Rockingham's campaign for merchant support now began to pay dividends. Bristol, Liverpool, Manchester, Nottingham, Leeds, and many other commercial centers sent petitions through their merchant committees. They complained of the disastrous state of trade. Unemployment had become so widespread, and the volume of their business so curtailed that there was distress in all commercial districts in the kingdom. This catastrophe they laid to the Stamp Act. Glasgow merchants, for instance, demanded immediate repeal as the only measure which could give them relief and bring order to America. They themselves held £1,500,000 in debts in Virginia and Maryland

---

[33] *Ibid.*, No. 256, the King to the Duke of York, through whom Bedford made his offer, February 18, 1766; see also No. 253, Egmont to the King, February 17, 1766.

alone, a sum they could not collect until the pernicious act was repealed.[34] These were arguments which would appeal mightily not only to the fifty-odd merchants in Parliament and to the representatives of the large commercial cities but also to the independent and unattached Members.

A third development now served further to bolster the ministry. Grenville committed a political blunder which went far to save the government he was seeking to destroy. His course now should have been obvious. He should have pressed for an amendment of the act. The King's Friends, knowing their royal master's views, would have supported such a motion. So would have the unattached moderates. The ministry could not have retreated from repeal. Even with Pitt and the merchant interest solidly in support, it is doubtful that the government would have been saved. Lacking political finesse when principle was involved, however, and outraged by the intention to repeal, Grenville, on February 7, suddenly moved an address to the King asking unqualified enforcement of the Stamp Act. No special arrangements had been made for a solid attendance of the Opposition. The division was crucial. Grenville's surprising and signal defeat amazed the ministry as much as it did the Opposition. The House divided against the motion by a vote of 274–134, providing the ministry with a majority twice as large as their most sanguine expectations. With drooping ministerial spirits brightened by the much needed fillip, Sackville reported to a friend, "The conversation is that the ministry may now stand their ground."[35] Grenville's uncompromising tone had thus failed to draw to his support that considerable number of Members who would have voted for an amendment; and a good chance to overturn the ministry had gone glimmering.

Events had conspired in favor of Rockingham and his repeal. When the issue came to a vote at half-past one on the

---

[34] Wentworth-Woodhouse, Burke Papers.
[35] RHMCR. *Stopford-Sackville Papers*, I, 106–108.

morning of February 22, the ministry, strongly supported by Pitt and the merchants, carried the resolutions for repeal in a division of 275–167. Of the eighty representatives of the counties, chiefly country gentlemen and Old Tories who were the most independent element in Parliament, only twenty-nine voted against the government.[36] The merchants responded solidly to the petitions of the commercial cities; and representatives from the larger urban constituencies had felt the pressure also. Pitt's friends had increased the ministry's majority. And, finally, a large majority of King's Friends had joined to carry the measure through. In the House of Lords, they performed a similar service, Lord Egmont speaking powerfully for the ministry.

Pitt, basking in "the Sun of liberty," was jubilant. The thanks of the mercantile interests poured in upon the ministry and the Great Commoner for the assistance given to "almost expired" trade.[37] There were disquieting aspects, however. The minority in the House of Commons had consisted of Grenville and Bedford followers firmly united with those of Bute. The forty-five Scottish Members had gone overwhelmingly against the ministry. Some fifty-two voting with the Opposition had been placemen, including many King's Friends such as Barrington and Sackville; and forty-one Old Tories had joined the protest against the repeal.[38] So the tide of conservatism had begun to flow. Henceforward it was to become increasingly strong. Opinion was growing that America's "flame is too permanent to be accounted for from the fury of the mob." Charges of "unsettled pusillanimity" were levied more often at the ministry, while Pitt had been guilty of "violence tinctured with his foible, a passion for popular applause." The debates on repeal had convinced King's Friends and independents alike that Grenville offered the securest harbor in the rising storm.

---

[36] Namier, *The Structure of Politics*, I, 187–88.
[37] Chatham Papers, 48, merchants of Liverpool to Pitt, March 11, 1766.
[38] Keith Feiling, *The Second Tory Party*, Chap. VII.

The repeal had scarcely been carried before they began to feel that the measure had been "merely a temporary expedient which will embroil us more and more in the process of time."[39] Meantime, both the Declaratory Act and the repeal received royal assent on March 18. The King breathed a sigh of relief; and Benjamin Franklin celebrated by sending his patient wife fourteen yards of pompadour satin.

Having made its supreme effort, the ministry now went to pieces. Pitt retired to Bath in early May, and so withdrew the last hope of bringing him into the government. Grafton promptly resigned as secretary of state, and while the office was hawked about, the King prayed only that the Old Whigs might hold together until the end of the parliamentary session. Then he could act more independently in the formation of a new ministry.

In their short year in office, the Old Whigs had shattered Grenville's imperial vision which had been based on an American financial contribution. The corollary of the repeal of the Stamp Act was an abandonment of all plans to organize the west. Always doubtful of the wisdom of keeping Canada in preference to the West Indies Sugar Islands, the Old Whigs now showed themselves willing to treat the west as an immense Indian reservation, to make permanent the boundary provisions of the Proclamation of 1763—which Grenville had accepted only as a temporary measure—and to remand to the Colonies control of Indian affairs.

On October 18, 1765, the Privy Council, considering a Board of Trade report dealing with settlements upon the Ohio River contrary to the Proclamation, had ordered additional instructions for the Governors of Virginia and Pennsylvania. Such illegal settlements were to be evacuated at once, and appropriate measures must be taken to prevent the like in future.[40]

---

[39] RHMCR. *Gray Papers*, 298–99, Thomas Falconer to Thomas Gray, March 18 and 19, 1766.

[40] Grant and Munro, *Acts of the Privy Council*, IV, 729–30.

Convinced as the Old Whigs were that inland colonies would be too independent of the mother country, it is doubtful that harmonious relations with America could have been long preserved, even if the Rockingham government had not fallen. Eventual conflict with the rapidly growing numbers of American frontiersmen and land speculators would have been inevitable.

The ministry quickly dismissed, because of the cost, all thought of implementing Hillsborough's plan (1764) for imperial control of Indian affairs. They had, nonetheless, to face the problem presented by the ten thousand troops already in America. Since no satisfactory solution to the financial question had been reached, it was necessary to make some new arrangement concerning them.

In May, 1766, Barrington, the secretary at war, reported on the situation. Although the Rockingham Ministry fell before the report could be considered, it may be accepted as a statement of their view of the west. Barrington proposed to evacuate it. Calling for the abolition of forts, garrisons, and settlements in the Indian country, he declared that it was unlikely that Britain herself would ever be in a state of hostility with the Indians. Should the Colonies become embroiled by their own misconduct, "let them get themselves out of it . . . or let them beg for military assistance, acknowledge their want of it, and pay its expense." New colonies would be confined to the Floridas, if the colonists were willing to erect them at their own expense. In any event, those already established offered room for expansion for "some ages."

The British troops in America, he urged, should be withdrawn from the western area and concentrated in East Florida, Canada, and Nova Scotia, leaving to the colonists the task of protecting the frontier. Troops so stationed could easily move to any point in North America where riot, tumult, or other contingency might require.[41] This report was a direct reversal of

[41] Fortescue, *Correspondence of George III*, I, No. 454; see C. W. Al-

Grenville's plan which had sought to transform the new conquests into valuable additions to the empire.

Time was now rapidly running out for the ministry, yet several other aspects of the American problem were treated before the Old Whigs fell. Truly commendable was their plan for Canada. Though never implemented, it foreshadowed the Quebec Act of 1774. In February, 1766, the Privy Council approved instructions to the governor of Canada which required him to grant to all Canadians, French and English alike, full and equal rights in courts of law, including the practice of law and jury service. A new and vigorous governor, General Sir Guy Carleton, who strongly favored a final settlement of Canadian affairs by Parliament, was appointed. Although the Old Whigs had neither time nor courage to carry out a parliamentary consideration of the state of the neglected province, they did indicate the course they would have pursued. Shortly before their fall, Attorney General Yorke and Solicitor General de Grey submitted to the Privy Council a report which suggested that French civil law be combined with the more humane English criminal law. Not daring to bring such a radical proposal before Parliament, the ministry decided to promulgate it through instructions to Carleton. Lord Chancellor Northington, the King's Friend, seized the chance, as he had done when Grenville was falling, to precipitate a cabinet crisis by violently opposing the plan. The King consequently called Pitt to settle a new administration.

Soon after the repeal had been carried, the united merchant support which had bolstered up Rockingham began to disappear. Rockingham was to learn upon what a shifting base of sand he had sought to build. In the closing months of their ministry, the Old Whigs had amended the Revenue Act of 1764, lowering the duty on molasses, British or foreign, from three pence a gallon to one penny. Bad feeling had immedi-

vord, *The Mississippi Valley in British Politics*, I, Chap. VIII, who dates the report May 10, 1766. A copy is in Chatham Papers, 97.

ately flared up between the American and the West Indian interests, and the alliance, born in common opposition to the Stamp Act, was so weakened that it became useless to Rockingham. The final and violent end of friendly co-operation came in April. The American merchants demanded a free port in the West Indies where the colonists might exchange surplus supplies and victuals for French and Spanish bullion. But British West Indians had to meet French and Spanish prices paid for American products; and a free port would facilitate the illicit purchase of foreign sugars which habitually undersold those of the English planters. When the free port plan gained Rockingham's support, the West Indian interest, led by William Beckford and Stephen and Rose Fuller, went into enraged opposition. Rockingham quickly moved to grant them comparable concessions, but the struggle had already exhausted the remaining energy of the ministry.[42]

Finally, it is important to note that while the duty on molasses was lowered, the act itself remained an act for revenue, indicating that, fundamentally, the Old Whig view of taxation did not differ from Grenville's.

In February, 1766, John Yorke complained to his brother Hardwicke that in Parliament "every point now turns immediately into something American."[43] With her resistance to the Stamp Act, America suddenly and unexpectedly presented herself as a problem of the first magnitude to British politicians. Having quieted her temporarily by repealing the Stamp Act, Rockingham had sought to walk the tightwire of commercial expediency between the views of Pitt and Grenville. He had sought to give the important question of right a mere academic answer, hoping to leave it actually in abeyance. But it had been raised on both sides of the Atlantic, and it would never be al-

---

[42] L. Stuart Sutherland, "Edmund Burke and the First Rockingham Ministry," *English Historical Review*, Vol. XLVII (January, 1932), 46–70.
[43] Add. MSS 35374, f. 286, February 14, 1766.

lowed to return to that comfortable obscurity whence it had sprung.

Pitt had sought a repeal on the ground of Parliament's incompetence to lay internal taxes, but far from adopting this view, the Old Whigs had brought forward the Declaratory Act. They had hoped that as a theoretical statement it would save the face of Parliament. In reality, it was the most explicit declaration and justification ever drawn up in support of Parliament's unbounded right to legislate for the Colonies. The repeal therefore represented no real departure from those traditions of eighteenth-century constitutionalism which formed the opinions of most parliamentarians. In the long run, the chief result of the repeal in England would be the alienation from America of a large body of moderate politicians, and their alliance with the conservatives. "I much fear," wrote Falconer to Gray, "the concessions to the Americans will have little effect. They did not complain of the weight of taxes, but of the power of taxing claimed by us."[44] In Great Britain, then, the repeal operated as an irritant and as a justification for later stringent measures against the "ungrateful" Colonies.

[44] RHMCR. *Gray Papers*, 299, May 11, 1766.

CHAPTER THREE

CHATHAM, FACTION, AND AMERICA

P ITT came into office in July, 1766, with three major objects: to smash "faction," to bring the East India Company under government control, and to settle the American problem. These objects were not unconnected.

His persistent refusals to associate himself with the Old Whigs or with any other political group, his friendly references to Bute during the late session of Parliament, and his call for a union of parties into a truly national government—all these had made him acceptable to the King. George III, however, had already gathered about him a group of Friends who formed a "faction" very like those he wished to crush. George, it would seem, did not understand the dual role he was playing, as domestic party leader and as imperial monarch. Indeed, by accepting the former role he made himself incapable of the latter one. He could not now rise above domestic politics to be a symbol of union in a "federalized" commonwealth, and his failure spelled disruption to the first British Empire.

The Rockingham Ministry had seen the emergence of the King's Friends as a full-fledged party. Chatham's administration was to let them rise to power and then consolidate their position. This loosely-organized body, consisting of all who looked immediately to the King for political leadership, was the precursor of the modern civil service, the "subministers."[1]

[1] See Jucker, *Jenkinson Papers*, xiii–xv; Namier, *The Structure of Politics*, I, 47.

Charles Jenkinson and John Robinson, who was to achieve amazing power as North's secretary of the Treasury, were prototypes. Usually without private fortunes, the men who became King's Friends longed for permanence in place and freedom from the ebb and flood of political fortune. The King could offer them this security if they would but support his measures in Parliament. Servants of the same master, these men naturally gravitated toward one another.

By the turn of 1766, the King's Friends were meeting in true party fashion. At that time, a dissolution of the Rockingham Ministry had seemed likely. The Friends had accordingly gathered to map out their course of action. Their deliberations cast a flood of light on the hardening of party lines and on the position achieved by the King since his accession. Should the Rockingham government fall, they stated, "the End to be wished is that His Majesty should have the free choice of his own Servants and that He should not put the management of His Affairs unconditionally into the Hands of the Leaders of any party." In an analysis of existing political conditions, they listed four parties. The first was their own. It was composed of "those who have always hitherto acted upon the sole Principle of Attachement to the Crown." Further, they were "probably the most numerous Body," and lacked only a parliamentary leader to undertake the formation of a ministry. Bute was ineligible because of his personal unpopularity. At any rate, his following, all but a few, were already counted among the King's Friends.[2] It was therefore necessary for the Friends to "be joined if it be possible to some one of the other Parties."[3]

[2] Romney Sedgwick (ed.), *Letters from George III to Lord Bute*, 255-58, Bute to the King, August, 1766. Bute complained that Chatham had disregarded the former Bute supporters because of his belief that they continued to constitute a Bute "faction." He had told his group, however, "Look to the King, not to me, I want no men to attach themselves to me, 'tis to him alone you should pay regard."

[3] Add. MSS 38338, ff. 307-10, "Observations on the probable dissolution of Lord Rockingham's [first] Administration at a Meeting of ——— [sic] King's Friends." Printed in Jucker, *Jenkinson Papers*, 404-408.

The three other parties were the Old Whigs, the Grenville-Bedford-Temple alliance, and the Pittites. The King's past experience ruled out the first two as possible allies. Pitt, however, presented no danger. His own strength was "merely ideal." His following rested "on no settled attachment and will be of no Importance if the Crown declares against them." Possessed of enormous personal prestige, he would yet be dependent upon the King's Friends for a majority. By declaring war against "faction," he had made himself acceptable to the King: George now felt, from Pitt's conduct during the past session, that he would work well with "those of my Servants who I have protected on every former change."[4] Pitt then was the obvious answer to their search for a parliamentary leader. George III, through clever appeals to patriotism and self-interest, had created just such a group as those he had called upon Pitt to combat. In effect, Pitt was to be set tilting at windmills. And the first of these would be the ramshackle structure of the Old Whigs which, almost miraculously, still functioned, albeit with many a creak and groan.

Pitt and the King in their initial conversations had agreed to accept the Rockingham Ministry as a basis whereon to build. From the first, however, Pitt showed such contempt for their "faction" that an open breach was not long to be postponed. The offer of the Treasury to Temple had been resented by the Old Whigs, and only Temple's refusal of it now prevented open hostilities.[5] Indignity after indignity was heaped upon them. Offices were filled without a word to them: Shelburne was made secretary of state for the Southern Department; Camden, lord chancellor; King's Friend Northington weathered yet another crisis and emerged as president of the Council; Egmont took the Admiralty, and Grafton the Treasury. Charles Townshend, at Grafton's express request, was forced

---

[4] Sedgwick, *Letters*, No. 339, the King to Bute, July 12, 1766.
[5] Add. MSS 35430, ff. 55–56, Rockingham to Charles Yorke, July 17, 1766.

to exchange the lucrative paymastership for the office of chancellor of the exchequer. Pitt himself took the privy seal and received the earldom of Chatham.

The new arrangement was thus an open affront to the Old Whigs. Conway, it is true, remained a secretary of state. Lord North, with Pelham family connections, was given Townshend's vacant post. A somewhat ungracious attempt was made to lay old Newcastle upon a "bed of roses" with a pension; but the veteran did not think he was "yet quite old enough to submit tamely to lie down on it, and be tuck'd up quietly."[6] Several other Old Whigs rested undisturbed in minor employment at various government boards. On the other hand, Pitt haughtily refused to place Dartmouth, erstwhile president of the Board of Trade, in a projected third secretaryship of state, that for America, although he had previously planned to create such a post. Dartmouth now resigned and was succeeded by King's Friend Hillsborough. Pitt offered the proud and ambitious Charles Yorke the honor of retaining his old office of attorney-general, but Yorke contemptuously declined. Dowdeswell was imperiously dismissed as chancellor of the exchequer to make room for Townshend. Rockingham immediately retaliated by refusing all personal communication with Pitt—now Earl of Chatham—and warmly asserted that only his friendship for Conway and Grafton kept him from calling for the resignation of all Old Whigs, even those in minor places.

Chatham's ministry as it now stood consisted of his own followers, the King's Friends, and the grumbling Old Whigs. This was a weak beginning. He was, moreover, faced with three dissatisfied factions: those of Bedford, Grenville and Temple, and Bute. Among his own people the Old Whigs were on the point of bolting, and several of the King's Friends, erstwhile followers of Bute—men like Charles Jenkinson,

[6] Add. MSS 35425, ff. 104–105, H. V. Jones to Hardwicke, July 26, 1766.

Thomas Whately, Sir Fletcher Norton, and Lord Darlington —had begun to resent his neglect for their interests.

Chatham, however, was moved by a higher consideration. He was preoccupied with the Old Whigs whom he thought the very embodiment of "faction." As long as they held office, that many more places were denied the King's Friends. Should they continue in place, however, and thus remain divided, some in office and some out, then a dissolution of the Old Whigs became a distinct possibility. Probably the King acquiesced in this reasoning. He was apparently willing to await the issue of the situation, gambling that in case of Old Whig resignations, the Bedfords, Chatham's choice as an ally among the hostile groups, would not come in. He could then bring in more of his Friends.

The conditions necessary for the success of Chatham's grandiose campaign were, however, not present. Group interests and loyalties had hardened too much, and after decades of vacuity, well-defined principles were re-entering politics. America and Wilkes had commenced to cut jagged lines across British political groupings.

Chatham took over the government intent on settling the affairs of America. He had fought passionately for the American cause during the two preceding sessions. That he was aware of the magnitude of the American problem and of the urgent need for its settlement is too evident. During the formation of his ministry, he had not only projected an American Department on a full parity with the older Departments of State but had contemplated taking its direction upon himself. However Temple's refusal of the Treasury had upset his outline of the new arrangement, and in the ensuing crisis, all idea of the new department had been dropped.[7] But just as Chatham had underestimated the strength of party divisions, he also failed to recognize the importance of the American issue as a divisive

[7] C. R. Ritcheson, "The Elder Pitt and an American Department," *American Historical Review*, Vol. LVII (January, 1952), 376–83.

force in British politics. He had wanted Temple at the Treasury, and Temple's opposition to the repeal of the Stamp Act had been notorious. Certain other elements in his cabinet possessed American views openly different from his own. In both cases—the campaign against party and the lack of attention to his colleagues' American sentiments—Chatham's attitude was a commentary on his monumental egoism which allowed him to believe that he would be able to impose his own ideas on the ministry and the nation. He had overestimated his own strength, political as well as physical.

When Temple had refused the Treasury in July, he had lashed out at the "new, virtuous, and patriotic administration." Consisting of Old Whigs and Chatham's friends, they were, he said, "all the most choice spirits who did in the last Session most eminently distinguish themselves in the sacrifice of the rights and honour of the whole Legislature and Kingdom of Great Britain."[8] America had thus united Temple and Grenville in firm alliance. Furthermore, certain of Bute's neglected followers, whom the Scot had willed the King while disclaiming his own party chieftainship, had already made approaches to Grenville. Sir Fletcher Norton and Lord Darlington were bade a cautious welcome. Grenville expressed his pleasure at their report that Bute had disavowed the new ministry. It was, Grenville told them, "certainly founded upon principles widely different from those which I am told he [Bute] laid down with such general approbation in the House of Lords last session."[9] The conservatism engendered by America's reaction to the Stamp Act was working rapidly now in the consolidation of the right wing of politics, and the process could not be stopped, even by a Chatham.

[8] Smith, *Grenville Papers*, III, 267–68, Temple to Grenville, July 18, 1766; 272–73, Temple to Gower.

[9] *Ibid.*, 273–77, Grenville to Thomas Whately, through whom the approaches were made, July 20, 1766. Chatham's only favor to Bute had been to restore his brother Mackenzie to the office of privy seal of Scotland, but the power of patronage had not been returned.

The American issue was of less immediate importance to the King's Friends and to the Bedfordites. The former group, whose American attitude at this point may be described as neutral, was now engaged in the practical struggle to achieve power. Without a definite American "plan," they were nonetheless confident that once they were in the saddle they could deal with the problem satisfactorily. "The Management of the American affairs," they admitted, "is certainly full of Difficulties but the House is so divided on that subject that whatever Sentiments are adopted, they will certainly find support from one side or another; and wherever the Crown casts its Influence there will be Success."[10] The King's Friends, then, had come to view themselves not merely as a separate political group but as the decisive one.

The Bedfords, too, were hungry for office and had hoped that Pitt would turn to them for support when forming his ministry.[11] In many ways, the Bedfords exhibited more signs of advanced party organization than any other group. Led by the Duke of Bedford, an honest, upright, conservative man of limited understanding, they worked together mightily to achieve one goal: office. That object being paramount, political principles were relative. Bedford himself was inclined to agree with Grenville in American affairs, but his friends, able talkers like Richard Rigby, Lord Weymouth and Lord Gower, could usually induce him to follow their lead. They themselves were capable of taking on any color that served their interest. So Bedford was soon reported as expressing himself in a friendly manner toward the new ministry: he would be perfectly satisfied, it seems, if he could but obtain office for a few of his friends.

In August, Egmont resigned the Admiralty. He had never liked Chatham, and he now declined to serve under him.

[10] Add. MSS 38399, ff. 307–10.
[11] Hinchingbrooke Papers, Sandwich to Augustus Hervey, July 15 and 23, 1766.

Chatham was at Bath, but Grafton, the titular head of government, immediately offered the vacant post to Bedford's relative Lord Gower. The Duke refused, averring his dislike of the measures pursued by many of the ministry during the last session—an obvious reference to the repeal of the Stamp Act—but it was clear that the offer had been merely insufficient. It would take more than this to tempt the Bedfords to break with Grenville.

The question of additional support for the ministry became a serious one before the meeting of Parliament, scheduled for November. Chatham, in August, had suffered a painful attack of gout—sinister portent of things to come—and had retired to Bath. While he was there, however, serious riots due to the grain shortage had occurred and had obliged him to hurry back to London. He and his ministry had then issued a proclamation prohibiting the export of grain. By doing so, they disregarded a law which allowed exportation of grain until a price higher than the prevailing one had been reached. Chatham had then returned to Bath. Grafton feared a strong attack from the Opposition for this exercise of the royal prerogative, and he longed for an accession of strength to meet it. By various half-hearted expedients he sought to quiet growing dissatisfaction. A Bute relative was made a Duke. One of Grenville's friends, Lord Buckinghamshire, was offered—but refused—the embassy to Madrid. Both Conway and Grafton suggested that the new Old Whig Edmund Burke be brought in. His oratorical skill would indeed have helped immeasurably, but Chatham, detesting all Old Whigs, would have none of him. His thoughts had returned to a Bedford accession. It would be a clever maneuver. That group possessed respectable strength, and they were the very center of opposition. Once they were drawn in, Rockingham and Grenville, diametrically opposed in American affairs, would find it exceedingly difficult, perhaps impossible, to unite. Furthermore, a new development was making a Chatham-Bedford *rapprochement* even more feasible: the disobedience of the New York Assembly was causing Chatham's own American views to stiffen.

Thus it occurred that Northington, representing the ministry, renewed the offers to Bedford while both men were at Bath. The Lord President called on the Duke on the nineteenth, expressed his desire to see Bedford in administration, and outlined Chatham's policy: to preserve the peace in Europe—an especially delicate point with the negotiator of the Treaty of Paris—to restore authority to government at home, and "to support the superiority of Great Britain over her colonies." A few days later, Chatham himself repeated the offer and elaborated upon his own plans. A chief point was that "measures for the proper subordination of America must be taken."

In a later interview, Chatham qualified this remark by declaring that he hoped he "was not understood to intend any violent measures toward the Americans at this time, unless absolutely necessary." It is apparent, however, that neither Chatham nor Bedford thought their American differences great enough to keep them apart. Bedford considered the openings so promising that he at once summoned his confidants, Weymouth, Gower, and Richard Rigby.

Chatham had promised the post office for Weymouth, an unspecified place for Rigby, and employment for Gower as master of the Horse. These, however, the Bedfords considered insufficient, and so negotiations failed. The first minister, though disappointed, parted with Bedford on "exceeding good terms," convinced that his party could be bought if more places were opened to them, and determined to create such vacancies as soon as he could.

Chatham had, in any case, driven a wedge between Bedford and Grenville. When Parliament opened on November 11, Bedford and his friends refused to join Grenville in opposing the loyal address. Next day, Bedford "went to the King's levee: was graciously received."[12] Meanwhile Chatham, now certain of an accession from the Bedfords, launched his most formidable attack upon the Old Whig "faction." Two days after the opening of Parliament, without previous warning, he demanded that one of them, Lord Edgecumbe, treasurer of the Household and possessor of several seats in Parliament, exchange his place for an inferior one in the Bedchamber. Deeply annoyed with Old Whig Edmund Burke and William Dowdeswell, who had spoken with Grenville for the necessity of a bill of indemnity to excuse those involved in the grain embargo, Chatham seemed determined to break Old Whig cohesion by a contemptuous display of his authority over them or else to drive them out, thereby creating the necessary vacancies for the Bedfords.

Old Whig leaders, Conway excepted, immediately consulted, and their decision was quickly made: mass resignation was necessary; "the Corps must be kept together." Portland, Bessborough, Scarborough, Morrison, Saunders, Keppel, and Meredith announced their withdrawal from the government. Only the fickle Conway remained, much to the disgust of his fellows, for he "doubted whether he would be justified in throwing the King's affairs into confusion."[13] Chatham's *coup de main* against faction was, in the end, an abysmal failure. The mass exit of the Old Whigs, binding its members in common adversity, saved that party from dissolution. They were to wander long in the wilderness, but they would live to fight another day.

Chatham had overreached himself, and he now saw his secondary object, an accession from the Bedfords, melt away. Immediately, the Bath offers had been renewed, but the Bed-

---

[12] Russell, *Bedford Correspondence*, III, 348 ff., Bedford's private journal. See also Smith, *Grenville Papers*, III, 337, Grenville to Temple, November 10, 1766.

[13] Wentworth-Woodhouse, Rockingham Papers, Dowdeswell to Rockingham, November 20, 1766; Hinchingbrooke Papers, Halifax to Sandwich, November 15, 1766; Albemarle, *Rockingham Memoirs*, II, 24, Hardwicke to Rockingham, November 20, 1766, 19–20, Rockingham to Scarborough, November 20, 1766.

fordites, realizing Chatham's exposed position, now proceeded to make the most of it. Their terms soared to shocking heights. Four more friends were to be provided for; three peerages were to be conferred; and the royal favor was to be manifested toward Sandwich. Thus, Chatham found himself faced with the same "evil" he had sought to extirpate. He had become a victim of his own highhanded ways. This painful situation might have been a demonstration to him that his campaign against faction was an attempt to sweep back the sea.

Both Chatham and the King denounced the Bedford's "extravagant proposals." But where were they to find the necessary support to replace that which Chatham had so haughtily tossed away? As soon as Rockingham's followers had resigned, Charles Jenkinson and Sir Fletcher Norton sent urgently to Bute's friend Sir James Lowther, begging him to urge Bute to hurry to London. Believing that the government was "drawing to a Conclusion," they represented the King as complaining of the apparent unwillingness of his Friends to come to his assistance. They warned Lowther that if immediate steps were not taken, the Friends would lose "an opportunity of the utmost Consequence."[14] Their worry was unnecessary. Chatham had no other recourse but the King's Friends. Robert Lord Nugent, whose connection with Grenville had always been amiable, became the first lord of trade. Sir Francis Dashwood, now Lord le Despencer, became a postmaster. Jenkinson went to the Admiralty Board. Hillsborough joined Le Despencer in the post office. The Duke of Ancaster, Lord Delaware, aged Sir Edward Hawke, Sir Percy Brett, and several others were called to minor offices. The first step toward the formation of the North Ministry had thus been taken. Those King's Friends now called into government in "subministerial" posts were to

14 Add. MSS 38205, ff. 108–109, November 27, 1766; printed in Jucker, *Jenkinson Papers*, 437–38. See also Add. MSS 35430, ff. 61–62, Rockingham to Charles Yorke, November 27, 1766.

form a nucleus within the government around which the new conservatism could gather.

Prospects for the new arrangement were not too bad. Grenville had become suspicious of Bedford. Their co-operation with Rockingham was highly improbable. Bute had been made easy. Affairs in Parliament, however, were to create a dangerous point of union for the Opposition, while at the same time, Chatham's ministry was to be so weakened that it could not recover.

The Seven Years' War had delivered up to the East India Company much of the great subcontinent of India, and had seen the company established in the territories of Bengal, Orissa, and Bihar. From these lands, the company derived a revenue, exclusive of its profits as a trading concern, of over a million pounds sterling a year. Abuses and cruelties to the native population, the rise of the "moguls," whose immense fortunes flooded England, a knowledge that the company would not have made its great conquests without extensive assistance from the royal army and navy—all determined Chatham to bring East India Company affairs before Parliament. An even more important consideration, however, was the pressing need of government for some new source of revenue.

Chatham, for all of George Grenville's criticism of his financial abilities, appreciated as much as did his brother-in-law the need for more government income. The nation staggered under enormous debts incurred during the war, and new revenue was necessary to effect any general American settlement. Indeed, Chatham saw in a parliamentary inquiry into the company's affairs a necessary prelude to the formation of a comprehensive American plan.

As early as October, 1766, Chatham's attention had been focused on India as a possible source of revenue. His friend Beckford had pointed out to him the worsening financial condition of Great Britain and had asserted that the only alternative to taxing America was an East Indian revenue. Beckford advised, "Unless you can procure a Revenue of a Million £ An[ually] without new Taxations, and oppressions on the people, there can [be] no salvation. . . . We must look to the East and not to the West."[15] An eastern revenue would bring relief to the suffering landowners and taxpayers of Great Britain and would finance the first expensive steps of empire building in the New World conquests. America would meanwhile be untaxed, and the distraught Colonies would enjoy a breathing spell. Then, in an atmosphere of peace and calm, the two countries could settle their differences and satisfactorily define their relationship.

Chatham's decision to inquire into the affairs of the East India Company was fully supported by the King.[16] Grafton therefore warned its representatives that steps would be taken to give the government the company's revenue.

The plan was, however, strongly opposed by Charles Townshend and General Conway, both members of the ministry. Townshend desired a ministerial negotiation with the company instead of a parliamentary inquiry. Conway, true to his Old Whig background, and believing that the principle of the sanctity of private property was involved, opposed any interference with the company whatsoever. Chatham, however, was insistent. He felt it was Parliament's duty to determine the company's right to the revenue—or lack of it. Moreover a successful ministerial-company negotiation, by giving the Crown control of a revenue independent of Parliament, would create a quite unconstitutional state of affairs.

The division in the cabinet soon became public knowledge, but Chatham was not one to brook opposition. On November 25, therefore, Beckford, at Chatham's prompting, moved in Commons to consider the East India Company's affairs. Succeeding here, he then demanded, on December 9, an account

<hr>

[15] Chatham Papers, 19, William Beckford to Chatham, October 15, 1766.
[16] Fortescue, *Correspondence of George III*, I, No. 437, the King to Grafton, December 9, 1766.

of the company's revenue and expenditures, and an inspection of its charters and treaties. On this occasion, it was feared that Townshend would bolt, but he stood with the government on the division. The central core of the Old Whigs had, however, joined with Grenville, although they were able to divide only 56 against 140. The Bedfords had found it prudent not to attend.

The Christmas recess now intervened. The company adopted tactics designed to reduce the ministry to making such demands upon it as would be a tacit admission of its right to the revenue. Offers were made to Grafton early in February, Chatham having returned to Bath to recoup his energy. Grafton, refusing to commit himself and faced with a wrangling cabinet, wrote frantically to his chief, begging him to come to London with all haste.

Chatham's tragic eclipse had begun already. His illness was becoming serious. In reply to Grafton he wrote in characteristic high style, but with a disconcerting vagueness: "As for the reviving hopes of particular Factions, I confess they but little engage my Thoughts. My whole Mind is bent on acquiring such a Revenue, as must give Strength, Ease, and Lustre to the King's Reign." East Indian affairs were "the Transcendant Object," he declared, but it had not been his absence which had ruined the "Great Transaction." Rather, it had been "an unfortunate Original Difference of Opinion among the King's Servants."[17] These words, however grandiose, were devoid of help to the distracted Grafton. To Chatham's mind, slowly descending into utter depths of melancholia, the great game had been lost. He collapsed completely in March, and the inquiry dragged on until May, when Parliament took the indecisive step of limiting the company's dividend to 10 per cent. Chatham's plan had thus been stopped in its tracks. This event was to have a profound effect upon America. Together with a

[17] Taylor and Pringle, *Chatham Correspondence*, III, 199–201, Chatham to Grafton, February 9, 1767.

reduction of the land tax, which was to be forced upon the government, it was to make a second attempt to tax the Colonies inevitable.

The ministry's treatment of the East India Company affairs is important in a second way. It served to demonstrate the rigidity of the lines dividing Grenvillites and Old Whigs. The Bedfords, fearing to offend either Chatham or Grenville, remained inconspicuous throughout the whole affair. Beckford's first motion had brought Grenville and Rockingham into an embarrassed agreement concerning East Indian matters alone. Various attempts from the fringe element in both parties to develop a full-fledged alliance proved absolutely futile. Rockingham, admitting that his party's prospect appeared forlorn when "viewed through political glasses," had already reconciled himself to a sojourn in the wilderness. Old Whigs had come to believe that "every dictate of honour and principle" called for complete isolation from Grenville. They had gained their reputation and credit with the public because they had opposed Grenville when he was minister and had reversed his measures when they had come to power. Not only did Rockingham and his friends scorn friendship with Grenville, but they insisted upon holding aloof from the Bedfords as well, for any Old Whig approach, they felt, would give the Bedfords a chance to acquire merit with either Grenville or Chatham.[18]

Impractical as his attitude may have been in the political sense, and motivated as yet by no "platform" save a vague and idealistic love of principle, Rockingham's action does demonstrate the sharply emerging lines of party development. The Old Whigs had come a long way from the Pelham "present system," when Newcastle would have made a coalition with Lucifer to maintain or achieve power. Indeed, at this point, it

[18] Wentworth-Woodhouse, Rockingham Papers, Rockingham to Dowdeswell, January 8, 1767. Extracts are printed in Albemarle, *Rockingham Memoirs*, II, 31–32.

Courtesy New York Public Library

LORD CHATHAM

is obvious that the King and his Friends had become the heirs of the "present system," while the Rockingham Whigs had begun to tread the lonely path toward a new basis of power—the people.

The Old Whigs voted with Grenville again in March in opposing the printing of the East India papers. Government triumphed by a slender majority of thirty-three, Charles Townshend having stayed away to avoid openly opposing his cabinet colleagues. Co-operation between the two Opposition groups was by chance, however, not by plan. What America had put asunder, East India affairs could not permanently unite. On the other hand a division in Chatham's cabinet had appeared, and it was never to be healed—a fact of great importance in that cabinet's effort to deal with the American problem.

After the Stamp Act, America was to know but little peace under the British Crown. With the repeal, the colonists, against the sensible advice of Old Whigs, had revelled in their "victory" over Parliament. They had thus alienated a growing mass of conservative opinion in Great Britain. Chatham had hoped that with the Stamp Act abolished, quiet would return, so that he could chart a reorganization of the empire on "Revolution principles." Whether or not he would have succeeded, however, is a matter for speculation, because he was never to have a chance to try. He was to be forced to utilize his few remaining precious months of health in an attempt to settle a temporary but violent dispute in America, a matter which only served to demonstrate the urgent need for a fundamental readjustment of the empire.

In this task, Chatham was gravely handicapped by that division of his cabinet which had arisen from the East India affair. In American matters, moreover, his ministry represented the most diverse views. He himself, Camden, and Shelburne had fought for the repeal of the Stamp Act and against the Declaratory Act. Grafton and Conway had voted for both. Townshend had been for both the Stamp Act and its repeal.

Barrington, the Master of the Ordnance Lord Granby, and Northington had opposed the repeal and supported the Declaratory Act. With such a motley crew at his back, Chatham had now to face the disobedience of the New York Assembly. The troublesome question of Parliament's right of taxation in the Colonies was about to be resurrected.

During Grenville's ministry, the Mutiny Act had been extended to America at the express request of General Gage and other military leaders there. Under Rockingham it had been amended to prevent the quartering of troops in private houses. Americans were required, however, to put them in barracks, empty houses, or barns, and to supply any troops within their colony, or passing through it, with kitchen utensils, salt, vinegar, small beer, cider or rum, candles, and firewood.

As soon as the new act was known in America, the Massachusetts Assembly characteristically entered into a long disputation with the governor. The New Jersey Assembly also proved recalcitrant, refusing Governor William Franklin's request that they insert the words of the Mutiny Act into their bill—which only partially complied with that Act of Parliament. In a strong representation to Franklin, they condemned the Mutiny Act as an internal tax and more unfair than the old Stamp Act, inasmuch as troops were kept constantly in some colonies and not at all in others.[19]

It was the assembly of New York, however, which caused the greatest concern. As a major port of disembarkation and a military center, New York would have to accommodate far more troops than any of her sister colonies. In June, 1766, her assembly refused to comply with the act. A month later, that body agreed to supply the required articles, except salt, vinegar, and beverage, but for only about eleven hundred men. Moreover, they still refused to accept the Mutiny Act, which they too deemed an internal tax.

[19] Chatham Papers, 97, William Franklin to Shelburne, December 18, 1766, copy.

News of this conduct was widely known in Britain by early August. Chatham, Shelburne, and their colleagues at once conceded the necessity of New York's obeying the act. It is thus evident that Chatham regarded that colony's action as radically different from the Stamp Act disturbances. The Stamp Act, Chatham had maintained, was an internal tax, and so beyond the power of Parliament. The Mutiny Act, he believed, was no such thing. It was designed to care for His Majesty's armed forces—always a point of special concern with Chatham. And those forces were in America to protect the Colonies. Nonetheless, it is difficult to justify Chatham's logic here. Grenville had tried to raise a revenue to help pay the cost of a military force in America. Chatham now sought the same object—albeit on a smaller scale. Was there really any difference?

Chatham met his cabinet on August 5 to consider New York's disobedience. Camden, Northington, Lord Granby, Conway, and Shelburne were present. No serious alarm was felt. They all believed that a stern admonition would suffice. It was then quickly decided that Shelburne, whose office of secretary of state for the Southern Department gave him responsibility for colonial affairs, should write to Governor Sir Henry Moore. He should state that "as It is the Indispensible Duty of His Majesty's Subjects in America to obey the Acts of the Legislature of Great Britain, His Majesty expects and requires all due obedience to the same. And It cannot be doubted that the Province of New York after the Lenity of Great Britain so recently extended to North America will not hesitate duly to carry into Execution the Act of Parliament pass'd last Session for quartering His Majesty's Troops."[20]

Much ill feeling remained on either side of the Atlantic as a legacy of the Stamp Act disturbances. In America, the repeal was already being denounced as a mere commercial expedient. More and more attention was being focused on the ominous import of the Declaratory Act. The colonies had gen-

[20] *Ibid.*, minute of cabinet.

erally evaded or only partially complied with the mother country's order to compensate riot victims. Massachusetts had
obeyed, but had added an Act of Indemnity for the participants,
in flagrant violation of the royal prerogative of mercy. There
were warnings that American "Demagogues" were "determined to bring all real power into the hands of the people."[21]
Still Shelburne did not think the situation critical. In September, he wrote to Chatham, now again at Bath to combat his
gout, calmly reporting that "at New York They have made
difficulties about quarters—but It appears to me by the Letters
that it's only the remains of the Storm, and wants a little good
humour and Firmness to finish."[22] It must have been an unexpected and unpleasant surprise to Shelburne and his colleagues
when, in spite of his stern letter, the New York Assembly
staunchly reiterated their refusal to comply. To do so would
"load them with Burthens they are incapable of supporting."[23]
Sir Jeffrey Amherst, who was in New York at the time, also
wrote to Shelburne warning that the assembly had no intention of retreating from their position: they feared an acceptance
of the act would be but a precedent for some new attempt to
tax them.

At no period in Shelburne's public life was he to appear to
less advantage. One of the most mystifying characters of the
eighteenth century, a man of undoubtedly great talent in public affairs, he was also one of the most despised men of his
time. Suffering a deep-rooted sense of inferiority about his
social and educational background, he sought psychological security in sly, hypocritical behavior. Unable to work on terms
of equality with his colleagues, he gave his complete devotion
to Chatham. Dependent upon his hero, he had only contempt
for those who did not come up to Chatham's high standards.

[21] *Ibid.*, Governor Bernard to Shelburne, December 6, 1766.
[22] *Ibid.*, 56, September 20, 1766. Quoted by R. A. Humphreys, "Lord
Shelburne and British Colonial Policy, 1766–1768," *English Historical Review*, Vol. L (April, 1935), 266.
[23] Chatham Papers, 97, address to the Governor, December 15, 1766.

Unfortunately, this included all his cabinet colleagues. When Chatham collapsed, therefore, Shelburne was set adrift upon a sea of his own fear and indecision. His confusion expressed itself partly in a cold silence toward his colleagues. He refused to believe that Chatham's illness would be of long duration. While it was Shelburne's job to find a plan for dealing with the New York Assembly, he maintained his aloofness even after it should have become obvious that Chatham was in no position to give direction to the cabinet. Shelburne's natural reticence, his reluctance to take any step without the most exhaustive researches, and his continued silence to the cabinet, resulted in his alienation from its other members. And so the initiative necessarily passed from his hands to those of one all too eager to employ it: Charles Townshend.

By the turn of the new year, 1767, Shelburne had begun to suspect that New York's disobedience would not be that simple matter he had previously imagined. In the same letter reporting the information from Amherst, he described the cabinet as in a "very weak state." Fearing that Grenville would brand New York's actions as rebellion, he begged Chatham to outline some proper mode of conduct.[24] Chatham, however, had already begun his descent into Inferno, and his answer—in tone much like that to Grafton on the East India Company— was specious, condemnatory, and quite unhelpful.

A few days later, Shelburne reported again to Chatham. He had had fresh word of New York's recalcitrance. Admitting that the act had many faults, he had directed Secretary at War Barrington to consider how it might better be adapted to colonial circumstances. Meantime, however, New York's obedience to the act as it stood was manifestly necessary. How that end might be obtained, he would not presume to suggest, for he looked to Chatham for guidance. "After a great deal

[24] *Ibid.*, 3; Taylor and Pringle, *Chatham Correspondence*, III, 182–88, February 1, 1767. Extracts are printed in Fitzmaurice, *Life of Shelburne*, I, 308–309, dated January 31, 1767.

of painful consideration on so disagreeable a Subject," he wrote, "I have nothing to submit to your Lordship, except what I took the Liberty to say to the King this morning, that I hop'd both He and Parliament would distinguish between *New York* and *America*."[25] Shelburne had conceded the necessity of parliamentary measures against that province.

Chatham's absence from London had by now nearly brought government to a standstill. Aware of the disastrous consequence of longer depriving the cabinet of his leadership, he girded himself for the grueling journey and set out on February 10. Unhappily, the effort proved too much, and he collapsed at Marlborough.

Meantime, events in America were forcing Shelburne willy-nilly toward a decision. On the sixteenth, he dispatched to Chatham a long and urgent letter. Some decisive action "as well on account of appearance here as effect there" was now so necessary that he had halted sailing of the American packet until Chatham's thoughts could be learned. Nor, although actual armed resistance in the Colonies was to be feared, had he laid the state of affairs before the cabinet, wishing first to learn his leader's wishes. He knew, however, that both the King and his own fellow ministers were "strong for enforcing," although nobody would commit himself to a definite course of action. Admitting the faults of the act, still the "infatuated conduct of the Assembly in refusing even present Obedience . . . precludes . . . all consideration of the Merits or Principles of it, by involving a far greater question." The act was then to be enforced. But how might this be done without creating a precedent which could be "turned to purposes of oppression"? The situation was in any case critical: "the public conviction goes so strongly to believing the dependence of the colonies at stake; and the opinion is so confirmed by their conduct since the repeal, which it must be expected will be both coloured and heightened by the

[25] Chatham Papers, 3; Taylor and Pringle, *Chatham Correspondence*, III, 191–93, February 6, 1767.

arts of their enemies, that, be the danger what it will, government appears called upon for some measure of vigour to support the authority of parliament and the coercive power of this country."

Under pressure from events in America and from a rapidly growing public conviction that the New York Assembly should be dealt with vigorously,[26] and fearful of the attacks of an anti-American Opposition, Shelburne had at last formulated a plan for Chatham's approval:

Governor Sir Henry Moore should be removed, partly for having transmitted the assembly's memorial against the Mutiny Act, and partly for certain irregularities in the granting of lands. As a successor, Shelburne suggested someone "of a Military Character, who might at the same time be entrusted with the Intentions of Government, and discretionary [power] to act with Force or Gentleness as circumstances might make necessary." (The idea of a military governor for a disobedient province did not, therefore, originate with Lord North.) Suggested now was Colonel John Burgoyne, or possibly General Monckton, "if his Mildness and Good Nature . . . is no objection." As for enforcing the act, Shelburne saw nothing to do but to let the governor billet in private houses if the assembly continued adamant.[27]

By this time, Chatham, quite beyond helping his troubled minister, could only reply that his shattered health prevented him entering "into any detail of things." He recommended merely that Shelburne and Grafton lay before Parliament both American and East Indian affairs.[28]

---

[26] On this point, see Chatham Papers, 3; Taylor and Pringle, *Chatham Correspondence*, III, 203, William Beckford to Chatham, February 12, 1767.

[27] Chatham Papers, 3, Shelburne to Chatham, February 16, 1767. Shelburne's plan has not been known hitherto. His letter is printed in a highly deleted form in Taylor and Pringle, *Chatham's Correspondence*, III, 206–11, the paragraphs in which the plan is outlined being omitted. Fitzmaurice, *Life of Shelburne*, I, 310–13, also deletes this very pertinent passage.

[28] Chatham Papers, 3; Taylor and Pringle, *Chatham Correspondence*, III, 214–15, Chatham to Shelburne and Grafton, February 17, 1767.

The cabinet was forced to meet without Chatham on March 12. All saw the intervention of Parliament as necessary to enforce the Mutiny Act. The provisions of an enforcing act were not, however, discussed at this time, and other matters now required all the attention of the cabinet for some weeks. There was a full cabinet on New York affairs on Friday, April 24.[29] Once again, Shelburne had an opportunity to act decisively, but as his alienation from his colleagues had meanwhile increased, he now suggested merely that the governor of New York be empowered to billet troops anywhere he saw fit—even in private houses—until New York should comply. His colleagues gave the idea no encouragement. Conway suggested a local extraordinary port duty, laid on the city of New York, which would be both a punishment and a source of revenue. This plan was vetoed, however, because it would have put a burden on British and West Indian trade to the colony. Anyway, it could have been easily subverted by smuggling.

It was Charles Townshend who now brought forward a proposal which was to serve as the basis for the measure finally adopted. He suggested a parliamentary address to the Crown asking that it assent to no laws whatever from the assembly of New York until that colony should obey the Mutiny Act. Shelburne wrote to Chatham of his dislike of the plan but weakly excused his failure to declare himself at the meeting by saying, "I did not care to dwell upon it." It was further suggested that the revenue of the colony be paid to the order of the governor. Thus royal officials could be paid no matter what retaliatory action the assembly might take. General approval greeted the proposal. However, Shelburne covered himself by writing Chatham, "I am far from satisfied with it."

Though Shelburne had refused to lay his own plan before

[29] For a report of the cabinet, see Chatham Papers, 56, minute of April 26, 1767. B. Tunstall, *William Pitt, Earl of Chatham*, 391, makes use of the letter, but misdates the meeting as April 26. Referred to by Humphreys, "Lord Shelburne and British Colonial Policy," *English Historical Review*, Vol. L (April, 1935), 257-77.

his colleagues, he did outline it for Chatham, now so ill that he could scarcely think, let alone direct affairs. The scheme was of so "reactionary" a nature that, had it been adopted, it would have given such a spur to colonial resentment and such aid to radicals that the Revolution would have been antedated by five years.

Since the Americans were generally questioning whether they were bound by Acts of Parliament, and since the cabinet had determined to enforce the Mutiny Act, Shelburne proposed that Parliament pass an act reciting the Declaratory Act—which he and Chatham had so bitterly opposed—and referring to the disobedience of New York as "an avow'd disregard of it." While pardon would be held out for past offenses, it should also be declared that from three months after the arrival of the new act, it would be high treason to refuse to obey or execute an Act of Parliament. Further, it would be misprision of treason for an American to write, preach or speak, publish or affirm that the King and Parliament did not possess power to bind the Colonies by their acts. Offenders would be tried either in America or Great Britain, and the act would be enforced by the military if necessary.[30]

It is most unlikely that the colonists, even in 1767, would have tolerated armed enforcement of the law, especially one openly based upon the detested Declaratory Act. At any rate, the plan was never presented to the cabinet. Townshend's suggestion was accepted, although it was to be embodied in an Act of Parliament, rather than in an address. On May 13, therefore, Townshend moved in the Commons for a bill forbidding the governor of New York to assent to any act of the assembly until the Mutiny Act should be obeyed. Parliament thus undertook to interfere in the internal polity of a colony. By doing so, it thought to demonstrate its authority to bind America in all cases whatsoever. Feeling against New York had begun to run high in British political circles. Nor was it improved when

[30] Chatham Papers, 56, Shelburne to Chatham, April 26, 1767.

the merchants of that colony chose to petition against the Revenue Act of 1764 and against certain other restrictions placed on their commerce by the Laws of Trade. The Old Whigs had established two free ports, in Jamaica and Dominica, but the New York merchants, some 240 in number, now asked for a whole system of free ports in America and the West Indies, warning that otherwise they would have to turn to manufacturing. Shelburne sharply rejected the petition and was sustained by Chatham, who wrote of the New Yorkers, "They are doing the work of their worst enemies themselves."[31] Both men thus stand revealed as good mercantilists, as good as Grenville or Rockingham. They had no intention of loosening the commercial bonds of the empire.

The disobedience of the Mutiny Act so soon after repeal of the Stamp Act, the bad grace with which riot victims had been compensated, the Bill of Indemnity passed in Massachusetts, and now this ill-timed petition "soured the minds of people here in general." Lord George Sackville—who had recently dropped his notorious surname and would hereafter be known as Lord George Germain—reported his own opinion that "the Colonys are growing worse and worse." Even men formerly inclined to defend, or at least to palliate, the American position were becoming critical. The Rockinghams, William Beckford, and even Lord Camden indicated publicly their growing dissatisfaction with the colonial attitude. Rumors circulated that Chatham himself "has changed his ideas about America, and means to act with vigour."[32] Such reports served to underline the rapidly growing opinion that the previous year's concession to America was unappreciated and that future attempts to placate her would be as futile.

In truth, however, save for that respect his name commanded, Chatham had ceased to exist as a political force. His

[31] *Ibid.*, 3, Shelburne to Chatham, February 1, 1767, and Chatham's answer, February 3, 1767; *Chatham Correspondence*, III, 182–90.
[32] RHMCR. *Stopford-Sackville Papers*, I, 119–20.

prolonged absence had reduced the cabinet to chaos. Grafton was too weak and too frightened of making his own decisions to exercise effective leadership. Shelburne had isolated himself from his colleagues. Conway was torn between his love of office and his obligation to his Old Whig friends. Camden was ineffectual without Chatham's leadership. Only Northington showed any degree of steadiness. And thus Charles Townshend, brilliant and erratic, found no real opposition from his colleagues.

Townshend had earlier been denied a place in the cabinet by Chatham himself. But with the great man absent, he had forced himself into its innermost council, and there was none to say him nay. Several points rankled in his breast. He had been forced to give up the lucrative paymastership and take the burdensome office of chancellor of the exchequer. He had been denied the lead of Commons and a seat in the cabinet. Furthermore, he soon found himself in fundamental disagreement with Chatham's East India Company policy. Of an irrepressible, spontaneous, and at times incorrigible nature, the youthful Townshend found in Chatham's absence from a "languid" ministry an occasion and an inspiration.

The opening debates of the first meeting of Parliament in January, 1767, saw him at his most irresponsible. His actions betrayed a complete absence of any concept of joint cabinet responsibility. For such a political idea—North was to enunciate it toward the end of his ministry—a necessary prerequisite would be well developed parties which could pledge their members to definite principles. Chatham's ministry was deliberately the antithesis of such an arrangement.

When the estimates for the military establishment in America were presented, the likely cost was found to be about £400,000, roughly equivalent to a shilling of the land tax. Grenville, insisting that the estimates be reduced by half, proposed that the remainder be borne by the Colonies and that a revenue be raised upon them for that purpose. Like a schoolboy on a lark, Townshend now rose declaring he would "assert his own opinions." Rejecting Grenville's suggestion, he nonetheless spoke warmly for America's bearing a part of the expense. Commending the Stamp Act ("only the heats which prevailed made it an improper time to press it"), he condemned "every word" of the doctrine of internal-external taxation. An astonished and delighted House then heard him pledge himself to find an American revenue nearly sufficient to cover all expenses there. "What he means," exclaimed Shelburne, "I do not conceive."[33]

Although Grenville's motion was defeated, Townshend's speech had reopened the whole question of taxing America. His own craving for attention and his desire to divert the House from its East India business now combined with the Members' irritation against the Colonies, their wish to assert the supremacy of Parliament once and for all, and with the nation's need for more revenue to make a new effort in this direction inevitable.

To oppose Townshend in his wild impetuosity should have been Shelburne's task. The Colonies were under Shelburne's care. He knew that Townshend had deliberately challenged the fundamental tenets of Chatham's policy and his own towards colonial taxation. However alone in the cabinet and distrusted by his colleagues, he cannot wholly be excused for the mildness and fatalism wherewith he accepted Townshend's action. Shelburne had been working for some time, methodically collecting information from every source, on his own plan for an imperial administration for the west. At this crucial time, when Townshend raised once more the fatal question of parliamentary right, Shelburne should have realized that the future of all British North America had been put to hazard. Perhaps he believed that Townshend's talk was merely talk,

---

[33] For an account of the debate, see RHMCR. *Lothian Papers*, 274–75, Grenville to Buckinghamshire, January 27, 1767; also Chatham Papers, 83, Shelburne's minutes.

but it was nonetheless incumbent upon him to act. Instead, he deliberately confined himself to his researches, never seriously attempting to combat Townshend's avowed intent which, if carried out, would make such painstaking efforts utterly futile.

An even more ominous situation now began to develop: one which would force Townshend to redeem his pledge of an American revenue. By mid-February, the ministry perceived they were to be faced with a combined Opposition attempt to reduce the land tax. The King testily ascribed this design to Grenville's "Hobby Horse, the reduction of expences," and to his "unbounded attachment to his own opinions and a desire of thwarting those of others." George III saw the Opposition's intent as mere false economy, writing somewhat naively to Conway that "the great acquisitions made by the Successful War must necessarily give rise to an encrease of expence in the Peace Establishment, which seems by them [the Opposition] unattended to."[34] Grenville was "attending to" it all too well.

Both King and ministry were as yet oblivious of their danger. Chatham's brother-in-law James Grenville sent urgently to the first minister—lying ill at Marlborough—warning that a move for reduction was imminent. The Opposition, he said, hard hit by the land tax, would be supported by the country members "in good number on the plea of the repeal of the Stamp Act."[35] It was not, however, until the very eve of the vote that a worried Grafton reported to his King the growing opposition to the ministry's four-shilling land tax. George III was bitter against Grenville. His conduct, the King wrote, was "as abundant in absurditys as in the affair of the Stamp Act; for there he first deprived the Americans by restraining their Trade, from the means of acquiring Wealth, and Taxed them;

[34] Fortescue, *Correspondence of George* III, I, No. 468, the King to General Conway, February 18, 1767. See also L. B. Namier, *Additions and Corrections to Sir John Fortescue's Edition of the Correspondence of George III*, 69.

[35] Chatham Papers, 35, James Grenville to Lady Chatham, February 23, 1767.

now he objects to the Public's availing itself of the only adequate means of restoring its Finances, I mean the taking such part that shall be judged expedient, out of the Territorial Revenues now received contrary to their Charter by the [East India] Company, and at the same time moves for a diminution of the Land Tax."[36]

His august wrath was, however, in part, misdirected. Rumors early in February that Grenville intended to move a reduction of the land tax had brought the Old Whigs together in party conclave. Grudging one iota of popularity to Grenville, they had decided to forestall him by undertaking the motion themselves. Altogether, it was a foolish decision. Sir George Savile, always full of common sense and good counsel, had warned them to think gravely on a plan which would cut the national income by £450,000. This would simply have to be made up from some source.[37] The Old Whigs themselves had helped to rule out the possibility of an East Indian revenue. What source remained—but America?

The debate began on February 25. From the first, Old Whigs stood shoulder to shoulder with Grenville, the Bedfords, and the country gentlemen. Townshend opened by proposing the land tax at four shillings, pledging that should he still be in office next year, he would move its reduction to three shillings. Old Whig Dowdeswell countered by moving an amendment immediately reducing the tax to the lower figure. He was seconded by Sir Edmund Isham, a country gentleman and Member for Northamptonshire. The Old Tory Sir Roger Newdigate, Member for Oxford University, declared for the amendment. A Grenville supporter, affirming the connection between this motion and Townshend's pledge of an American revenue, reminded him of his promise and by it justified the tax reduction.

[36] Fortescue, *Correspondence of George III*, I, No. 471, the King to Grafton, February 24, 1767.

[37] Albemarle, *Rockingham Memoirs*, II, 37–39, Savile to Charles Yorke, February 11, 1767.

Still, the administration did not believe itself in danger. And when the vote came, on February 27, their defeat by 188 to 206 surprised all parties. The country gentlemen had tipped the scales for the Opposition.

Although Sir George Savile thought the defeat of the ministry due solely to an approaching election and a desire to curry favor with landowning electors, yet it was a major catastrophe for the ministry—and for America. Coming as it did before they had got a revenue from the East India Company—Chatham's cherished plan for relieving his country's finances—the land tax reduction made imperative Townshend's early redemption of his pledge. Indeed, funds were so short that Grafton had to ask Chatham, quite against the usual practice, to pay some ninety thousand pounds which the first minister had held unaudited since his paymastership of the forces.

Chatham, shocked by news of the tax reduction, drove himself on to London, arriving on March 2, but once there was too ill to deal with either domestic or American matters. There was an abortive attempt to oust the captious Townshend by offering the exchequer to Lord North, but that noble lord refused because of the unclear political situation. Chatham, his strength and mind now failing rapidly, withdrew to his house on Hampstead Heath. From this time onward, he was no longer the effective head of an administration, but his colleagues and his King unfortunately refused to accept this fact for many months.

As chancellor of the exchequer, Townshend was directly faced with the nation's financial problem, a problem created by the delay in gaining a revenue from the East India Company and the unexpected reduction of the land tax. Nor was he long in bringing matters to a crisis. At the cabinet meeting on March 12, still smarting from the attempt to replace him, Townshend declared that if the estimates for the American extraordinaries were not reduced, he would resign. Well he knew that such action would overturn the ministry. To achieve the reductions, he could afford an ultimatum. British troops in America must be withdrawn from the frontier toward the larger cities. New port taxes must be laid upon America for revenue. Thus, to offset the decrease in national income and to pay even the reduced cost of the ten thousand troops in America, the colonists had to be taxed and the last remnant of Grenville's imperial scheme abandoned. Western forts, Indian trade, the disposition of troops, "in short the whole arrangement," must be reconsidered so as to cut expenses. American duties would do the rest. In effect, then, Townshend urged a western policy based on the principles set forth in Barrington's report of May, 1766.[38]

Plagued with an apparently insoluble domestic financial problem, Townshend was determined to force an American settlement upon the hesitating government and a slow-moving secretary of state. Shelburne, badgered by an insistent Townshend at home and beseiged with urgent calls for direction from royal officials in the Colonies, was at last obliged to act.

On March 30, therefore, he read a paper to the cabinet. Making no effort to combat Townshend's avowed intent to derive a revenue from America, he fixed his efforts on saving the west to the empire. He advised caution and begged his colleagues to be patient while he gathered the data whereon to base a western plan. The cost of his eventual plan, he thought, might be borne by a revenue from the quitrents and land-grant fees, augmented by a system of annual requisitions. Despite the cabinet's personal hostility towards him, Shelburne won his point, and his report was accepted.

Shelburne's victory, however, was a shadowy one; Townshend's the substantial one. Shelburne had asked for time to evolve his policy. There was no time. Time had run out at the reduction of the land tax. Townshend, on the other hand,

---

[38] Chatham Papers, 3; Taylor and Pringle, *Chatham Correspondence*, III, 231–32, Grafton to Chatham, March 13, 1767, 232–33, Shelburne to Chatham, March 13, 1767.

had presented a feasible, positive policy ready for immediate execution. Furthermore, it coincided with a general opinion among government and Opposition alike that "something must be done in support of the authority of the Mother Country." Townshend's taxes would produce a revenue, but more than that, they would be an exercise of British sovereignty—which most home politicians thought long overdue. When Townshend opened his budget on April 15, therefore, he "adopted most of Mr. Grenville's ideas, and spoke as freely of Administration as if he had not been in office"[39] To such an end had come Chatham's campaign against faction.

A full cabinet on American affairs, chiefly concerned with New York, was held on April 24. Shelburne, secure on the laurels of what he thought a long-range victory, made no effort to combat Townshend's American tax proposals or even to bring him to an explanation of them. The Chancellor of the Exchequer accordingly redeemed his promise on May 13, the day he moved for the bill suspending the New York Assembly. By his second and third bills, he proposed to establish a Board of Commissioners of the Customs in America, better to execute the Laws of Trade and to receive the revenue from the new duties, about forty thousand pounds annually. To avoid an American objection to internal taxes, these were to be port duties on tea, glass, paper, printer's colors, and red and white lead. To make smuggling unprofitable, the duty on tea was to be reduced from one shilling to three pence per pound. Coffee and cocoa imported from Great Britain were to be tax-free, but the drawback on china earthenware exported to America was to be withdrawn. The act would further empower the Superior Court in each province to grant general writs of assistance. These would allow officers of the customs to enter any house or shop by daylight to search for prohibited or smuggled goods. In his speech, Townshend scouted Shelburne's suggested use of

[39] RHMCR. *Stopford-Sackville Papers*, I, 121–23, letters of Lord George Germain.

a requistion system and affirmed that the time had come to assert British sovereignty by an Act of Parliament.

Townshend's plan, however, differed radically from Grenville's earlier one. The Stamp Act revenues were to have been applied solely to imperial defense. Now, Townshend proposed to create an American civil list whence governors, judges, and other royal officials would be paid. Such a provision cut violently across the lines of political evolution in America, where the power of the purse was as well understood and as jealously guarded by colonial assemblies as in the mother country by Parliament. The controversy between the Colonies and Great Britain was therefore to move to the highest constitutional level, even as Franklin had predicted in his testimony to the Commons during the Stamp Act crisis.

Opposition to Townshend's plan being weak and desultory, the resolutions were agreed to and reported on the 15th. At one stroke, then, America was taxed, an American Board of Customs set up, and the assembly of New York suspended—all this under a ministry which bore the name of one who had stood foremost in denying Parliament's right to tax the Colonies for revenue.

Townshend had sponsored the new taxation of America, but in doing so he had reflected the majority of opinion in Great Britain. Faced with an intolerable situation as chancellor of the exchequer, he simply put into legal form a deep-seated belief that Great Britain was entitled to financial help from her colonies. A minister more forceful than Shelburne might, by resolutely opposing his proposals, have driven Townshend from office. But at a moment when decisive action might have saved the first British Empire, he showed himself hesitant to stand forward. He failed to support those principles which he and his stricken chief had so long maintained. Here then he committed a cardinal error of statescraft and politics: he allowed the initiative to pass from his hands.

Grenville had aimed at creating an imperial system, partly

supported by funds from America. No similar grand motive influenced Townshend. He was indifferent to imperial plans, although his actions had the deepest imperial ramifications. The end product was as much a negation of Grenville's concept of empire as the Old Whig ministry had been. Grenville had seen the vision of an orderly and steadily expanding commonwealth; Townshend saw only an imperial budget. This much, however, Grenville, Townshend, and nearly all parliamentarians had in common: they believed America a proper object of imperial taxation and Parliament possessed of competent authority to tax her.[40]

[40] Franklin expressed the opinion that the anti-American sentiment in Britain was so great that it did not matter if Townshend was in or out of office. In all fairness to the Chancellor of the Exchequer, it must be remembered that he wished to allow colonial ships to sail directly from Spain and Portugal to the Colonies with wine, fruit, and oil. He was forced to drop this concession in the face of great opposition from British merchants. See Sparks, *Franklin's Works*, VII, 338–44.

CHAPTER FOUR

THE FALL OF THE CHATHAM SYSTEM

C HATHAM was gone, and without his leadership his government seemed on the verge of a breakup. Shelburne, considered a "secret enemy" by his colleagues, remained in office solely for Chatham's sake. Conway, under great pressure from his Old Whig friends, declared he would resign at the end of the session. Charles Townshend was flirting with the Old Whigs, and Northington announced that health obliged his retirement. Camden was helpless and ineffectual without his chief's support; and Grafton himself made it known that he would follow Conway out of the government.

The situation in Parliament was equally discouraging. On a division in the House of Lords in April, the government had been saved by a majority of only three. Evidently the Opposition was achieving a formidable measure of union.

The repeated appeals of the King and Grafton to the prostrate Chatham, urging him to chalk out a new ministerial arrangement, met with reiterated declarations of his incapacity to do so. Finally, on May 31, Grafton was allowed to see Chatham for a short time. He obtained however only a suggestion that he treat with the Bedfords or the Rockinghams, preferably the former. Grafton was, moreover, profoundly shocked at Chatham's condition; the more so as he realized that now his titular leadership of the ministry had become a real one. It is to the young Duke's credit that he rose to the challenge.

The King clung pathetically to a belief that if only Chatham would revive, all would go well. He was willing to gamble, as was the younger Pitt at a later date, on the chance of a sick man's recovery. Grafton knew all too well, however, that an accession of strength or, at least, the dispelling of the threat of a united Opposition was imperative. As soon, therefore, as the session ended, on July 2, Grafton, following the King's preference, not Chatham's, approached Rockingham about a coalition. The ensuing negotiations furnish an opportunity to appraise both the importance of the American problem as an issue in domestic politics and the development of lines of party division.

The three Whig "splinter groups" in Opposition, the Old Whigs, the Bedford group, and the Grenville-Temple supporters, possessed in reality only one common trait which might form a basis for union. This was a mistaken belief that the King's Friends belonged to Bute and that Bute himself was a secret adviser to the King. Bedford had shown a disposition to unite with the Rockinghams in order to extirpate Bute's supposed influence, that is, to pull down the ministry. Grenville, too, had expressed his desire to join in such an attack. And Newcastle was eager for a conjunction on this basis, for he was astute enough to see that an anti-Bute "platform" was the only foundation on which a united Opposition could stand.[1] Here then was a force working for Whig union and against those which were widening party divisions. How strong was the force? And what had happened to the American issue?

First, the inner council of the Old Whig party was split. The old corps, led by Newcastle, Albemarle, and Portland, looked nostalgically to the past when a united Whig party had held undisputed sway. They strongly desired an alliance with Bedford, and with Grenville, too, should that be possible. Control of the group had passed from their hands, however, and

[1] Wentworth-Woodhouse, Rockingham Papers, Newcastle to Rockingham, July 8, 1767.

now rested with the "boys," led by Rockingham, Burke, and Dowdeswell. Rockingham was not sanguine for an alliance built on so negative a ground as mere hatred of Bute. Indeed, he declared himself unwilling to treat the King's Friends harshly, and in fact he coveted their support should he come again to power. Underlying this reluctance to draw nearer to the other Opposition groups, however, was a consideration which the old corps could not be expected to understand. The "boys" feared that a Bedford alliance would draw them closer to Grenville whom they detested.[2] From the outset, then, this tendency toward union was not as strong as it looked.

Still, when Grafton approached Rockingham in July, the Marquis insisted that the Bedfords be included in the negotiations. Bedford, in turn, would not move without Temple and Grenville. The conversations which followed were two-sided, Rockingham holding talks with Grafton and the King on the one hand, and with Bedford, who was acting for Temple and Grenville, on the other.

On July 20, Bedford, Weymouth, and Rigby met Rockingham, Newcastle, and other Old Whig leaders at Newcastle House. Bedford immediately threw a bombshell by informing the Old Whigs that Grenville and Temple, besides certain other vague demands, required a declaration of intent "to assert and establish the rights of Great Britain over her colonies." Rockingham flew into a rage, denying that he and his friends had ever given ground for a suspicion that they intended giving up British sovereignty over the settlements. The Grenville demand he denounced as a trap for his own party and as a proof of the bad faith of theirs. The meeting would have ended then and there had not Bedford urged that the declaration be taken as a mere formula. Despite Rigby's warning that the Grenvilles would be satisfied with nothing but the words as

---

[2] Add. MSS 35430, ff. 834, Rockingham to Charles Yorke, July 18, 1767; Wentworth-Woodhouse, Rockingham Papers, William Dowdeswell to Rockingham, July 23 and 24, 1767.

they stood, a compromise was eventually reached, whereby the phrase "maintain and support" was substituted for "assert and establish."

So it was not the American issue that ruined the Rockingham-Bedford negotiations. Rather it was an irreconcilable difference over General Conway. Despite this person's weak and fickle conduct—he had not resigned from Chatham's ministry with his friends—Rockingham insisted that in any new arrangement he have the lead of the House of Commons. The Bedfords demanded his exclusion, and the meetings then broke up. On July 23, therefore, Rockingham told the King he was unable to form a new administration.[3]

Newcastle and the old corps were thrown into despair, and the Duke wrote bitterly to Rockingham of the latter's misplaced loyalty. While Newcastle and Albemarle fervently advised him "for God's Sake my dear Lord don't loose sight of the D. of Bedford," the "boys," particularly Burke, were congratulating him on his escape from the alliance and for refusing to enter office but "in corps."[4] America had not kept Rockingham apart from Bedford. Even old Newcastle saw that "as to the Declaration proposed by Mr. Grenville, relating to America, It was so whittled down by the Duke of Bedford, That It could not *finally* have created any Difficulty."[5] Rather, it was Rockingham's insistence—quixotic to the old corps—upon viewing his party as founded upon principle and a community of interest which took precedence over the love of office.

The American issue had, however, kept the Old Whigs irreconcilably apart from Grenville and Temple. Early in the negotiations, Grenville had informed Rigby that America was

[3] Russell, *The Bedford Correspondence*, III, 82–87.

[4] Wentworth-Woodhouse, Rockingham Papers, Newcastle to Rockingham, July 22, 1767, Albemarle to Rockingham, July 22, 1767; C. Williams, Earl Fitzwilliam, and Sir R. Bourke (eds.), *Burke Correspondence*, I, 132–37.

[5] Wentworth-Woodhouse, Rockingham Papers, Newcastle to Rockingham, July 22, 1767.

the great point. To other friends, he reiterated his intent never to retreat from his demand that Britain assert and establish her sovereignty over the Colonies.[6] Nor was he deceived when the negotiations failed. He knew well that Bedford and Rockingham had reached agreement about America, and that, consequently, his own connection with Bedford was weak indeed.

In September, Charles Townshend died, and was succeeded at the exchequer by the former paymaster Lord North. The whole political situation again became fluid, most of the Opposition expecting a renewal of offers from Grafton. Again, Newcastle and Albemarle preached to Rockingham the gospel of a Bedford alliance and the necessity for pulling down the *"Bute* Administration."[7] But Rockingham had taken his stand in July. Once more, now, he tried to explain himself to the old corps. He feared a Bedford alliance because the Old Whigs might thereby be pulled into alignment with Grenville and Temple, whose acid account of the July negotiations, now published, had fanned his hatred to new heights. His party, Rockingham stated, was eternally committed against joining a ministry in which Grenville might have a major part. The Old Whigs had won their honor and credit with the public by overturning Grenville's American plan. To admit him now as an ally would be the ruin of them, and a union with Bedford might well bring him in.[8] Rockingham's conception of "party" was thus taking on a surprisingly modern tone. While the old corps poured out a stream of advice, threats, and entreaties, he was writing to Dowdeswell of Newcastle's "hurries and Impatience and want of Steadiness to adhere strictly to . . . one of the Fundamental Principles on which we have acted."[9] Indeed, in the

---

[6] Smith, *The Grenville Papers*, IV, 48–52, Grenville to Suffolk, July 14, 1767; RHMCR, *Lothian Papers*, 277–78, Grenville to Buckinghamshire.

[7] Wentworth-Woodhouse, Rockingham Papers, Newcastle to Rockingham, September 11, 1767.

[8] *Ibid.*, Rockingham to Portland, September 15, 1767; Albemarle, *Rockingham Memoirs*, II, 57–59.

[9] Wentworth-Woodhouse, Rockingham Papers, September 14, 1767.

consolidation of the right wing of politics, the Old Whigs were in danger of being pulled to pieces. But by rejecting Newcastle's advice and by adopting a standstill policy, Rockingham, though he doomed his party to tedious years out of office, saved it from dissolution. The failure of the negotiations in July and September, 1767, indicated that a reunion of the Old Whig party was a dream that was past. Henceforward, the modern party system was to develop without hindrance from a half-century-old myth.

For the Bedfords, the American issue, due to Grenville's insistence upon "the asserting and establishing the lawful authority of the King and Parliament of Great Britain over every part of our dominions in every part of the world,"[10] meant that a united Opposition was impossible. Motivated by no principle but love of office, they now turned their thoughts to a possible coalition with the Grafton Ministry. On December 11, Grafton learned from Weymouth that the Bedfords had "the greatest Desire . . . to make no Difficulties," and that their only condition for an alliance was the removal of Shelburne. Grafton eagerly began negotiations upon the basis of this offer.[11]

The point concerning Shelburne—now cordially disliked and distrusted by his colleagues—was, however, a rather delicate matter. He was Chatham's man. So how was his retreat to be achieved without offense to Chatham? The Earl might recover at some future date and demand a reckoning. With these considerations in mind, Grafton agreed to a shameful Bedfordite proposal that Shelburne's office, that of secretary of state for the Southern Department, be divided and that a new secretaryship of state for the Colonies be created. Such a humiliation, it was agreed, would force Shelburne to resign. The King too, loathing the Secretary, heartily concurred in the proposal.

[10] Russell, *The Bedford Correspondence*, III, 396–99, Grenville to Bedford, November 6, 1767.

[11] Fortescue, *Correspondence of George III*, I, No. 567, Grafton to the King, December 11, 1767.

The utility of a third secretary of state for the colonies had long been acknowledged. Both Rockingham and Chatham had thought seriously of such an arrangement. Grafton's decision now to create such an office was, however, one of pure political expediency and had nothing to do with improving the administration of the Colonies. It therefore came as a great disappointment to the King, Grafton, and the Bedfords when Shelburne, from his attachment to Chatham, reluctantly agreed to the division. Moreover, he chose to remain southern secretary, although Grafton, perhaps fearful of the Bedfords' American views, urged him to take the new office.

The Bedfords, however, would not allow the frustration of their plan to ruin so promising an opportunity for office. With the entire cabinet against him, Shelburne would scarcely be an important factor. The alliance was accordingly concluded. Observers then were convinced that American affairs had played a large part in the political "jobbing" which had produced it.[12] However, there is no evidence that any comprehensive American policy was insisted upon by either party, and the question was more likely set aside and left to the dictate of future events.

The consolidation in office of the conservative element in British politics had begun with Chatham's use of the King's Friends to replace the Rockinghams. A second great step in the process was the Bedford accession. In the coincident cabinet shuffle, Conway resigned his position as secretary of state for the Northern Department, but, retaining a seat in the cabinet, remained on friendly terms with the government. Bedfordites Weymouth and Gower became secretary of state and president of the Council respectively, old Northington retiring from the latter post. Sandwich was made a postmaster, and Rigby vice treasurer of Ireland with a promise of the paymaster's

---

[12] Smith, *Grenville Papers*, IV, 197–207, Whately to Grenville, December 25, 1767; 205, Lord Trevor to Grenville, December 29, 1767; 249–53, Lord Lyttelton to Temple, January 1, 1768.

office. King's Friend Hillsborough took the new office of secretary of state for the colonies. The original elements of Chatham's "mosaic," Camden, Shelburne, Grafton, Granby, and Hawke, still held a nominal majority in the cabinet, but unity and determination were on the side of the new members.

How would the incoming ministry handle the American issue? Franklin was pessimistic. Conway and Shelburne, whom he accounted friends to the Colonies, were no longer in a position to shield them from those who might counsel stern measures. This much was evident, however: some action about the Colonies was pressingly necessary. In December, it was known that America had not accepted the Townshend taxes quietly. Reports that Boston had adopted a nonimportation agreement put the newspapers "in full cry against America" and produced "a prodigious clamour."[13]

From the collapse of Chatham to the Bedfordite accession, Grafton and his government had seemed inert. Secretary at War Barrington had written his kinsman Bernard of the disgraceful confusion among the ministers. They feared, it seemed, to take any steps about America, lest Chatham, when he did emerge, would disapprove.[14] It was during these months, however, that Shelburne was working up a comprehensive policy for the American west. His slow and painful methods, his great personal unpopularity, and the division of his office were yet to render his efforts nugatory.

As soon as Shelburne had taken office, his mind had turned to the western problem, and he had begun to collect his information. In autumn, 1766, he had written to General Gage, the commander-in-chief in America, revealing the direction his plan was taking: "The forming an American fund to support the exigencies of government in the same manner as is done in Ireland, is what is so highly reasonable that it must take

[13] Sparks, *Franklin's Works*, VII, 371–73, Franklin to William Franklin, December 19, 1767.

[14] Channing and Coolidge, *Barrington-Bernard Correspondence*, 127–28, July 8, 1767.

place sooner or later." Shelburne's colonial ideas were none the less in harmony with Chatham's in that he felt Parliament had unlimited power within the Colonies to secure the British trade monopoly but none to levy taxes there for revenue. Where then did he propose to find that "American fund" which Grenville had sought to raise by a Stamp Act and Townshend by his port duties? Part of it would come from a diligent collection of the quitrents on both past and future land grants. In a paper read to the cabinet on March 30, however, he revealed that the fund would rest "chiefly on requisitions from the different provinces to be granted annually by their assemblies according to their respective abilities."[15]

This was the interim report which Shelburne had read to the cabinet during those weeks when Townshend was ramming through his taxes. In the intervening months, Shelburne had continued his work. It was thus not until September, 1767, that his final report was ready. In it, his basic hypotheses were that it was impossible to prevent westward expansion in North America and that to allow it would be to postpone colonial manufacturing. Further, the Colonies should be permitted to regulate Indian affairs because they were familiar with the problem. The imperial Indian establishment could then be abolished.

Two new colonies were to be formed, one at Detroit and the other in the Illinois country. Eight forts, manned by British troops, were to be maintained in the area. Thus betraying the influence of Franklin and Richard Jackson, the plan also stated that a fixed boundary line and a clarification of Indian rights were urgently necessary.

This plan was never implemented, although the Privy Council accepted the proposed boundary line, somewhat to the west of the older Proclamation Line, in January, 1768. Shel-

---

[15] Fitzmaurice, *Life of Shelburne*, 305–307, Shelburne to Gage, November 14, 1766; extracts of this letter and of Shelburne's paper of March 30, 1767, are printed in Alvord, *Mississippi Valley*, I, 282–83, 334.

burne was soon to lose control of American affairs; and Hillsborough, his successor, was to reject totally his proposal for a rapid settlement of the west. In any event, one doubts that the plan would have succeeded had it been adopted. It went quite against the grain of eighteenth-century British imperialism, and it was based financially on quitrents and requisitions which probably could not have been collected. A revival of the question of right would have followed.

Shelburne's plan held, however, the seeds of a concept of empire radically different from that then prevailing. It is not too much to say that the plan is one of Shelburne's best claims to greatness as a statesman. For the first time since Grenville, a scheme had been presented which envisaged the creation of a new imperial system and full utilization of the North American conquests. Grenville would have had a centralized empire minutely administered from Whitehall. His plan was in full accord with the eighteenth-century persuasion that a widespread empire had to have somewhere a center of supreme power. Shelburne, however, had now brought forward the idea of a decentralized empire. Had it been implemented, it would have spared Britain decades of bitter political controversy and the alienation of her colonial peoples everywhere. It would have been a tremendous step towards the modern Commonwealth of Nations. Shelburne believed that if the Colonies were given management of their own internal affairs, and if the westward movement should be allowed to develop naturally, colonial affection for the mother country would secure perpetual empire. His time, however, had run out. He was replaced by Hillsborough, and the uneasy calm of autumn gave way to mounting storms on either shore.

The new Board of Commissioners of the Customs appointed under Townshend's Act had held their first meeting in Boston on November 18, 1767. No overt indignity had been offered them, but the townspeople had left no doubt about their opinion of the proceedings. The board had immediately undertaken a reorganization of the entire customs service. New officers were added and a better system of accounting adopted. Further, a network of revenue cutters and royal naval vessels was established. The molasses tax had been reduced to a penny. This, with the increased efficiency of the new organization, cut illicit trade until it became negligible. For the first time, the entire system of trade and navigation laws, evolving since the reign of Charles II, was put into efficient operation. American merchants now suddenly found themselves bound and checked on every side. Some drastic countermeasure was manifestly necessary if American trade were to escape from strangulation.[16] A great majority of American merchants therefore threw themselves wholeheartedly into the nonimportation agreements. It was soon obvious, too, that the revolutionary apparatus developed during the Stamp Act crisis was very much alive. Mob violence and intimidation again became the order of the day in Boston. Bernard was so frightened that he refused to ask for troops which the commissioners desired, so that he might be able to swear that he had never called for them. Nevertheless, his letters to England were but thinly disguised appeals to the government to take the initiative and to send the troops anyway.[17]

Obviously, the situation was rapidly worsening. In January, 1768, Bernard forwarded to Barrington a copy of the "Letters of a Pennsylvania Farmer," written anonymously by John Dickinson. The American readily admitted the right of Parliament to regulate trade. America was "as much dependent on

---

[16] See Channing, *History of the United States*, III, 87 ff. The new system was a success in the immediate sense. In contrast to the small amounts collected before the Townshend Acts, thirty thousand pounds was collected annually between 1768 and 1774, at a cost of only thirteen thousand pounds a year. Channing states, however, "The hardships of the regulations put an end to existing modes of trade in many cases and the profits in foreign commerce dwindled to so low a figure that importers were far readier to sign non-importation agreements in 1769 than they had been in 1766." (p. 90.)

[17] Channing and Coolidge, *Barrington-Bernard Correspondence*, 141–45. See also 147–50, Bernard to Barrington, March 4, 1768.

Great Britain as a perfectly free people can be on another." The important point, however, was the disappearance of the confusion concerning internal and external taxes. Parliament, the Farmer declared, had no right to levy any taxes for revenue.[18] In British eyes, Dickinson's position was illogical and contradictory, besides being highly disrespectful to Parliament, but it cannot be doubted that Dickinson had presented the current American view.

In February, Bernard reported that the radicals in the assembly had gained control of it. They had then proceeded to expunge a previous adverse vote from their journal and had carried a resolution calling for petitions to the home government and a circular letter to the assemblies of the other North American Colonies. In such a letter, they would ask for cooperation and consultation in forming a program of "legal" resistance to the Townshend Acts. At the beginning of March, the distressed Governor could write only that the nonimportation agreements were gaining new supporters daily, and that it had been generally resolved in his province that the new duties would be disregarded until repealed.

Nor could Grafton take much comfort from the news, which arrived in April, that the New York Assembly had "complied" with the Mutiny Act. That body had indeed voted a sum of money to the Crown, but, bent upon minimum retreat, had refused to specify its use or otherwise acknowledge the act. This was at best a compromise which, in view of the increasingly violent disturbances at Boston, had barely the appearance of a government victory.

At that place, the commissioners had taken the step which Bernard had feared to take himself. Informing the home government that the revenue laws could not be enforced without assistance and that Boston was on the point of rising against them, they had sent to Commodore Hood at Halifax for warships. Hood had replied by sending them the fifty-gun "Rom-

[18] S. E. Morison, *Sources and Documents*, 34–54.

ney," but the Commissioners considered their situation so serious that they requested him to send an additional force.[19] This sense of danger was by no means confined to the commissioners. Indeed, all officers of the Crown and friends of government were in "a distressed State," and Bernard was in a fever to resign his burdensome office. Obviously, concerted and decisive measures were necessary if the cause of royal government were to be saved in Massachusetts, and probably in the other colonies as well. But Grafton did not act.

Affairs of empire had to await the result of a domestic political upheaval. On March 11, Parliament was dissolved, and a general election followed. It worked no radical change in the composition of the House, although 164 of its Members were elected for the first time, one of whom was Charles James Fox. The election was observed by Benjamin Franklin, and while it was in the main an average one, it served to point up his consciousness of American virtue and English corruption. In the critical days to come, a conviction in the Colonies that Old England, venal and degenerate, was unfit to rule an empire went far to render compromise impossible.

The election of 1768 was distinguished by the return from exile of that outlawed scapegrace John Wilkes. Having unsuccessfully sought pardon from both the Rockingham and Chatham Ministries, Wilkes now took the bull by the horns. He appeared suddenly in London, petitioned the King for pardon, and announced himself candidate for the city of London. Failing of that seat, he promptly stood for the radical county of Middlesex which on March 28 returned him at the head of the poll. Grafton's inclination was to pardon Wilkes and let him take his seat, so that his own character might sink him to a deserved obscurity. The King, however, remembering the *North Briton*, No. 45, vetoed such a solution. George III's obstinacy was to lead the government and Parliament into a

[19] Add. MSS 38340, ff. 309–10, memorial of the commissioners to the Lords of the Treasury, July 11, 1768.

Portraits courtesy New York Public Library

EARL OF SHELBURNE   DUKE OF GRAFTON

headlong collision with the radical element and to make them ridiculous in the eyes of the country.

Wilkes' imprisonment for seditious libel and blasphemy, and the ministry's refusal to release him—so that he might take his seat in the new Parliament on May 10—led directly to a nasty outbreak of riot and violence among the London mob. These formed the great mass of Wilkes' supporters. Troops actually clashed with rioters in St. George's Fields, but the "horrid massacre," far from restoring quiet, merely inflamed the situation. Many of the mob had been rendered desperate by unemployment, commercial depression, poor harvests, and high prices. Wilkes served as the focal point of their accumulated discontents.

Confronted with radicalism and tumult both at home and in the Colonies, the Grafton Ministry was at a loss which way to turn. The result was confusion and indecision at a moment when strength and diplomacy were needed on both "fronts." When the Lords of the Treasury, with Grafton presiding, met to consider the reports from the harassed Customs Commissioners of Boston, their only answer to the inflamed situation in America was to ask the American Secretary of State, Hillsborough, to send "most positive Instructions" to Bernard and to the other colonial governors, requiring them to aid the commissioners in the execution of their duty.[20] Such inanities were ill designed to encourage officials who felt their very lives in danger.

Hillsborough, however, sought to take more decisive action. The American Secretary, whose pomposity and determination to play the strong man could not conceal his want of talent, now wrote to Bernard in the King's name: he must order his assembly, on the pain of dissolution, to rescind their vote for the Circular Letter. Foolishly drawing in all the North American provinces, he told the other governors that they too must dissolve their assemblies should these be inclined to go

[20] *Ibid.*, ff. 314–19, Treasury minutes, January 26 to July 28, 1768.

along with Massachusetts. It was further implied that force, if needed, would not be lacking.

Before this order could reach America, however, yet more serious affrays had occurred over the seizure of John Hancock's sloop, "Liberty." The persons and property of the commissioners were assaulted by the Boston mob, and these unfortunate officials—all but one—together with their families, sought refuge first on the "Romney" and later at Castle William. Thence, they had appealed to Gage for troops and to Hood for more naval aid.[21]

Furthermore, Bernard was required to inform the home government at the end of June that despite the presence of two more armed schooners lately sent, the assembly had refused by a vote of ninety-two to seventeen, and "in a very offensive manner," to rescind their Circular Letter resolution. He consequently dissolved the Massachusetts Assembly on July 1. Henceforward, however, "ninety-two" was to form a rallying cry in Bernard's province similar to "forty-five" among Wilkes' admirers in Britain.

Indeed, attempts were going on to link up the radicalisms growing on either shore. A Committee of the Boston Sons of Liberty, for instance, wrote to the jailed but "Illustrious Patriot," acclaiming him a savior of the Constitution and sending him a monetary token of their esteem.[22]

In February, 1769, the House of Commons had declared Wilkes expelled the House, thereby seeking to invalidate his election for Middlesex. Then followed a scene without parallel in British political history, one that would have been ludicrous had not the constitutional implications been so serious. Twice was Wilkes re-elected by the voters of Middlesex, and twice more expelled the House. After a third contest, which saw Wilkes far ahead of his opponent, a Colonel Lut-

[21] *Ibid.*, f. 285, commissioners to Gage, June 15, 1768, copy.
[22] Add. MSS 30870, f. 45, signed by Benjamin Kent, Thomas Young, Benjamin Church, Jr., John Adams, and Joseph Warren.

trell, the House took the highhanded measure of declaring Luttrell duly elected. Radical ferment in the London area increased ominously with Wilkes again its focal point. From this time dates the rise of "The Society for Supporting the Bill of Rights," among whose founding members were the radical parson of Brentford, Horne Tooke, and several Members of Parliament. Three decades hence, radical ferment, engendered by the French Revolution, would find expression in similar organizations and would pose a serious problem to the home government. Now, however, fortunately for the ministry, the society did not long survive the blow of its hero's release from "martyrdom." When Wilkes had served his sentence and was freed, the society fell into the bitterest internal wrangling because Wilkes saw in it no other object but his personal welfare.[23] It was therefore incapable of seriously affecting the course of events, save by intensifying the conservative reaction now steadily growing as a result of the American disturbances.

American radicals, however, saw in the persecution of Wilkes and the disregard of the rights of the electors of Middlesex proof of their worst suspicions. For them it indicated that the ministry had openly abandoned any pretense of respect for constitutional government. Wilkes' letters to them confirmed their fears that the ministry was deep in a plot against all liberty and theirs in particular. Had Wilkes been less a charlatan, more diabolically clever, and less preoccupied with making money on his misfortunes, he might have played the role of a British Samuel Adams. He might have welded British radicalism into a potent political force, joining hands with that across the Atlantic. Crafty and shrewd Wilkes was, but he was no revolutionary. Lacking any motive but self-interest, he dallied with the American radicals, accepted their presents, laughed at their gullibility, fed them on hackneyed phrases, fanned the coals of their resentment against the home

[23] See Alexander Stephens, *Memoirs of John Horne Tooke.*

government, and encouraged them so long as he thought they might be of service to him.[24]

Grafton's position in the summer, 1768, was assuredly an unenviable one. Faced with riots at home and in the Colonies, and with a growing conservative demand that parliamentary supremacy be vindicated, he had also to reckon on the chance of Chatham's recovery. The fear of his master's disapproval of measures which might be adopted was a heavy burden for the young Duke, and he was fully resolved to avoid responsibility all he could. Hillsborough had written his stern letter; Bernard had dissolved the Massachusetts Assembly. The home government had ordered Gage to collect and make ready his troops at Halifax and to hold them there until Bernard should request them. These were steps forced by the weight of events upon a reluctant Grafton. Desperately, the Duke longed for the meeting of Parliament in the autumn, so that if necessity should require it, responsibility for American measures could be shifted from himself to that body. For instance, when Grafton's Treasury Board met on July 5 to consider the disastrous American situation, they did no more than send to the London Commissioners of the Customs asking how past obstructions had been dealt with. Not till more than two weeks later, on July 21, did they consider the "Liberty" riots. They then decided to lay the whole affair before the law officers of the Crown for an opinion on the legality of the Boston Commissioners' seizure of the vessel.

Such procrastination could not go on indefinitely in the face of repeated colonial insults to legal authority. And, at the end of the month, Grafton and his board wrote the Boston Commissioners that their "complaints" had been sent to Hillsborough to be laid before the King. Concern was expressed that they had been forced to retire to Castle William, but the Treasury Board had no doubt that they would soon return to

[24] For a sampling of Wilkes' correspondence with the Boston Sons of Liberty, see Add. MSS 30870, ff. 75–76, 135–36, and f. 166.

Boston and execute the revenue laws with "firmness and resolution." Only toward the end of this communication were the commissioners told that their urgent pleas had been heeded and that two regiments were bound for Boston to protect them.[25]

While Grafton dallied, British political opinion was solidifying. The desire was for some vindication of Parliament's supremacy over the Colonies. The new disorders in Massachusetts seemed to show that indulgence of the Colonies, as in the repeal of the Stamp Act, had been futile and that a settlement with the Americans was overdue. Grenville declared that a return to the requisition system or any effort to derive a revenue from quitrents would violate the Constitution. (The Crown would thereby derive an income independent of Parliament's control.)[26] This pronouncement summed up what had become accepted doctrine; and it was now adopted as an irrefutable answer to colonial demands for the abandonment of parliamentary taxation in favor of requisitions.

The conservative reaction was running strongly among the Old Whigs, too. Rockingham was as angry with "the dangerous madness of some in America, as at the passion and obstinacy of some at home." America's outbursts were "most dangerous and offensive," and, fearing the Colonists were impugning the Declaratory Act, he proclaimed his eternal support of that piece of Old Whig legislation.[27]

That country gentleman Thomas Falconer might consider Massachusetts' refusal to rescind her Circular Letter a "signal

---

[25] Add. MSS 38340, ff. 314–19.

[26] RHMCR. *Knox Papers, Various Collections,* 95–98, 101–102, Grenville to Knox, June 27, July 15, 28, October 9, 1768. See also Smith, *Grenville Papers,* IV, 316–19, Grenville to Thomas Pownall, July 17, 1768.

[27] Albemarle, *Rockingham Memoirs,* II, 78–81, Rockingham to Collector of the Boston Customs, Harrison, October 2, 1768; see also 76–77, Rockingham to Dowdeswell, August 11, 1768. Add. MSS 35374, ff. 350–53, John Yorke to Hardwicke, July 28, 1768; Wentworth-Woodhouse, Rockingham Papers, Sir George Savile to Rockingham, July 31, 1768.

for war,"[28] but he had even ruder shocks in store. Bernard had dissolved the Massachusetts Assembly, but he was powerless to prevent that unique New England institution, the town meeting. Before the arrival of the troops on October 1, such a conclave had resolved that the regiments could not be kept in the colony without the consent of the assembly. It was further recommended that the people procure arms on the pretext of an apprehended French invasion. Action was also taken for calling a "convention" in September, to be composed of delegates from the towns. Massachusetts was thus rapidly approaching a revolutionary state and was busily setting up an effective government independent of royal authority. In the autumn, a new assembly was elected to replace that which Bernard had dissolved. It was soon found, however, that it was as radical as the last had been. It promptly refused to provide barracks in the town of Boston, maintaining that quarters were available at Castle William. From such a point, its members knew, troops could not act effectively. A gloomier consideration for the mother country was the growing scope of the controversy. Within a few months' time, the assemblies of Virginia, Maryland, Georgia, North Carolina, and New York had been dissolved because they had exhibited too much inclination to follow the lead of Massachusetts.

By 1768, then, the great question of parliamentary right had obscured the home government's original purpose—the creation of a coherent imperial system. With near-anarchy in the eastern colonies, the west had become a secondary problem. Even so, the Board of Trade under Robert Nugent, now Lord Clare, presented a report on the west on March 7, 1768. Calling for a reduction in the imperial Indian establishment, a paring of expense to the minimum, and the control of Indian trade by each colony, the report went strongly against new inland settlements, thereby blasting the hopes of several colo-

28 RHMCR. *Gray Papers*, 302–303, Falconer to Thomas Gray, September 19, 1768.

nial land companies. In the long run, however, the report was to have little influence except to alienate American speculators. Moreover, the westward movement had already assumed the character of a force of nature, and it was not now to be stopped by even the most solemn orders from the mother country. In the end, then, curtailment of imperial activity in the west would merely clear the way for a showdown between the Indians and the westerners.[29]

As summer turned into autumn, Grafton, still fighting to postpone a full-dress treatment of the American problem until Parliament should meet, had to face another unpleasant development on the domestic scene. The conservative elements in his ministry, the Bedfords and the King's Friends, were beginning to exert pressure against those farther to the left. The ministry now began to loose all pretext of existence under the name of Chatham. In August, Thomas Townshend, Chatham's friend, resigned from the Treasury Board. Demands by Sandwich for a place of greater power brought from Grafton the promise that Shelburne would soon be dismissed. Then followed a sordid intrigue which drove Chatham and Shelburne from office, both resigning in October.

Chatham's action came as an unpleasant surprise to Grafton, but the Opposition was elated. There were immediate attempts to unite the separate groups into an effective weapon against the ministry. These were, however, premature. Chatham was still ill and in retirement. Further, he had pleaded reasons of health as the ground for his resignation, an excuse not openly hostile to the ministry. Most of his friends therefore could be persuaded to remain in office. Furthermore, the Opposition, caught between the two millstones of radical disorders in America and in Britain, was in a declining state. Several of Grenville's friends were being drawn over to the Court. Lord Powis put his considerable Parliamentary interest at the dis-

[29] The report is printed in Morison, *Sources and Documents*, 62-73. See also his excellent introductory essay.

posal of the ministry. Rigby would soon capture Alexander Wedderburn. Sir Lawrence Dundas, the Scottish magnate who controlled several seats in Commons, let it be known he would not decline to support government. Far from overturning the ministry, then, Chatham's resignation merely pointed up the growing stability of a consolidating conservative bloc.

With the conservative tide running thus strong, Parliament met on November 8. Grafton, having now won his summer's battle to delay treatment of the American problem, was only too happy to turn that irksome task over to the representatives of the nation. Colonial affairs took precedence over all others. The two houses heard the King, in his speech from the throne, declare that a new "spirit of faction" was arising in North America. Actual violence had occurred in some colonies, and Boston seemed intent on throwing off her dependence altogether.[30] From the debates which followed it soon became obvious that Parliament would demand a new and sterner policy toward those Americans so presumptuous as to question Parliament's supremacy. It was equally apparent that the great majority of the ministry were also so inclined.

The Old Whigs immediately demanded a comprehensive parliamentary inquiry into the causes of the American disorders, but a week after the meeting of Parliament, Lord North, now chancellor of the exchequer and leader of the Commons, announced that the House's attention would be focused on Boston. Such a limitation was, of course, an attempt to localize the controversy and to isolate the captious town as much as possible. From the subsequent debates, two pertinent facts emerged. First, American violence had cut the ground from under Members who in the past had inclined to defend the colonists. Secondly, Parliament had firmly determined to vindicate the principle of its supremacy. When John Huske, American by birth and now a London merchant and Member

[30] Henry Cavendish, *Debates of the House of Commons*, I, 30–32, speech and debate.

of Parliament, tried to present a petition from the Pennsylvania Assembly against the Townshend taxes, the House resolutely refused to accept it because it contradicted the Declaratory Act.

The Boston papers were also being read in the House of Lords, and as the American Secretary, Hillsborough, was a member of that chamber, it was to be expected that the ministry's plans would first be presented there. Anti-American views were so prevalent among the peers that Rockingham sent urgently to his friend Dartmouth, asking him to hurry to London and lend his weight to the Old Whigs. Very soon after the meeting of Parliament, therefore, Grafton and his cabinet colleagues knew that any policy of stern American measures which they might choose to adopt would be supported by solid parliamentary majorities.

The inquiry in the Lords ended on December 15, and the ministry's American plan was then revealed in a series of resolutions moved by Hillsborough. Shelburne, seconded by the Old Whig Duke of Richmond, could put up only a token resistance. The Circular Letter of the Massachusetts Assembly was declared subversive of the Constitution, tending to create "repugnant combinations." The Council and civil magistrates of the province were charged with negligence in putting down riots. The resolutions of the town meeting of Boston were declared illegal. Summoning a convention manifested a design to become independent. The election of delegates to such a meeting was a "daring insult" to royal authority and "audacious usurpations of the powers of government."[31] Here, then, was Parliament's answer to American pretensions. To make it the more impressive, an address to the King, moved by Bedford, pledged the House's support to all measures designed to secure royal government and parliamentary supremacy in the Colonies. Having given the ministry a free hand, the address went on to call for the transportation of American traitors

[31] Cobbett and Wright, *Parliamentary History*, XVI, 477–80.

to England for trial—under an ancient Treason Law of Henry VIII. After the Christmas holidays, the Commons, by great majorities, voted their concurrence in the Lords' actions. Thus Hillsborough's plan had gained the united sanction of both Houses.

Harsh as the Americans might think this new policy, the prevailing opinion in parliamentary circles thought it moderate. Many thought it too much so. One who did was Secretary at War Barrington. The American Secretary, Hillsborough, was another. In reality, the adopted plan was merely a preamble to Hillsborough's intentions. There is evidence that the rump of Chatham's cabinet, Camden, Granby, and Conway, had a hand in frustrating a strong inclination within the ministry to adopt yet sterner measures.[32] The man chiefly responsible for vetoing Hillsborough's worst suggestions was, however, one whom the Americans would soon consider the very image of a tyrant. He was King George III.

Soon after the holiday recess, Hillsborough, adopting several suggestions from Barrington and Bernard, formulated and sent to the King new proposals for America. Intending to submit them at the next cabinet on American affairs, he desired first the royal approval. His plan recommended first that the Council of Massachusetts be appointed by the Crown and not elected as hitherto. Secondly, that any further vote or resolution of the assembly which denied or questioned Parliament's authority to bind the Colonies in all cases whatsoever should automatically cancel the charter. Thirdly, that four councilors of New York be removed for their radical sympathies. The

[32] Channing and Coolidge, *Barrington-Bernard Correspondence*, 182–83, Barrington to Bernard, January 2, 1769: "I wish there were a better prospect of such measures at home as will tend to preserve the Obedience of the Colonies, and such have been proposed; I can moreover assure you that they have been relish'd by the majority of the cabinet; but by some fatal catastrophe, two or three men there, with less ability, less credit, less authority, and less responsibility than the rest, have carry'd their point and produced that flimsey unavailing Address which has past the Lords."

governors of Georgia and South Carolina were to call their assemblies and lecture them on their duty to Parliament.

Two points in this plan had come from Barrington. First, the Townshend taxes should be repealed for Virginia and the West Indies, which had already made ample provisions for a civil establishment. They would be repealed for the other colonies as soon as these did the same. Finally, the Mutiny Act was to be altered to allow quartering of troops in public houses, or, if such were not available and if the colonists refused to provide barracks, in private houses.

Hillsborough told the King that the entire cabinet, except Camden and Conway, had approved the plan, although Grafton had had doubts about the alteration of the Massachusetts Council. The American Secretary was strong for this measure, however, declaring—with supreme and foolish optimism—that he was "almost convinced it will be generally approved at Home, and be popular in the Colony."[33]

Probably this inflammatory plan would have been adopted had it not been for the King. He approved the removal of the four New York councilors. But he considered Virginia's conduct in the spring so offensive as to make it improper to repeal the Townshend duties for that colony. He was willing to consider a repeal in 1770, however, should Virginia remain quiet and peaceful in the meantime. He further agreed that it might be necessary someday to vest appointment of the Massachusetts Council in the Crown if that province should persist in her unruly conduct. Until that time, however, such a step should be avoided, for "the altering Charters is at all times an odious measure." Never very confident in Hillsborough's ability, the King now directly opposed his suggestion that questioning the authority of Parliament work immediate forfeiture of Massachusetts' Charter. Such a procedure, the King felt, "seems cal-

[33] Fortescue, *Correspondence of George III*, II, No. 701, Hillsborough to the King, February 15, 1769.

culated to increase the unhappy feudes that subsist than to asswage them."[34]

While the King and the remnant of Chatham's cabinet could thus exercise a moderating influence upon Hillsborough and the Bedfordites, the Opposition was weak, divided, and ineffectual. It is interesting to note, however, the American issue was now bringing together a new group. Unfortunately for the colonial cause, it was always to remain on an informal basis and small in number, never breaking down previously existing interests. Nonetheless, it was a creative minority; and from some of its members arguments were heard which, had they been accepted by a Parliament all too determined to defend its total supremacy, might well have saved the first British Empire. First, there was the small Chatham contingent, led by his friends Barré, Thomas Townshend, and Frederick Montagu in Commons, and by Shelburne and Camden in the Lords. At the present conjunction, this group was usually joined by the Old Whigs Burke, Dowdeswell, Sir George Savile, and their friends. Both these parties were, however, preoccupied for the moment with defending their own past administrations and exculpating themselves from charges of having caused the American disorders. Barré, for instance, had found it necessary—at the beginning of the parliamentary inquiry into the Boston disturbance—to defend Chatham's view that taxation formed no part of the legislative power of Parliament. Similarly, when Burke and Dowdeswell had spoken against Hillsborough's American plan, it had soon become evident that Old Whig efforts were primarily bent toward a defense of the repeal of the Stamp Act.

A small group of Americans also sat in Parliament in those crucial years between 1763 and 1783. The group totalled only five Members, however, and never more than three held seats at any one time. One of these, Paul Wentworth, of New Hampshire, would become a staunch loyalist. Another, Henry Cru-

[34] *Ibid.*, No. 701 A, the King's memorandum, February, 1769.

ger, of New York, proved remarkably inept in presenting the American thesis to his colleagues. Two others, John Huske and Barlow Trecothick, did yeoman service, but, unfortunately, they died or left Parliament before the outbreak of hostilities.

More important than these was the "Jamaica cousinhood," consisting of some thirteen Members headed by William Beckford and Stephen and Rose Fuller. The West Indians had often offended the aims and aspirations of the North American merchants. In days to come, however, they would rally to the support of the American constitutional position.[35]

Finally, a small but important group—if two can constitute a group—opposed to the American measures were the former colonial governors Thomas Pownall and William Johnstone. Of the two, Pownall was the more capable. He had become famous as a colonial authority with the publication of his *Administration of the Colonies*. On April 19, 1769, Pownall moved for a repeal of the Townshend duties. In a very capable, if not brilliant, speech he displayed a deep understanding of the Anglo-American controversy and a fund of personal knowledge and experience with colonial affairs.[36] It may well be that Pownall's speech determined the ministry's decision in the following month to repeal the duties, except that on tea.

Pownall began by declaring that his motion was not an attack upon the administration and that he himself was associated with no party. The controversy, he said, was one in which only power could now operate. Both sides had taken up absolute and mutually exclusive positions. Compromise was therefore necessary. The taxes were, he believed, unjust in that they were for the purpose of creating a civil list independent of the control of the assemblies. At any rate, some colonies—Virginia and several of the West Indian governments—already pos-

[35] See Namier, *England in the Age of the American Revolution*, Chap. 4, and p. 278.
[36] Henry Cavendish, *Debates of the House of Commons*, I, 391–401.

sessed adequate civil lists. He then adduced a profound argument. Great Britain had an undoubted "right" to lay the Townshend duties, but to do so operated as a revocation of those rights and privileges the colonists had hitherto enjoyed. To tax America for revenue was contrary to the practice of Parliament. Unfortunately, the binding force of "parliamentary convention" was still far in the future. Yet it is significant that only a few months later, Hillsborough, in his private correspondence, stated views very similar to those here presented by Pownall. From the debates of the session, however, it was clear that the groups opposing the ministry's American measures were in a decided minority. Critical divisions, those on the presentation of American petitions or on Hillsborough's plan, stood at 70–133, 80–213, and 89–155.

Pownall had sensibly tried to destroy the strict legalism which, if persisted in by the home government, would make a headlong clash with the Colonies inevitable. He had also sought to remove America as a party issue. He would fail because the whole weight of domestic political development was against him; and America had become the strongest dividing principle in British politics since the Jacobite rebellion of 1745. Some months before, Franklin had already shrewdly noted that colonial affairs had become "one of the distinctions of party here." Burke, in supporting Pownall's motion, might lament that America was being "beat backwards and forwards, as the tennis ball of faction." Yet, in days to come, it would be the Old Whigs, and Burke in particular, who more than any other group would factiously spirit up America to resist a ministry they themselves could not overturn. Preoccupied with their own virtue, they sought to teach the Americans that only an Old Whig ministry could give them relief from the measures of an oppressive and tyrannical government. When, for instance, Rockingham learned of the Grafton Ministry's intention to repeal the Townshend taxes, he immediately wrote to a friend in Boston, urging the Americans to be quiet and that "tho' they might have no Reason to trust to Vague assurances from *this Administration,* yet it would be wise for them to act so, as might enable us to take some Steps in their behalf."[37] Lacking power and prestige at home, Old Whigs looked to the Colonies for the support they craved. They thought to be swept into office on the mounting waves of colonial dissatisfaction and disturbance. Old Whig attempts to make domestic political capital of the troubles of a distracted empire would grow to shocking heights in the years ahead. From that party, the colonists were to learn lessons of hate never to be forgotten.

The Old Whigs also courted extraparliamentary support at home. Decisively beaten in Parliament, they launched in the summer of 1769 a campaign to capture popular support by taking the Wilkes affair to the freeholders of the country. Working on the county and local level, Old Whig agents were indefatigable in their attempts to win petitions for the dissolution of Parliament. Furthermore, Grenville and Temple brought their support to the campaign; and when Chatham suddenly reappeared in July, he informed the King that he could not approve the ministry's measures concerning either Wilkes or America. It therefore seemed that a united Opposition was at last possible.

The Grenville-Old Whig working alliance was free of any American implications. Nor did Chatham's reconciliation with Grenville and Temple, in August, in itself touch the American question. Because of the grave constitutional issues then raised by the Wilkes affair, America had for the moment receded as the great dividing factor among Opposition groups. When, however, Rockingham sought to infuse the American issue into the campaign for petitions, calling it "aggravating circumstances," Grenvillite Whately gently, but firmly, rebuked him.[38] All knew that the alliance was but a temporary

[37] Wentworth-Woodhouse, Rockingham Papers, Rockingham to Dowdeswell, May 26, 1769.

[38] *Ibid.,* Rockingham to Crofts, his Yorkshire agent, July 11, 1769; Thomas Whately to Burke, August 30, 1769.

stratagem. The Old Whigs, in the very midst of it, could not overcome their deep suspicion of Grenville, while Burke's hatred for Chatham was almost pathological. They deliberately kept co-operation with Chatham and the Grenvilles at a minimum, therefore, because they were determined to monopolize the campaign and to capture support for themselves.

Although the joint Opposition campaign for petitions did not achieve its object—the dissolution of a Parliament corrupted by the expulsion of Wilkes and the consequent violation of the rights of the freeholders of Middlesex—yet it did profoundly stir the country and worry the ministry. At least fifteen counties, numerous cities, and many boroughs sent petitions. The government's strenuous efforts to get counterpetitions were successful only in the two universities, four counties, and three or four cities.

Furthermore, on the international scene, there was developing a crisis with Spain over the Falkland Islands. Rumors of war grew steadily stronger. Sir Edward Hawke, Chatham's friend and first lord of the Admiralty, caused considerable uneasiness by selling out his public stocks. There were fears for Gibraltar and Jamaica. There were reports that France had smuggled ten thousand troops to the West Indies. In addition, Ireland was in great unrest, with Lord Lieutenant Townshend barely able to cope with the unruly Parliament. At home, Grafton knew that Chatham's friends were on the point of resigning and that the ministry would have to bear the brunt of the great man's wrath at the opening of Parliament. In this troubled state of affairs, the "terrible shadow," Junius, in his letters to the London *Public Advertiser*, was adding his carefully distilled drops of venom to the steaming brew.

The direct result of all this was a desire on the part of the ministry to leave America alone. There could be indeed no retreat from the great principle of parliamentary supremacy, yet there was a clear disposition toward some peaceable solution of the knotty problem. Nor was such a wish confined to the ministry. Franklin reported to his colonial constituents that a spirit of moderation toward the Colonies was developing throughout the country. He pointed out that the petitions from Middlesex and London during the summer had listed "the unconstitutional taxes on America" as a grievance, and he assured them that if America would only persevere in her nonimportation scheme, repeal would be within her grasp.[39]

Chatham's return to the political scene had aroused among the British public almost a feeling of relief.[40] Suggestions were heard that British consuls in foreign ports be allowed to act as customs officers and empowered to clear American ships for their home ports after payment of legal duties. This would relieve Americans of lengthy and expensive trips to English ports to pay them. Further, there were those who counseled a return to the requisition plan; and Dartmouth had been given an outline of a new system of colonial government. Coming from an anonymous West Indian merchant, the proposal had included "a Lord Lieutenant and Parliament in America similar to that in Ireland." Dartmouth, declaring his own liking for the plan, sent it on to Rockingham for that leader's perusal.[41]

The new spirit of moderation was also conditioned by the considerable success of the colonial nonimportation agreements. In spite of government propaganda to the contrary, British trade was being seriously affected. In 1768, the value of goods exported to North America had been set at nearly £2,500,000. In 1769 it fell to £1,635,000.[42] Although this loss was being offset by the opening up of new channels of European trade and British merchants from this time onward were correspondingly reluctant to be drawn into a clamor on behalf of the

[39] Sparks, *Franklin's Works*, VII, 447–48, Franklin to James Bourdain.
[40] See RHMCR. *Weston Papers*, 416, Edward Sedgwick to Edward Weston, July 19, 1769.
[41] Wentworth-Woodhouse, Rockingham Papers, Dartmouth to Rockingham, October 21, 1769; see also Add. MSS 38341, f. 104.
[42] Add. MSS 38341, f. 119. The paper is in Jenkinson's hand.

Americans,[43] the decrease was nevertheless a problem of primary concern to the ministry.

In view of all these considerations, therefore, Grafton and his ministry decided in May, 1769, to repeal all the Townshend taxes except that on tea. Since British products were taxed, the arrangement was "uncommercial." Tea, not being of British manufacture, would continue to bear a tax and would thereby serve to uphold the principle of the Declaratory Act. Although no immediate action could be taken to repeal the taxes until Parliament should meet in the winter, it was hoped that the Americans would remain quiet so that the mother country might make her conciliatory step with dignity.

Thus the Colonies were at once informed of the ministry's intentions. When the new governor of Virginia, Lord Botetourt, went out to his post, he carried with him a circular letter from Hillsborough announcing in the King's name that the ministry had no intention of proposing any new taxes for America for purposes of revenue, and, indeed, that the Townshend taxes, except that on tea, would be repealed. At home, the American Secretary, speaking of the Colonies, let it be known he had "no apprehensions of everything doing well, if they be let alone by Parliament, and their affairs not intermixed with opposition points." Privately, he expressed sentiments similar to those of Pownall in his great speech at the preceding session. The proposed repeal, he said, was based on "principles of justice, that as the colonies are obliged to take our manufactures and cannot have others, we ought not to tax them." His correspondent William Knox declared himself agreed, adding, "I like the idea of letting the colonies alone."[44] Apparently, then, the time had come—if indeed it was ever to come—for a peaceable solution to the imperial problem. The mother

[43] Add. MSS 38577, ff. 9–10, Israel Mauduit to Thomas Hutchinson, November 4, 1769.

[44] Smith, *Grenville Papers*, IV, 479–81, Knox to Grenville, November 10, 1769.

country was frankly in a mood for compromise, and she would take the first step toward conciliation.

The American position had not, however, remained static. In November, William Strahan, busybody printer to the King and friend of Hillsborough, wrote to Franklin, probably at the American Secretary's suggestion, to ask his views on how a pacification of the Colonies might be accomplished without sacrifice to the honor, dignity, and supremacy of Parliament. In his answer, Franklin put forward a view which was already gaining wide acceptance in America: that the King governed the Colonies in a capacity independent of Parliament. It had been only with Cromwell that Parliament had usurped a sovereign power over the Colonies. Finally, Franklin affirmed that only a complete repeal of the Townshend taxes and a withdrawal of the troops from Boston could bring quiet to America.[45] Great Britain was to be forced to make periodic retreats from the position she took up in the spring of 1769. As often as she did so, however, American demands were to be at least one step ahead. A heartbreaking decade lay ahead for those who now struggled to preserve the empire.

Meantime, Chatham had declared war on a ministry which he felt had betrayed him. To make his assault more effective he was also resolved to form a strict union with Rockingham, employing to this end his friendships with his old admirals Keppel and Saunders.[46] Although Burke and the Yorkes continued to advise caution, it was soon clear that Rockingham and Chatham would stand together at the opening of Parliament.

The King began the new session on January 9, 1770, with his famous "horned cattle" speech. Besides giving a Wilkes wit occasion to suggest that the speech would have sounded

[45] Sparks, *Franklin's Works*, IV, 258–69, William Strahan to Franklin, November 21, 1769; Franklin to Strahan, November 29, 1769; VII, 475–79, Franklin to Samuel Cooper, June 8, 1770.

[46] Chatham Papers, 25, Calcraft to Chatham, November 22, 1769; 23, Sir Alexander Hood to Lord and Lady Chatham, December 3, 1769.

better sung to the tune of "Roast Beef of Olde England," the King called attention to the grave American situation. He asked Parliament to give it serious attention and admitted that his own efforts to restore obedience in North America had failed.

However the American question had now become a side issue with the Opposition. In the Commons, Old Whigs, City Radicals, and Chathamites excoriated the ministry for its violation of the rights of electors. In the Lords, Chatham blasted them with bombshell oratory. While expressing the hope that America would never return to tranquillity until the invasion of her liberty had been redressed, he made his primary concern the expulsion of Wilkes. His attack on this occasion brought Camden back to the fold, and there followed several minor resignations among his friends in the ministry.

On January 22, Chatham and Rockingham united again to assault what appeared to be a disintegrating ministry. Again, however, it was not America which provided Chatham's ammunition. "I need not look abroad for grievances," he proclaimed. "The grand capital mischief is fixed at home."

The debates of the session indicated that both Old Whigs and Chatham had begun to see confusion in America as but part of a wider and more unwholesome situation created by the steadily growing influence of the Crown. From this time dates Chatham's increasing preoccupation with the cause of Parliamentary reform. The joint assault against the irresistible consolidation of a new conservatism, called forth by Wilkes and America, was, however, the frenzied attack of an army near exhaustion. Failing to grasp the nature of this consolidation, Chatham and the Old Whigs could but attribute it to secret influence.

Chatham's nonpartisan illusion had been forever shattered. No longer was he the champion against party connection. In brilliant and glowing phrases he admitted that the necessity of party originated in nature itself: "There is a distinction between right and wrong—between Whig and Tory." Thus his merciless attack was an admission that he had formerly proceeded on the basis of a false principle—or at least one too ideal to be realized in his time. He could call for violence, could criticize the Old Whigs for their moderation, could bring down the stunned Grafton, but his attack had come too late.

The events following Grafton's resignation on January 28, 1770, indicated that government, after ten years of administrative chaos, had at last gained stability. There was no general overturn. North succeeded quietly. The King and his Friends had moved to center stage.

The North Ministry represents the final success of George III's long struggle to escape "capture" and to regain what he thought his rightful place in British politics. Henceforth, the government would be, in very truth, His Majesty's Government. The royal party leader had become in fact the chief executive. Unfortunately, he wore a crown, the touchy dignity of which would not, in the days to come, allow those compromises which less exalted politicians might have found so easy.

CHAPTER FIVE

PRELUDE TO CIVIL WAR

ORTH's quiet accession to power was possible because America and Wilkes had called into being a new conservatism supported not only by the King's Friends but by members of every other major group. Those means of corruption at the Crown's disposal did not create North's steady majorities. Rather they arose out of a frightened reaction against radicalism at home and abroad.

North became first lord of the Treasury and chancellor of the exchequer. The Great Seal was temporarily put into commission after the suspected suicide of Charles Yorke. Hillsborough remained as colonial secretary; and Lord Rochford, the veteran diplomatist, occupied the Northern Department of State. North's uncle Halifax came in; and Edward Thurlow buttressed the Bedford interest as attorney general. Among those who took minor office was Charles James Fox. This arrangement was the strongest and most stable the new reign had seen. It possessed a unique vigor and was quite determined to solve the ills of the empire.

North had been head of the ministry only a month when, on March 5, 1770, in accordance with the cabinet decision made before his elevation, he moved to repeal all of the Townshend taxes but that on tea. Refusing "to run after America

---

[1] In 1761, there were about 170 placemen; in 1774, about the same. See Feiling, *Second Tory Party*, Chap. 8.

in search of reconciliation," North made it clear to the Commons that the step was not undertaken because of American pressure. Nor was it to be interpreted as compromising the great principle of Parliament's supremacy and her right to tax America for revenue. The preamble of the act, providing for the creation of an American civil list, would remain, as would the tax on tea, which, North assured his listeners, could be brought to produce considerable sums.[2]

It is interesting to speculate upon the probable course of the Anglo-American conflict had there existed then the means of rapid communication available today. Time after time, irrevocable decisions were made during the "time gap" necessary to the transit of news from one country to the other. Had intelligence of North's motion on March 5 been known in Boston on the same day, would the clash between British troops and townspeople have occurred?

Be the answer what it may, this "bloody massacre" formed another step in the growing alienation of two kindred peoples and gave the Boston radicals grist for their propaganda mill. However, speedy action by Governor Hutchinson prevented a final crisis. Yielding a point for which the people had agitated ever since arrival of the troops, he quickly removed them from the city to Castle William. Such speedy compliance with a popular demand deprived the radicals of their chief grievance, and an uneasy quiet followed. The radicals continued to work for a system of Committees of Correspondence throughout the province.

Meantime, Franklin, in London, was claiming for the American cause "the body of Dissenters throughout England, with many others, not to mention Ireland and all the rest of Europe." It is significant that he did not mention either the merchants or any group in the Opposition. Indeed, from the American standpoint, an ominous change was occurring in Britain. The support of the American demands among the

[2] Cavendish, *Debates of the House of Commons*, I, 483–500, debate.

merchants and manufacturers, so helpful during the Stamp Act crisis, was no longer to be counted on. The merchants of London had with difficulty been brought to offer a weak petition against the Townshend taxes. Those of other cities now bluntly refused, asserting that they had enough trade without America, and that in any event, her nonimportation agreements would soon break down.

As for the Opposition, Americans had begun to feel that even should Rockingham or Chatham come to power, the situation would improve but little. Both men insisted upon the supremacy of Parliament, although they would not venture to exercise it in taxing the Colonies. In his speech on March 2, before proceeding to his main attack against secret influence, Chatham had uttered a somber warning that the Americans "must be subordinate. In all laws relating to trade and navigation especially, this is the mother country, they are children; they must obey and we prescribe."[3] In the early days of the new year, mutual consultation among Chatham, Camden, and Shelburne, Rockingham, Dartmouth, and Richmond, and Temple and Suffolk had been common. As the session wore on, however, Chatham's very violence on the threadbare issues of the Wilkes affair began to alienate the Old Whigs. Meanwhile the increasingly bad state of American affairs was turning the Grenville group toward the ministry.

By mid-February, Opposition numbers were dwindling rapidly. Sir Lawrence Dundas and his friends went over to Court. In March, the City Radicals led by Beckford and Trecothick, and those of Westminster, under the influence of Horne Tooke, were alienated permanently from the Old Whigs. As mayor, Beckford had presented a very strong remonstrance from the City to the King on the incapacitation of Wilkes. When he was called to explain his action by the Commons, the Old Whigs refused to come to his support. Total alienation resulted. Henceforward, the Old Whigs equally

[3] Viscount Mahon, *History of England*, V, Appendix, xli–xlii.

fearful of Chatham's violence and domination and of the City's radicalism, pursued an independent course. Their break both with Chatham and with the Radicals became irreparable when, in the summer of 1770, Burke published his "Thoughts on the Cause of the Present Discontents."

In this pamphlet the justification of party received classic statement. Lashing out bitterly at Chatham's "cant" of "not men, but measures," Burke called the Old Whigs to battle. The ideal he set up was that of a House of Commons responsible to the nation, and a ministry responsible to the House. It was an attempt to justify his own party's increasing inclination to look outside the doors of Parliament for its support. By deifying the constitutional arrangement which had existed, though but superficially, during the two previous Hanoverian reigns, he unconsciously projected the line of constitutional development several decades into the future. Prevailing constitutional doctrine in his own time was exactly what he said it was not: the freedom of the monarch to appoint his own ministers.

The chief weapon by which the Court had revived the power of the prerogative, he said, was "influence," wielded by a "junta" of persons holding "secondary, but efficient" posts in government and in the royal household, "so as on one hand to occupy all the avenues to the throne; and on the other to forward or frustrate the execution of any measure, according to their own interests." Burke was here describing the King's Friends. His observations were accurate, but his eagerness to present the Old Whig party as a spotless innocent, the victim of insidious and subterranean forces, led him too far in his interpretations. His *idée fixe* of a secret and wicked "Court system" was, however, at once seized upon by American radicals who saw in it a true account of domestic political conditions. Here then was their justification for resistance to measures carried out, it would seem, by a tyrannical ministry independent of constitutional checks.

Just as Burke's pamphlet was putting an end to united Opposition, the Grenvillites were about to make their peace with the Court. Grenville himself had become an old man since his wife's death a year before; and he now sought only retirement and quiet. In July, he sent William Knox his blessing upon that Grenvillite's accepting office as undersecretary of state for the colonies. In October he fell seriously ill, and his friends, fearful of his death, began to wonder "what part we are then to take?" What indeed could be the object of continued opposition? "I hope," exclaimed Lord George Germain in answer, "not to make Lord Chatham minister."[4]

Opposition was thus disintegrating rapidly. Chatham forsook the City Radicals, whose fight against press warrants had offended him. The City itself was soon to resound to the battle between Horne Tooke and Wilkes. This squalid struggle, together with the presence among the Radicals of such "crackpots" as Lord Buchan, ruined them with the public, and they never again could seriously affect the political balance of power.

Before Parliament could meet in the autumn, Beckford, Granby, and Grenville had died. Temple was so affected that he withdrew from politics, thus ending a career of sordid intrigue and self-aggrandizement. Beckford's death deprived Chatham of his chief contact with the City and removed one of the few men able to keep the City Radicals under a semblance of control.

The announcement in January, 1771, of a peaceful conclusion to the Falkland Islands dispute further weakened the Opposition cause. Chatham, intransigently attacking the convention with Spain, now saw his numbers melt away. Support simply could not be had for his thesis that a war would have been preferable to the compromise reached by the ministry. Chatham, gloomy and depressed, felt himself losing contact with affairs: "The Ministers are pretty much at their ease;

[4] RHMCR. *Stopford-Sackville Papers*, I, 131–32, letters of October 23, 25, 1770.

the *Public* is, I believe, a Scurvy Rascal, as I have long known it to be."[5] Thus discouraged and defeated on every hand, the leaders of Opposition went their separate ways. North and his ministry possessed the field.

Grenville's death made the defection of his friends to the Court a foregone conclusion. The Falkland Islands dispute had produced the resignation of Bedfordite Weymouth as secretary of state for the Southern Department. He had wished for war and felt himself overruled in his own office. The resulting shuffle gave the Grenvillites their opportunity, and they came over "en masse." Lord Suffolk, generally accepted as Grenville's successor, became lord privy seal, an office vacated by King's Friend Halifax who now became northern secretary of state. Bedfordite Sandwich took up at the Admiralty the place he was to hold so long. Grenvillite Wedderburn became solicitor general, and Thomas Whately a commissioner of trade. When, in June, Halifax died, Suffolk moved to the Northern Department, and Grafton, mortally offended at Chatham, took the vacant privy seal, although with a proviso that he be not of the cabinet. This accession of the Grenvillites was the last great step in that consolidation of the new conservatism which was preparing the advent of a new Tory party.

Now so well established in power that no Opposition could touch them, the North Ministry turned to the task of evolving a comprehensive American policy. Although all but one of the Townshend duties had been repealed, the past behavior of the Colonies suggested that the American problem would not be a transient one. That quality most lacking in the mother country's past efforts to deal with colonial outbursts had been firmness: the North Ministry now proposed to remedy this omission at the earliest possible moment. The American bluff was to be called.

[5] Chatham Papers, 4, Chatham to Lady Chatham, January 25, 1771. The quotation is deleted from the printed version. See Taylor and Pringle, *Chatham Correspondence*, IV, 86–88.

In January, 1770, when Lord Dunmore became governor of New York, his instructions clearly indicated an intent that he and other Crown officers of the province should have their salaries from a colonial revenue. In April, the Privy Council annulled an act of the South Carolina Assembly passed in the preceding year. It had provided for a present of £1,500 to a radical London organization, the Supporters of the Bill of Rights. Moreover the Privy Council forbade the assembly ever again to issue money in so illegal a manner and ordered the province attorney general to prosecute the treasurer.

These were but symptoms of the ministry's new firmness. In June, a committee of the Privy Council undertook to canvass the entire state of affairs in Massachusetts, the very center of American unrest. When Hillsborough laid before that body transcripts of earlier testimony and reports, the picture that emerged confirmed the belief that some fundamental readjustment of American affairs in general, and of those of Massachusetts in particular, was urgently needed. Maltreatment of customs officers, intimidation of royal officials, the appointment of committees to enforce the nonimportation agreements, riots, which, as Customs Officer John Robinson pointed out, could not "be properly called Riots as the Rioters appear to be under Discipline," all foreshadowed the dissolution of civil government. Testimony from Governor Bernard confirmed such fears. Since the Stamp Act, he told the investigators, an accepted doctrine in Massachusetts was that the colonists were not subject to parliamentary taxes. Ever since May, 1768, he had considered "all Government as at an end," for it was impossible to enforce laws against the will of the mob. Warning that his former province could produce forty thousand fighting men, all of them now armed by a law of the colony, he declared that the only cure of this unhealthy situation was a decisive intervention by Parliament.

In light of these disquieting facts, the Privy Council Committee concluded that despite a present calm in Massachusetts, further outbreaks were to be anticipated. Indeed, the proceedings of both the assembly and the town meetings demonstrated "an evident Disposition to support by force the unconstitutional Doctrines, which have been inculcated." The committee then made a series of recommendations, all soon to be adopted and implemented by the ministry. The rendezvous of the Royal Navy stationed in North America—hitherto at Halifax—should now be Boston harbor. Castle William should be put into a state of defense and fully garrisoned with regulars. More troops should be sent to America. Finally, as past disturbances demanded the "interposition of the Wisdom, and Authority of the Legislature," the King should recommend to Parliament a consideration of the state of Massachusetts.

The committee's report having been accepted, orders based upon it were issued on July 6 to the Admiralty, to the Ordnance, and to the secretary of war.[6] It was in keeping with the new policy when in January, 1771, Hillsborough refused to receive Franklin as agent for the Massachusetts Assembly, a post to which he had but recently been appointed. His Lordship maintained that Franklin could not legally represent the assembly because he had not been named agent by an act of that body duly concurred in by the council and the governor. The Privy Council, sustaining Hillsborough, in March issued instructions to Hutchinson forbidding his concurrence in the voting of a salary to any agent not appointed by an act of the assembly.[7]

The Falkland Islands crisis and the near war with Spain made it necessary however to postpone parliamentary intervention, and on May 15, 1771, Franklin reported to the Massachusetts Assembly that Parliament had been prorogued without taking notice of American affairs. The international situation thus brought a period of quiet to both sides of the Atlantic.

[6] Grant and Munro, *Acts of the Privy Council*, V, 247–65.

[7] Sparks, *Franklin's Works*, VII, 506–12; Franklin to Samuel Cooper, February 5, 1771. See also Grant and Munro, *Acts of the Privy Council*, V, 264.

In America there was a general feeling that a "pause in politics" had been reached; and it was hoped that the acquittal of Captain Prescott, commander of those troops involved in the "massacre," would make a good impression on the mother country. The nonimportation agreements were breaking down despite the tax on tea, and it was believed that "administration has a fair opportunity of adopting the mildest and most prudent measures respecting the colonies, without the appearance of being threatened or drove."[8]

Hillsborough seized this opportunity to attempt a solution of the western problem. Here, however, he was to be no more successful than his predecessors and would achieve, indeed, only his own overthrow and fall from office.

Hillsborough was in agreement with the report of the Board of Trade in 1768. That report had been a compromise, following neither Grenville's plan to imperialize the west, allowing orderly expansion, nor with Shelburne's more radical scheme for rapid and decentralized exploitation. It had deprecated new interior settlements and had assigned the management of Indian trade to the Colonies. The home government would maintain the boundary line.

In November, 1768, the Indian Superintendents, Johnson and Stuart, had concluded the Treaty of Fort Stanwix by which a boundary line had been settled and some Indian land had been ceded to the imperial government. Samuel Wharton, of Pennsylvania, present at the time as the representative of a group of merchant land speculators, had managed to obtain from the Indians a particular cession as compensation for those merchants who had suffered during Pontiac's Rebellion. Because this transaction had been unconfirmed by the imperial government, Wharton's associates had sent him to London to obtain the necessary ratification. There, failing in his intended mission, he became involved in a scheme to purchase from the government that area lawfully acquired by the treaty. Thanks

[8] Sparks, *Franklin's Works*, VII, 499–500, Samuel Cooper to Franklin, January 1, 1771.

to his friendship with Franklin, he soon met and managed to interest such highly placed politicians as Lords Gower, Rochford, Hertford, Temple, and many others. To the first petition of this new group, asking a grant of 2,500,000 acres, Hillsborough gave an encouraging answer but suggested they buy a larger tract, enough for a new colony.

In December, 1769, therefore, this group, enlarged and reorganized, emerged as the Grand Ohio or Walpole Company. They at once petitioned for a grant of 20,000,000 acres, offering £10,460 7s 3d., the exact amount paid by the imperial government at Fort Stanwix. Competing claims of other speculator groups—such as the Old Ohio Company and the Virginians, whose spokesman was George Washington—were quieted by the simple expedient of admitting them all to partnership in the new company.

Hillsborough's encouragement was strange in view of his long opposition to new inland colonies. In July, 1770, the American Secretary asked General Gage, then in America as commander-in-chief, for his personal views on the west. Gage's reply seems to have confirmed Hillsborough's own opinion. He was convinced that interior colonies would be disastrous, that the forts in the Indian country were of little value, and that the west could be adequately protected by troops stationed at the mouths of the avenues of commerce.

Hillsborough then proceeded to submit to the Privy Council a report which directly contradicted his encouragement of the Grand Ohio Company. (He was later to maintain that he had deliberately appeared favorable to the petition, believing that the magnitude of the request would of itself defeat it.) The report was accepted. Forts de Chartres and Pitt were ordered abandoned and the Ohio Valley sealed off. Only fur traders were to be admitted to the area. Here then was a willful shattering of the imperial vision.[9]

[9] RHMCR. *Dartmouth Papers*, II, 81, Hillsborough to Gage, December 4, 1771. See also Alvord, *Mississippi Valley*, II, Chap. 2.

Hillsborough now became the center of a political intrigue which amply repaid his two-faced conduct toward the Grand Ohio Company. The Bedford element in the cabinet, lead by Gower, sought nothing less than his overthrow and through him that of North. For while the new conservatism had driven many groups to take refuge with the Court, it had by no means wrought a complete amalgamation of interests.

When the Grand Ohio Company's petition was presented to Hillsborough, he promptly sent to the Privy Council an adverse report. On July 1, 1772, however, that body took the almost unprecedented action of rejecting the report and deciding in favor of the petitioners. Gower, as president of the Council, had engineered this maneuver. As North had asked him to delay bringing up the report, it was unmistakably an affront not only to Hillsborough but to the head of the ministry as well. Indeed North was so offended that he almost resigned, being dissuaded from that action only by the King himself. For Hillsborough, however, the humiliation was simply too great, and he resigned in August, salving his wounds with an English earldom.

The American seals North then offered to the Bedfordite Weymouth who refused them. Reasoning that he had done his duty by the Bedfords, he now gave the office to his half-brother, that erstwhile Old Whig the Earl of Dartmouth. Thereby North strengthened his own position in the cabinet. His ministry had successfully weathered its first storm of internal intrigue.

When the new session of Parliament had opened on January 21, 1772, Franklin had written home that he saw no disposition to "meddle" with American affairs, and that, indeed, he anticipated no such a desire for at least a year.[10] In Massachusetts, the response to Samuel Adams's and Joseph Warren's efforts to establish a network of Committees of Corre-

[10] Sparks, *Franklin's Works*, VII, 534–38, Franklin to William Franklin, January 30, 1772.

spondence throughout the province was apathetic. The nonimportation agreements were being dropped, although the tea tax had indeed created associations pledged to drink none of that beverage unless smuggled in tax-free. Nor did Hutchinson's announcement that he and other Crown officers would henceforth be paid from the colonial revenue rouse great excitement. Samuel Adams was, however, able to draw the Governor into an undignified debate with the assembly on the theory of government, an interesting dispute in that it showed a growing acceptance of the theory which Franklin had expressed to William Strahan: that the Colonies were bound to Britain only through the person of the King.

This suspicion-laden calm was shattered in America in the early hours of the morning of June 10, 1772. On the tenth—the same day that the King ended the parliamentary session in London thousands of miles away—a band of from 50 to 150 irate Rhode Islanders boarded the revenue cutter "Gaspée," aground not far from Providence, severely wounded the captain, and burned the vessel. Captain Dudingston, who had previously incurred the wrath of the Rhode Islanders by his overzealous enforcement of the Laws of Trade and Navigation, barely escaped with his life.

Here, then, was an open challenge to North's policy of firmness. Parliament was not in session, but the ministry acted at once. On July 30, Hillsborough laid before the cabinet an angry report from Admiral Montagu, the naval commander-in-chief in America. Although the opinion of the law officers was requested, Hillsborough was authorized to take certain immediate steps. The Governor of Rhode Island and the Admiral were to be ordered to discover the guilty parties and, under a recent act for securing the royal dockyards, send them to England for trial. Letters were at once dispatched to appropriate colonial officials, but on August 10, the law officers reported that American offenders could not be tried under this act although indictments might be had for treason. A few days later, Hillsborough resigned, and the direction of American affairs passed to Lord Dartmouth. Both the change and the adverse report of the law officers required a new approach to the problem. Meantime, public indignation mounted in Britain. Thurlow, the attorney general, considered the affair "five times the magnitude of the Stamp Act."[11] The King advised Secretary of State Rochford to moderate his attitude toward France whose *quai* at Dunkirk remained undemolished despite the Peace of 1763. "We must," said the King to North, "get the Colonies in order before we engage with our Neighbours."[12]

At the cabinet on August 20, a new plan was presented and adopted. Hillsborough's previous letters were cancelled. A commission would be issued to Governor Wanton of Rhode Island, to the admiralty judge at Boston, and to the chief justices of Massachusetts, New York, and New Jersey bidding them seek out the identity of the criminals. Once their identity was established, the civil magistrates of Rhode Island would be called upon to arrest them and deliver them to Admiral Montagu. General Gage would be ordered to furnish military assistance at need.[13] Six days later, the King duly approved the commission and a proclamation for apprehending the offenders.

It is difficult to believe that the ministry expected their plan to succeed. The Governor of Rhode Island, as an elected official, could hardly be expected to act with zeal under the commission. Further, the whole plan rested ultimately upon the civil magistrates of Rhode Island who would be asked to arrest their compatriots and turn them over to Montagu. That the commission proved a fiasco should have surprised no

---

[11] RHMCR. *Dartmouth Papers*, II, 91–92, John Pownall to Dartmouth, August 29, 1772.
[12] Fortescue, *Correspondence of George III*, II, No. 1102, the King to North, August 1, 1772.
[13] RHMCR. *Dartmouth Papers*, II, 88, minute of cabinet, August 20, 1772.

one. Two sessions, one in January and another in May, 1773, established only that no evidence of the identity of the mobsters could be found.

The colonists, not only in Rhode Island but throughout America, viewed the commission with "abhorrence." Chief Justice Smythe, of New Jersey, was convinced it would have required armed might to commit any of the offenders to Montagu's custody.[14] So probably the failure of the commission postponed the outbreak of hostilities in America. In England, however, it served to intensify the growing determination to bring the Colonies under effective control.

In the Colonies, the net result of the North Ministry's effort to vindicate law and order was three-fold. First, colonial unity was reaffirmed and strengthened. No longer could the ministry or Parliament delude themselves that Massachusetts was the sole disturber of the imperial peace. "If anything therefore be done by Parliament respecting America," Hutchinson wrote home in April, "it now seems necessary that it should be general and not confined to particular Colonies."[15] Secondly, the imperial government was further discredited. A royal commission had been made an object of ridicule, and American radicals were confirmed in their belief that royal government was too ineffectual to be feared. Finally, the commission lessened Dartmouth's initial popularity at a critical moment: when he was urgently needed as a bridge between the colonists and the ministry.

Lord Dartmouth was a sincere friend to the Colonies. Amiable, pious, and commonplace, the former Old Whig desperately wanted a peaceable settlement of the American problem. He found himself, however, surrounded by colleagues who disagreed with his American views, treated him as a well-meaning nonentity, and sought to engross American business

[14] Smythe is quoted by Channing, *History of the United States*, III, 127.
[15] RHMCR. *Dartmouth Papers*, I, 335, Hutchinson to John Pownall, April 19, 1773.

all they could.[16] Often circumventing these colleagues by seeking an accommodation outside the cabinet framework, Dartmouth would then encounter the stone wall of colonial hatred
for the ministry of which he was a member. Measures pursued
by the home government since the end of the war, and a constant confirmation of their view received from men like Wilkes
and Burke, had convinced most Americans that a wicked "Court
system" was plotting their enslavement. Indeed every new in-
cident in America had evoked an increasingly authoritarian reaction in the mother country. This, in turn, was then taken
as a further step in the ministerial design. Dartmouth found
himself involved in this tragic spiral.

It is impossible to say that Edmund Burke caused the colonists generally to harbor such thoughts and suspicions. There
is no doubt, however, that he had a hand in the formation of
New York's opinion of the North government. And as he
permitted the assembly of that province to circulate his letters
to them, he must also have had a part in the forming of American opinion at large. Burke had become colonial agent for the
New York Assembly at the turn of the decade. His violent and
passionate nature, his hatred of the King's Friends and the
North Ministry, his conviction that only the Old Whigs were
fit to govern an empire, and their discredited position which
he could but attribute to some dark influence, all led him to
seek among his American constituents that support so lacking
at home. When, for instance, in 1771, Hillsborough refused
to receive as colonial agent any person not duly appointed by
a full act of assembly, Burke immediately wrote, "This I consider in Effect, as destructive of one of the most necessary me-
diums of communication between the Colonies and the parent
Country. The provinces ought in my opinion to have a *direct*

[16] Bamber Gascoigne at the Board of Trade and Suffolk especially
constantly attempted to undermine Dartmouth. The Bedfords and Rochford
sided against him. Indeed, he had only one supporter in the cabinet, North,
and he was not always to be depended upon. See RHMCR. *Knox Papers,
Various Collections*, 110, John Pownall to Knox, July 23, 1773.

intercourse with Ministry and Parliament here, by some person who might be truly confidential with them who appoint him." Intervention of the governors in naming an agent "would totally frustrate" this end, and the agent would become a mere officer of the Crown. In short, the plan for Burke was so "ministerial" that if the government insisted upon carrying it into effect, he would, he declared, resign as agent. If the Colonies needed any encouragement to resist Hillsborough's new measure, Burke had given it. Only Hillsborough's fall prevented the development of a first-rate crisis.

In his reports to the assembly, Burke rarely confined himself to attacks upon the ministry's American policy. The Royal Marriage Bill, "little conformable to the Spirit of our Laws, and the genius of the English constitution," called forth a long tirade. To explain the weakness of his own party, he invoked time after time the bogey words, "Court Scheme," "all-prevailing influence," "well-formed and well-paid Bands of the Court," each designed to persuade the colonists that the Old Whigs, their only British friends, were fighting valiantly against ministerial werewolves.[17]

While Burke, unbeknownst to Dartmouth, added fuel to a fire soon to be grown beyond control, internal troubles had come to the Colonies. Hard times and depression, widely viewed as direct results of the ministerial American policy, were disrupting colonial life. Class war threatened, indeed in North Carolina actually broke out in the War of the Regulators. Never more than in these years just before the Revolution had frontiersmen and poor farmers been so hostile to eastern merchants and aristocrats who held them by the double bonds of debt and political domination.

In Massachusetts, which was especially hard hit by the de-

[17] Wentworth-Woodhouse, Burke Papers, Letterbook, Burke to the Committee of Correspondence of the New York Assembly, December 4, 1771; Burke to James Delancey, same date; Burke to the Committee, June 30, 1772; Burke to Delancey, August 20, 1772, December 31, 1772; Burke to Speaker Cruger, April 16, 1773.

pression, unrest took the form of a mounting discontent with the home government. The assembly sent two petitions and remonstrances against the decision to pay Crown officers from the American revenue. The old dispute between Hutchinson and his assembly flared again, and such contempt was expressed for parliamentary authority that Dartmouth told Franklin he saw no way to avoid bringing the affair before Parliament. The American Secretary's position had become very delicate. Fearing that Parliament's intervention would merely inflame the situation, he strongly opposed such a step. Yet, should he not lay the American papers before them, he risked being charged with criminal neglect and dereliction of duty.

In the summer of 1773, therefore, taking advantage of Parliament's absence, Dartmouth sought to stem the rising tide of ill-humor in Massachusetts by extracabinet means. Bypassing the usual chain of authority, he addressed himself directly to Thomas Cushing, the speaker of the assembly. Delighted colonial leaders saw in Dartmouth's action only an insult to Governor Hutchinson; but the American Secretary's real purpose was to establish contact with the malcontents and then use his personal prestige to procure some peaceable settlement. In his letter, Dartmouth expressed great concern at colonial unrest. Refusing to involve himself in a discussion of parliamentary right, he went straight to the heart of the dispute. Let such theories be what they might, he believed that the right to tax should be "suspended and lie dormant till some occasions should arise, if any such can be, in which the Expediency and Necessity of such Exercise should be obvious to every considerate Man in every Part of the Dominions of Great Britain." In contrast to his view, Dartmouth pointed to the "wild and extravagant Doctrines" put forward by the assembly in their disputes with the governor, terming them "a most serious (I had almost said, an insuperable) Bar" to the return of tranquillity. Only by their own actions, Dartmouth said, could that bar be removed. In return, he promised his aid and support in a general settlement of their complaints.

Such an attitude expressed by a secretary of state even two years earlier would probably have quieted America. Now, however, Cushing, while firmly denying that his assembly had rejected Parliament's supremacy, reminded Dartmouth that the Colonies were already laboring under an imperial revenue tax, and that only a repeal of it would bring peace.[18] Thus each side demanded a prior concession of the other, and concession itself would not come until too late.

Dartmouth's attempt at personal intervention consequently failed. Even before his letter had arrived in Massachusetts, events in that colony had blasted any hope there might have been for his success. The assembly had come into possession of Hutchinson's confidential letters to England and those of Lieutenant-Governor Oliver. Franklin had obtained the letters in London from an anonymous friend under certainly questionable circumstances. Both officials now stood revealed as favoring more rigorous measures by the home government, enforced by troops if necessary, in order to prevent colonial independence. The letters provided a fillip for the radical cause, and soon the whole colony was ablaze with indignation against two men whose confidence had been betrayed. The assembly, evading with sophistry Franklin's injunction that the letters not be published, immediately circulated copies throughout the colony and its neighbors. Soon, they had voted them as designed "to subvert the constitution and introduce arbitrary power," and a petition went to England asking the removal of both Hutchinson and Oliver, probably crossing paths with Dartmouth's letter to Cushing. Not only did Dartmouth's well-meaning attempt fail, then, but colonial radicalism got such a spur that

[18] B. F. Stevens, *Facsimiles of MSS in European Archives Relating to America*, No. 2025, Dartmouth to Cushing, draft; No. 2028, Cushing to Dartmouth, August 22, 1773.

Joseph Ward, writing from Boston in June, warned Dartmouth that "the System for a commonwealth in America seems by every appearance to be ripening fast."[19]

New events were to drive spiraling antagonisms to the breaking point. Once more, the history of the East India Company crossed that of the American Colonies. Chatham, during his ill-fated ministry, had hoped to derive a revenue from the company, thereby saving the Colonies from taxes. His collapse had brought failure to this plan, and Townshend, desperately needing funds, had substituted the Colonies for the company as more proper objects of imperial taxation. Subsequently, the government had arrived at an agreement with the company by which that body paid into the exchequer £400,000 a year. By then, of course, the Townshend taxes had been levied, and the controversy over right between the mother country and the Colonies had grown to such proportions that retreat was impossible.

Since their agreement with the government, however, the company had become increasingly embarrassed. Much of the parliamentary session which opened in November, 1772, had to be spent investigating the company and passing legislation to govern its operations. It was now brought directly under government control, but so critical were its finances that far from augmenting government revenue, it had to borrow a great sum to avoid total collapse.

Ironically, in view of what followed, Franklin sought to use the bad state of the company as an argument for the repeal of Townshend's tea tax, the "splinter in the wound." He pointed out to Dartmouth that the government had just lost a sizeable revenue from the company, while there had been numerous private bankruptcies because of the drastic fall in East India stock. The public credit itself had been shaken, and the failure of fifteen banking houses in Amsterdam had caused

[19] RHMCR. *Dartmouth Papers*, II, 158, Joseph Ward to Dartmouth, June 26, 1773.

what the King described as "a fresh stagnation of Credit." Yet in the company's warehouses lay four million pounds sterling in tea while the American market was being supplied by French, Dutch, Swedish, and Danish smugglers.[20] Should the tea tax be repealed, Franklin intimated, the whole American market would become available to the company.

This was a cogent argument. North was not unaware of the company's assets in tea, but he proposed to use them in quite a different manner from that Franklin had suggested. His policy of firmness forbade a repeal of the American tea tax. That would have to be maintained as a matter of principle. There remained however, a way in which he could relieve the company, maintain the principle, and, he thought, exploit the American market too. On April 27, 1773, therefore, North rose in the Commons and proposed that the company be allowed to export tea directly to British America. It should be free of duties payable in Britain, though still subject to the Townshend duty of three pence a pound in America. The price of the tea in the Colonies would then be substantially lower than that of the smuggled article.[21] Economic interest would induce the colonists to accept the taxed tea, thereby tacitly admitting Parliament's right to raise a revenue from them. The House accepted this plan and resolved that it take effect from May 10.

In America, the news of Parliament's boon to the company was a signal for renewed outbursts of violence. To American radicals, it was obviously a ministerial design to undermine the colonial determination to take no article taxed for revenue. Crown officials in Boston were soon warning the home government of a new "trumpery Spirit of independency" there springing up, with resistance to the landing of the tea fully to be

[20] Sparks, *Franklin's Works*, VIII, 28–31, Franklin to Cushing, January 5, 1773; see also Fortescue, *Correspondence of George III*, II, No. 1182, the King to North, January 1, 1773.

[21] Cobbett and Wright, *Parliamentary History*, XVII, 840–41.

expected.[22] Hutchinson reported in mid-November that conditions had become so chaotic, and the council so backward in putting down the new riots, that he despaired of restoring order. Indeed, riots in Boston, late in the month, drove the Customs Commissioners and five of the tea consignees to Castle William. On December 14, Hutchinson wrote that the radicals planned to prevent any landing of tea from the three tea ships which had just arrived.

Up and down the Atlantic seaboard, the tea had met with firm refusals. It had indeed been landed at Charleston but had been promptly stored, and was to be auctioned three years later for support of a rebel government. Philadelphia and New York had obliged reshipment of the tea to England. At Boston, however, Hutchinson felt that the time had come for a showdown with the radicals. Firmly believing that established government was at hazard, he now determined not to retreat an inch. Despite—or perhaps because of—ominous signs that a crisis greater than that of '65 was imminent, he refused to allow the ships to depart until they should discharge their cargo. Thus he forced the issue.

On December 17, therefore, it was his unhappy duty to report to Dartmouth that during the preceding night, a band of Boston "Indians" had boarded the tea vessels, had seized 340 chests of that article, and had thrown them into the harbor. Neither Admiral Montagu nor the temporary military commander, Colonel Leslie (Gage had returned to England), had been called upon for aid because the council had refused to sanction military intervention. Hutchinson was aghast. Here was a determination equal to his own. "At and near Boston," he wrote, "the people seem regardless of all consequences. I may not presume to propose measures. To enforce the duty appears beyond all comparison more difficult than I ever before imagined."[23]

[22] Stevens, *Facsimilies*, No. 2029, Benjamin Hallowell to John Pownall; see also Add. MSS 38207, f. 304, General Haldimand to Dartmouth, November 3, 1773, copy.

Thus a final crisis had come. Both sides were now committed to doctrines whence there was no retreat. To yield would be to forfeit all. Previously, Parliament had postponed a comprehensive treatment of the American problem. Now, however, a new chapter in Anglo-American relations was at hand—the era of parliamentary coercion.

"The popular current," Burke wrote to the New York Assembly soon after the Boston Tea Party, "both within doors and without, at present sets sharply against America." To make certain that the colonists should harbor no thoughts of a compromise, he added, "That you may not be deceived by any Idle or flattering report, be assured, that the Determination to enforce Obedience from the Colonies to Laws of Revenue, by the most powerful means, seems as firm as possible, and that the Ministry appears stronger than ever I have known them."[24]

Public opinion had in fact turned universally against the Bostonians. While Alderman Bull, radical Member and ardent admirer of Wilkes, might wish Boston cleared of British soldiers—"brutes that have too long been suffered to live there"—his voice was the exception.[25] The Opposition, weak and divided, was stunned. "The conduct of the Americans cannot be justified," wrote Rockingham to Burke, although he declared he would never sanction the use of force against the colonists.[26] Chatham himself branded the destruction of the tea as "certainly criminal." Moreover the King's own attitude had changed greatly. Receiving advice from General Gage, who had assured him that the Americans would be "lyons, whilst we are Lambs," and that four regiments of troops would quick-

[23] RHMCR. *Dartmouth Papers*, I, 342–44, Hutchinson to Dartmouth, December 17, 1773.

[24] Wentworth-Woodhouse, Burke Papers, Letterbook, Burke to the New York Assembly's Committee of Correspondence, April 6 and May 4, 1774.

[25] Add. MSS 30870, ff. 228–29, Bull to Wilkes, December 5, 1773.

[26] William, Fitzwilliam, and Bourke, *Burke's Correspondence*, I, 448–50, Rockingham to Burke, January 30, 1774.

ly bring Massachusetts to submission, the King now laid the blame for the renewed violence to "the fatal compliance in 1766." Believing that America had declared for independence, George was ready to endorse the use of force if necessary.[27]

Within the ministry, Dartmouth, hating the thought of military coercion as much as did his former chief Rockingham, soon found himself, in his plea for moderate measures, alone or supported only by a wavering North. The Bedfordites, erstwhile friends of Grenville, the King's Friends, and the King himself saw the Tea Party as utterly the last straw. Both Dartmouth and North, however, hoped to confine coercive measures to Boston. Both accepted the necessity of punishing that city, but beyond this they did not wish to go. They were nonetheless to be forced, by a cabinet solidly ranged against them, down a path for which neither had any inclination.

Of the four so-called Coercive Acts—a fifth, the Quebec Act, so regarded by the colonists may not be properly considered with the others—only the first derived from Dartmouth's American plan. Acting on a suggestion from his undersecretary, John Pownall, Dartmouth proposed to the cabinet on February 4 that both the Customs House and the assembly be moved from Boston until that city submit to Parliament's supremacy. Boston would cease to be the political and mercantile center of New England, and economic distress, he believed, would bring her to obedience. It should be noticed at this point that Dartmouth supposed—and it was a belief shared by all the cabinet even after the Coercive Acts had been broadened to include the whole of Massachusetts—that, for so patently criminal an act as the Tea Party, Boston would be condemned by the rest of the American settlements. No colony would intervene in behalf of the transgressor. So firm was this belief that the situation was not even seen to involve a calculated risk. Only Chatham, perhaps, was aware that colonial

---

[27] Fortescue, *Correspondence of George III*, III, No. 1379, the King to North, February 4, 1774.

resistance might become general. "The violence committed upon the tea-cargo is certainly criminal; nor would it be real kindness to the Americans to adopt their passions and wild pretensions," he wrote. Boston certainly owed reparation; but he feared, with reason, that Britain would lose her moral advantage if she sought by this opportunity to enforce her "general declared rights." Rather she ought to seek satisfaction merely for a specific wrong. Her demand for reparation and their refusal of that demand should, he believed, precede coercive measures.[28] An accumulated discontent and irritation against the Colonies, both in the cabinet and in Parliament, however, ruled out so wide a mode of action. The coercive measures were not, in fact, intended to win compensation for the East India Company: they were to punish "the last overt act of high treason, proceeding from over lenity and want of foresight." Great Britain would thus cross the Rubicon, and the colonists—not only those of Massachusetts but of all America—would know that the mother country could temporize no longer, and that the time for debate had passed.[29]

As soon as the cabinet had accepted Dartmouth's suggestion of a port bill for Boston, North and the American Secretary, aided by John Pownall, hoping to forestall harsher measures, quickly drew up the bill for introduction into Parliament. Until this time the two half-brothers had worked well together, but on February 25, North, suffering a chance defeat in the Commons on a relatively unimportant point, experienced one of those attacks of melancholia which were to become increasingly frequent during his ministry. So despondent was he that it was with the greatest difficulty that Suffolk, acting at the King's request, prevented his resignation. When, as soon became obvious, his colleagues demanded more stringent Ameri-

[28] Taylor and Pringle, *Chatham Correspondence*, IV, 336–38, Chatham to Shelburne, March 20, 1774.

[29] The quotations are from Mansfield's speech in the Lords during debate on the port act which was reported to Chatham by Shelburne. See Taylor and Pringle, *Chatham Correspondence*, IV, 339–41, Shelburne to Chatham, April 4, 1774.

can measures, he had neither the energy nor the courage to support Dartmouth. The temper of his colleagues had been demonstrated when on January 29, the Privy Council, under Gower, suddenly resumed consideration of the Massachusetts petition for removal of Hutchinson and Oliver. The hearing had been but an elaborately staged expression of imperial wrath, with Franklin as its target. Solicitor-General Wedderburn, by his splendid, malevolent, and venomous invective denouncing Franklin for his part in making public the Hutchinson-Oliver letters, had delighted thirty-five privy councilors and a large audience. The petition had then been contemptuously dismissed, and the next day, Franklin, who had resigned his agencies, was summarily turned out of his office as deputy postmaster for North America. The day's work had cost Britain much, however: she had made an implacable enemy.

It is impossible to gauge with precision Dartmouth's resistance to the subsequent Coercive Acts. Certainly, his task was not rendered easier by Boston's unrepentant belligerency. Far from seeking the forgiveness of Parliament, the people, on March 9, made a second raid upon a newly arrived tea ship and destroyed thirty more chests of that commodity. In any case, Dartmouth was brought to agree to the second act, that for regulating the government of Massachusetts. For that purpose, it was deemed necessary to alter the charter of the colony, long a favorite measure of that new baronet and old governor of Massachusetts Sir Francis Bernard, with whom North was in close communication at this time. Dartmouth wished to limit the changes to Hillsborough's old proposal of vesting the appointment of the council in the Crown. Probably at Bernard's suggestion, however, other "improvements" were incorporated in the act. North described it as designed "to take the executive power from the hands of the democratic part of government." The legislative power of the council and assembly would remain as they were. The governor would appoint magistrates, judges, sheriffs, and all civil officers except justices of the Supreme Court. Jurymen, no longer to be elected, would be summoned by the sheriffs. Town meetings were to be practically forbidden. Dartmouth, however, won a minor victory against a proposal that the tea rioters be tried for their crime in Great Britain.[30]

With the second measure, North had reached the limit of his own intentions. Serious tensions were now developing within his cabinet. Dartmouth and Suffolk, in violent disagreement on American measures, were at daggers drawn. The American Secretary told Shelburne of the great difficulties under which he labored but declared he was determined "to cover America from the present storm to the utmost of his power." Barré reported that North, too, was moderate. But extremely noticeable in parliamentary debate was "a more than disregard to Lord Dartmouth, and somewhat of the same sort towards Lord North" on the part of the other ministers.[31] It was apparent that the Bedfordites and Suffolk were trying to seize the initiative from the American Secretary.

The third Coercive Act had its origin in a cabinet meeting of March 30. It is significant that Bedfordite Sandwich, rather than Dartmouth, kept the minutes of the meeting. Sir Jeffrey Amherst and General Gage were examined. Under questioning, they declared that if British soldiers should be taken by the Bostonians during the suppression of a riot and after bloodshed and should then be tried by a local jury, they would have no fair chance for their lives. It was consequently decided that an act for the impartial administration of justice was indicated. Should British soldiers be charged with crimes committed in Massachusetts, they were to be tried in some court other than those of the province.[32]

---

[30] RHMCR. *Dartmouth Papers*, II, 198, cabinet minutes, February 16, 19, 1774. See also Fortescue, *Correspondence of George III*, III, No. 1416, the King to North, March 14, 1774.

[31] Taylor and Pringle, *Chatham Correspondence*, IV, 334 ff., Shelburne to Chatham, March 15, April 4, 1774.

[32] Hinchingbrooke Papers, Sandwich's cabinet minutes, March 30, 1774.

The Boston Port Bill received the royal signature on March 31, and Gage, now ordered back to Massachusetts as governor and captain general, was instructed to carry it with him and to put it into effect on June 1. The government would be transferred to Salem. Since the bill changing the charter had not yet become law, Gage was authorized to veto election of any member of the council. Concluding his instructions, Dartmouth made another bid to stave off the outbreak of hostilities: "Every care is to be taken to quiet the people by gentle means, the troops over whom the Governor has the command are not to be called out unless absolutely necessary."[33]

The fourth coercive measure was the Quartering Act, which improved upon the Military Act. It provided that where —as in Boston—barracks were not conveniently located, the province itself should provide accommodations. Should it refuse, the governor might seize unoccupied houses or barns, for which a reasonable compensation would be paid. The last of the acts became law in May.

It was with fear that Dartmouth viewed the future, and with pathetic eagerness that he sought a peaceful solution. In his correspondence with American friends, he argued that if only Massachusetts would submit, he was certain all grievances could be settled to colonial satisfaction.[34] For the colonists, however, Acts of Parliament spoke louder than one man's voice.

For the Opposition, the American problem had become difficult, indeed. They had heard North solemnly declare that at Boston, America and Britain were already considered separate and independent states, and that "we are no longer to dispute between legislation and taxation, we are to consider only whether or not we have any authority there."[35] Both Chathamites and Old Whigs were unwilling to identify them-

---

[33] RHMCR. *Dartmouth Papers*, I, 351–52, Dartmouth to Gage, April 9, 11, 1774.

[34] *Ibid.*, I, 354–55, Dartmouth to Joseph Reed, May 30, 1774, draft.

[35] Cobbett and Wright, *Parliamentary History*, XVII, 1159.

Courtesy Library of Congress

CHARLES TOWNSHEND

Courtesy New York Public Library

LORD NORTH

selves with Boston's cause, and felt it necessary rather to present apologies for measures pursued during their ministries. Shelburne, for instance, told Chatham in February that "the great object of my parliamentary conduct would be to prove, that if the King had continued his confidence in the sound part of his administration of 1767, the East Indies might have proved the salvation of this country, without injury to the Company, or to any individual; and that peace might have been preserved in Europe, and in America."[36] Both Shelburne and Barré subsequently supported the Boston Port Bill, in order, they said, the more effectively to counter future stringent measures. It was not, indeed, until the third coercive measure—that for the impartial administration of justice—that Barré raised his voice. He now warned the House that they were goading America into rebellion and that they were becoming the aggressors.[37] Chatham's own objections to the coercive system were made when, at the invitation of the ministry on May 27, he attended the debate on the Quartering Act. Still in a weakened condition, the sick man attacked the whole plan because it punished the innocent as well as "a few lawless depredators and their abettors."[38] He could do nothing, however, to stem the tide now running so strongly.

The Old Whigs, thwarted in their attempt to identify themselves with the public, had practically withdrawn from politics. On March 19, however, Burke presented his great apologia for his party in his speech on American taxation.[39]

Condemning the ministry for their but partial repeal of the Townshend taxes, Burke called for an honest and forthright repeal of the whole act. He then traced the rise of Amer-

[36] Taylor and Pringle, *Chatham Correspondence*, IV, 322–26, Shelburne to Chatham, February 3, 1774.

[37] Cobbett and Wright, *Parliamentary History*, XVII, 1205.

[38] *Ibid.*, 1356. Chatham was in constant communication at this time with Franklin; the radical American sheriffs of London, William Lee, brother of Arthur Lee, and Stephen Sayre; and with Samuel Wharton. See Chatham Papers, 48, 55, 66, *passim*.

[39] Cobbett and Wright, *Parliamentary History*, XVII, 1216 ff.

ican resistance from Grenville's administration forward. Internal taxes for revenue, he declared, were contrary to principles of commerce and political equity. For that reason his party had repealed the Stamp Act. So eager was he to justify the Old Whigs and to magnify their success in quieting the empire, that he denied Chatham's aid in winning the repeal.

The Townshend taxes had but revived the controversy, and now the only way to restore peace was to repeal those duties too. Striving with the paradox of the federal principle, stating it, but refusing to accept its implication—a limiting of Parliament's supremacy—Burke told his listeners that Parliament possessed two characters, one imperial, and the other local. In her relations with local assemblies, "she is never to intrude into the place of the others, whilst they are equal to the common ends of their institution." On the other hand, Great Britain, in her imperial character, superintended, guided, and controlled the inferior legislatures "as from the throne of heaven." Parliament had the power to say, if necessary, " 'Tax yourselves for the common supply, or parliament will do it for you.' " Her power of taxation, however, should be "an instrument of empire, and not . . . a means of supply." Requisitions, not internal taxes, were the constitutional mode of raising aids from America.

Involved in a basic contradiction of the federal principle, Burke sought to bury the inconvenient question of right. His speech did not touch the problem immediately at hand, nor did it attempt a defense of Boston. Furthermore, it did not offer a practical means for settling the troubles of the empire. Burke shut his eyes to the fact that Massachusetts had already proceeded beyond the question of taxation and had, at least in the opinion of most British politicians, actually denied the supremacy of Parliament.[40]

[40] See James Wilson, "Considerations on the Authority of Parliament," and John Adams, "Novanglus," extracts of both in Morison, *Sources and Documents*, 125–36. See also Thomas Jefferson, "Summary View." All appeared in 1774.

The colonists and the Old Whigs mistakenly accepted the Quebec Act as one of the coercive series. Yet the ministry had taken up the neglected affairs of Canada well before the Tea Party. In early December, North had suddenly called for, and William Knox had prepared, a précis of the affairs of the Province from the time of its first establishment.[41] A regulation of Canadian affairs, however, involved the whole of western policy.

Dartmouth's western views were almost identical with those of Shelburne. The new American Secretary firmly intended to create a new colony in the Ohio country and in March, 1773, actually offered the post of governor to a relative.[42] It would seem, therefore, that in view of the Privy Council's rejection of Hillsborough's earlier report against a grant to the Grand Ohio Company, and with a sympathetic Secretary presiding over colonial affairs, the Grand Ohio Company was upon the verge of success. Their grant, indeed, was ordered made out, but both the Attorney and Solicitor Generals, not usually on such terms of unanimity, joined to throw obstacles in its way, raising questions of law and procedure.

Dartmouth, however, supported by North and Mansfield, was determined to solve a problem which had been handed on to so many successive ministers. In the spring of 1773, he returned to Shelburne's idea of a regulation of the quitrents as a source of funds for developing the west. Consequently, the Privy Council received a report from the Board of Trade on June 3: lands on the Ohio were to be divided into lots of 100 to 1000 acres and were to be sold at auction, subject to a quitrent of a half-penny per acre. This proposal, had it come sooner, would probably have resulted in a final settlement of the vex-

[41] RHMCR. *Knox Papers, Various Collections,* 111, Pownall to Knox, December 3, 1773.
[42] RHMCR. *Dartmouth Papers,* I, 335, Dartmouth to Major Legge, March 17, 1773. The salary would have been £1,000 per annum, but Legge preferred to take the office of governor of Nova Scotia.

ing problem; now, however, it was too late.[43] Although the report was accepted, and the Privy Council ordered additional instructions to the governors based upon it, the net result was merely an intensified resistance to the mother country. Virginia's claim to the Ohio territory had been ignored, driving Jefferson to the radical assertion, in his "Summary View" of 1774, that vacant lands in America were not of the King's domain. Governor Dunmore, who found his own speculative schemes threatened, short-circuited the plan in that same year by leading an army of Virginians into the back country, defeating the Indians, and wresting from them a new boundary, the Ohio.

Dartmouth understood that any settlement of the western problem must include Canada as well. Since he had come to power, he had carried on a very full investigation of that province, consulting a wide variety of authorities. Among them were Maurice Morgann, Shelburne's former undersecretary and his confidential adviser on Canadian matters; Gage; Thurlow; Wedderburn; Hey and Maseres, the Canadian law officers; and many others. Even the Tea Party did not cause Dartmouth to drop his grand design. The results of his researches are to be found in the Quebec Act.

This act sought primarily to remedy the faults of the Proclamation of 1763. Bold and statesmanlike, it provided for a military governor and council nominated by the Crown and fully possessed of legislative power. Until the inhabitants of Canada, the great majority of whom were French and without experience in representative government, could be indoctrinated in parliamentary processes, the blessings of a colonial assembly would have to be foregone. Furthermore, English criminal and traditional French civil law were combined to form a legal system more satisfactory and more humane. Roman Catholics were given complete toleration and full legal rights, including that of jury service. Tithes were legalized.

[43] See Alvord, *Mississippi Valley*, II, 237 ff.

The act was, then, a sincere attempt to right the wrongs inflicted upon a great body of alien people absorbed into the empire through conquest. No longer would a handful of English merchants and fur traders, constituting a "representative Assembly," rule a population who outnumbered them a hundredfold and yet were politically incapacitated.

The religious provisions greatly offended the ardently protestant seaboard colonies, but their chief outcry was raised because of the extension of the Canadian boundaries southward to include much of their own hinterland, the present states of Wisconsin, Michigan, Illinois, Indiana, and Ohio. The reason for such an extension was obvious. It was to bring that territory under the jurisdiction of some established government for purposes of law and order. It was a necessary step toward eventual settlement of the territory. The colonists, however, did not so regard it. Already on the brink of revolution, they saw in this act an insidious attempt to create a powerful French-Canadian and Indian threat on their frontiers. Such a belief was supported out of the words of various political figures in England. Lord Lyttelton had in debate delivered a philippic against the colonists and praised the Quebec Act for just such reasons. Burke, too, confirmed colonial apprehensions.

The Quebec Act so enraged him that his violent misinterpretation of ministerial policy reached new heights of fantasy. The act, he informed New York politicians, aimed at nothing less than to confine the Colonies' growth and so keep them weak and subordinate. He had fought the extension of Canada's boundary, but he had lost out to a ministry eager to extend prerogative over as much territory as possible.[44] Thus interpreted, the Quebec Act was of vast importance in swinging New York into line with the other colonies.

Burke apparently did not realize that his letters were inflaming a situation rapidly getting beyond control. One of the

[44] Wentworth-Woodhouse, Burke Papers, Letterbook, Burke to the New York Assembly Committee of Correspondence, August 2, 1774.

more curious misapprehensions of this time was a widespread conviction, especially apparent among the Old Whigs, that neither America nor Great Britain would proceed to the last resort. Sir George Savile predicted to Burke in September, 1774, that colonial affairs would not cause sufficient trouble to make the first session of the new Parliament one of great activity. Rockingham, confused and uncertain, thought America would soon grow quiet. Even Burke agreed that "the American and foreign affairs will not come to any crisis, sufficient to rouse the public from its present stupefaction."[45]

The Coercive Acts passed, Parliament was prorogued on June 22. The ministry had now to await America's reaction. There was abroad a general optimism. It was widely felt that since Britain had at last called the colonial bluff, the fractious Colonies would subside. Hutchinson, newly arrived from Boston, reported such would be the case and went on record with an opinion that Americans would never dare resist British troops. Rumors had it that her sister colonies had abandoned Massachusetts to her fate. Congratulations poured in upon the ministry for so happy a beginning of their American plan.

Soon, however, the news took a change for the worse. It became known that a general congress had been summoned in America. Gage reported from Boston that civil government was near an end, and that he despaired of a peaceable outcome unless the congress should recommend submission. In August, he published his list of "Mandamus Councillors." A meeting of delegates from the towns at once voted them unconstitutional, denied the supremacy of Parliament, and suggested a provincial congress to take charge of government. The new councilors, hunted out of their home towns by angry mobs, were forced to resign or to flee to Boston for protection. Gage, foreseeing an armed clash, did not think his troops sufficient

---

[45] *Ibid.*, Savile to Burke, September 13, 1774; William, Fitzwilliam, and Bourke, *Burke Correspondence*, I, 469–82, Burke to Rockingham, September 16, 1774.

to restore civil government until reinforcements should arrive.[46] A more sinister consideration for the ministry was the fact that the other colonies were rallying to the support of Massachusetts. Dartmouth pinned his rapidly declining hopes on the congress. Believing it illegal, he was nonetheless eager to use it in any way that might bring peace. He stood alone, however. Both sides had reached a point of no retreat: "The dye is now cast," the King told North; "the Colonies must either submit or triumph; I do not wish to come to severer measures but we must not retreat."[47]

To prepare for any contingency, the King determined upon an early dissolution of Parliament. North finally yielded despite misgivings about the government's unpreparedness, and against a background of a deepening Anglo-American crisis, the general election of 1774 proceeded. Although Gower wrote that affairs in America were "of a very alarming nature, and big with mischief to the two countries, for I am sure they may too properly be called two now,"[48] and although reports circulated with truth that American vessels at Southampton and Amsterdam were loading quantities of gunpowder and war stores, the American issue played a surprisingly small part in the general election. Burke came in at Bristol on a moderately pro-American "platform" based upon his concern for the welfare of the merchants of the kingdom. The electors in London, Westminster, the borough of Southwark, and the county of Middlesex—all radical strongholds—obliged candidates to sign a test which, among other things, bound them to work for the repeal of the Coercive Acts and for a reconciliation with America. The great majority of election contests were fought, however, along traditional lines of difference and were free

[46] RHMCR. *Dartmouth Papers,* I, 361–62, Gage to Dartmouth, September 2, 1774.

[47] Add. MSS 38208, f. 100, Israel Mauduit to Jenkinson, September 15, 1774. See also Fortescue, *Correspondence of George III,* III, No. 1508, the King to North, September 11, 1774.

[48] RHMCR. *Dartmouth Papers,* I, 364, Gower to Dartmouth, October 6, 1774.

of American implications. The colonists had counted on the general election for an overthrow of North and the adoption of a conciliatory policy, but the new Parliament represented an unqualified victory for the King, Lord North, and the latter's indefatigable secretary to the Treasury, John Robinson. The steady friends to government were calculated at 321, a more than comfortable majority. The contest produced no startling change or upheaval. David Hartley, a nephew of Lord Mansfield, came into Parliament in the Old Whig interest. Sheriff Stephen Sayre, although with Chatham's blessing, sought a seat unsuccessfully, and Lord Clare by declining the poll at Bristol inadvertently made room for Burke's colleague, "a hot Wilkite and American Patriot, Mr. Cruger."[49] It was, however, obvious that North and his ministry had retained a comfortable majority within Parliament and among the electors.

The meeting of the first Continental Congress in September, with delegates from all of the thirteen colonies but Georgia, indicated for Gage that he was up against a united resistance and made him painfully aware of his own helplessness. In September, he urged the hiring of Hanoverian and Hessian mercenaries, [advising the home government that "these provinces must be first totally subdued before they will obey." Until Great Britain was actually prepared to crush resistance, he suggested a suspension of the Coercive Acts] For this seemingly pusillanimous suggestion, the King and a majority of the cabinet never forgave the hapless general. Even more disturbing to Gage, however, was the "considerable" number of desertions both from his small force and from the navy. Graves, the incompetent protégé of Sandwich, who had succeeded Montagú as naval commander-in-chief, joined with Gage in calling for reinforcements.[50]

[49] Add. MSS 35427, ff. 6, 8, 11–12, Hutchinson to Hardwicke, January 5, April 19, May 5, 29, 1775; Fortescue, *Correspondence of George III*, III, No. 1518, North to the King, September, 1774.

On October 3 the cabinet met to consider the dispatches from the two commanders. Rejecting Gage's diagnosis of affairs, they insisted upon believing that Massachusetts could be isolated. Indeed, this was a necessary premise to the success of their intended action. Should colonial resistance become general, it was admitted, Gage would "certainly want a much greater force than can well be spared here." Until future events should bear out his pessimistic forecast, however, it was decided to undertake no general mobilization of the country's military and naval power, although three ships of the line, with marine detachments amounting to some six hundred men, were to be sent to bolster both Gage and Graves. Underlying the cabinet's unwillingness to send greater reinforcements was the stark fact that no regiment could be spared from the home scene.[51]

Even at this early date there existed within the ministry a fundamental cleavage which was to become of great importance. From the first, Lord Sandwich, first lord of the Admiralty, and Barrington, secretary at war, were skeptical of sending large reinforcements to North America. Each saw France as potentially the main danger, and each wished to build up strength to counter any sudden attack from the House of Bourbon. United on this point, they nevertheless worked against each other, Sandwich preferring to send troops to North America while he husbanded British naval strength in European waters. Barrington, on the other hand, wished to make the struggle in America primarily a naval one and to avoid stripping Great Britain of her troops. Time after time, Barrington, who held no seat in the cabinet, advised withdrawing the troops from Massachusetts, "where at present they can

[50] RHMCR. *Dartmouth Papers*, II, 226, Gage to Hutchinson, September 17, 1774; Hinchingbrooke Papers, Lord Lisburne, a lord of the Admiralty, to Sandwich, October 1, 1774.

[51] RHMCR. *Dartmouth Papers*, I, 364, Rochford to Dartmouth, October 5, 1774, 228, cabinet minute, October 3, 1774; Hinchingbrooke Papers, George Jackson, a lord of the Admiralty, to Sandwich, October 8, 1774.

do no good, and without intentions, may do harm." Limited as he may have been in ability, he nonetheless recognized the North American continent for the quagmire it was and knew that British armies would be swallowed up in its immense expanses.

The conduct of Massachusetts, Barrington asserted to Dartmouth, merited military conquest, but he considered it highly doubtful that conquest could be achieved. Even should that happen, occupation would be a constant and ruinous expense, and attended with all the horrors of civil war. Let the troops be withdrawn from Boston, he pleaded, and stationed in Canada, Nova Scotia, and Florida. Then let a tight naval blockade be established on the coast, and within a few months the Colonies would consent "probably to submit to a certain degree; and in my humble opinion, the whole is then over, for with dignity we may make them concessions. I repeat it, our contest is merely a point of honour." Experience had proved that "we have not strength in that part of our dominions to levy such taxes, against an universal opinion prevailing there that we have no right to lay them. Besides, many among ourselves, though persuaded of the right, doubt at least the equity of such taxations; as Parliament is less acquainted with the state of the Colonies than of Great Britain, and as Members of neither House are to bear any part of the burthen they impose." When the Americans could be brought "to submit to a certain degree," then "if we are wise we shall for the future abstain from all ideas of internal taxation."[52] Barrington's sensible suggestions carried, however, too much an aspect of compromise. A point of honor was not to be dismissed so lightly. The supremacy of Parliament had to be vindicated. "The New Eng-

[52] Channing and Coolidge, *Barrington-Bernard Correspondence*, x–xi, Barrington to Dartmouth, November 12, 1774; RHMCR. *Dartmouth Papers*, II, 243, Barrington to Dartmouth, December 24, 1774. Knox and his fellow undersecretaries agreed with Barrington as to giving up the exercise of the right of taxation. See RHMCR. *Knox Papers, Various Collections*, 257–58, "Secrets of proceedings respecting America in the new Parliament."

land Governments are in a State of Rebellion," wrote the King; "blows must decide whether they are to be subject to this Country or Independent."[53]

Logic was nonetheless clearly on the side of Barrington. Great Britain was primarily a naval power: her rise to world power had been a brilliant illustration of that very fact. Why, then, was she to allow herself to slide into a land war which would mean her defeat and her disgrace? The answer is simple: her great naval strength was still not sufficient to meet at one time European and American commitments.

The blame for Britain's unreadiness at sea has traditionally been saddled upon North's first lord of the Admiralty, John, fourth Earl of Sandwich. His profligacy and his immoral private life have been allowed to blacken his name as a minister. His family life disrupted by a mad wife and a spendthrift son, he commonly sought diversion in the abbey at Medmenham. Hated by Wilkes because he had been elected a senior member in the Medmenham secret society before that worthy himself, Sandwich was set at target both by Wilkes and by his friend Churchill, whose brilliant satire helped to drag His Lordship's name through the mud of centuries. And yet, be Sandwich's private life as it may, and it was probably no worse than that of the average eighteenth-century nobleman, he never allowed such vagaries to interfere with his work as a minister of the Crown. One of the most experienced members of North's Ministry, and indifferent to slander, he preferred to devote his time and a very real talent to the progress of the King's affairs rather than to making what replies he could to these attacks against himself. Furthermore, he was ever watchful and solicitous for the welfare of the Royal Navy. The blame for Britain's naval unpreparedness must, then, rest upon Lord North and his royal master themselves.

During the first session of Parliament in 1772, North had

[53] Fortescue, *Correspondence of George III*, III, No. 1556–57, the King to North, November 18, 1774.

held out to the House a hope that £1,500,000 might be applied annually to the decrease of the public debt. Considering himself so committed, he then determined upon a reduction of the navy and discussed it, upon several occasions, with a resolute and resisting Sandwich. He stated his fear that the revenue for 1772 would fall by £400,000. This figure can be no accident. It was the sum which the East India Company was bound to pay annually into the exchequer. In 1772, however, with the company near bankruptcy, North knew that such payments could not be kept up. In short, if North were to pay £1,500,000 on the national debt that year, £600,000 would have to be found someplace, and he now proposed that a lion's share of that sum be withheld from the navy. This would mean decommissioning four of the twenty guardships, the very cornerstone of British naval might. Should that reduction not be sufficient, more decommissionings would have to follow. In words that are hard to credit, with the burning of the "Gaspée" fresh in all minds, and when within three years the mother country would be straining every nerve to put down colonial rebellion, North declared, "I do not recollect to have seen a more pacific appearance of affairs than there is."

Sandwich fought North's proposal with all the power and eloquence at his command. He pointed out to his chief that foreign affairs by no means wore so peaceable an aspect, and he called to aid his friend Secretary of State Rochford. North was, by such resolute opposition, indeed forced to give up his plan, but meantime, an increase in naval power was effectively vetoed. Sandwich felt lucky to hold on to what he had.[54]

Moreover the Admiralty Lord had to contend with other difficulties which rendered a solely naval war in America impossible. Britain's supply of seasoned wood, used in naval construction and repairs, had been exhausted during the late war. Thus unseasoned timber had to be used, and this caused many

<hr>

[54] Hinchingbrooke Papers, North to Sandwich, September 5, 1772; Sandwich to North, September 10, 1772.

breakdowns and lengthy dry-docking.[55] Furthermore, North, desperately afraid of offending France, continued to block Sandwich's moves to increase the navy. In 1774, however, with reports that France was fitting out a fleet at Toulon, North began to take alarm. By that time the school of thought, formerly led by that minister himself, which so greatly deprecated any affront to France had gained a powerful supporter. The King himself warned North against measures likely to annoy the Bourbons, since "the conduct of our Colonies makes Peace very desirable."[56] Naval preparedness was therefore still allowed to slide. A "war of nerves" had started in Europe even before the outbreak of hostilities in America.

Faced with a full-scale rebellion, and with a call for reinforcements from his beleaguered commanders ringing in his ears, North now took a step imprudent to the point of folly. Bemused by his hope that there would yet be no general colonial war, and wishing to pay some of the national debt, he moved in the Commons (on December 12, 1774) for only 16,000 seamen in the following year, 4,000 less than in the previous year. As the East India fleet under Admiral Harland had been recalled, North convinced himself that this force, when augmented by the 16,000 sailors now requested, would be sufficient for any contingency. At this, even the Opposition was taken aback, Lord John Cavendish charging that it was a ministerial trick designed to surprise the House at some future date into "grants of a very improper and burdensome nature." At North's behest, Barrington moved for only 17,547 men for the army. Seven battalions and five companies of artillery, he revealed, were already in America, and three more battalions were ordered to join those at Boston. Ignoring information received, and speaking with almost unbelievable lack of foresight, North declared "the forces now demanded were suffi-

<hr>

[55] Navy Record Society, LXIX, *Sandwich Papers*, I, Introduction and Chap. 1. See also R. G. Albion, *Forests and Sea Power*.

[56] Fortescue, *Correspondence of George III*, III, No. 1436, the King to North, April 3, 1774.

cient, unless from the conduct of the other colonies it should be judged necessary to extend the line with respect to them."[57] Despite the meeting of the Continental Congress, despite the petition from that body, and despite constant reports that the colonists were busily preparing for war, North apparently refused to believe that the cause of Massachusetts had become the cause of America. Yet it had been none other than he who had written the speech with which the King opened the new Parliament on November 29—a speech which had referred to "a most daring spirit of resistance and disobedience to the law" which still prevailed in Massachusetts. "These proceedings," the speech continued, "have been countenanced and encouraged in other of my colonies and unwarrantable attempts have been made to obstruct the commerce of this kingdom by unlawful combinations."[58] This speech clearly recognized that the conflict had now broadened far beyond Massachusetts. The reason North apparently refused to accept the facts was that he was considering a proposition to the Colonies of a conciliatory nature. He was therefore hesitant to plunge the country into an expensive mobilization.

The greatest obstacle to a conciliatory proposition at this time must have been the proceedings of the Continental Congress, news of which arrived in England early in December. The Congress had met in September. Its early sessions had been employed chiefly in a consideration of Joseph Galloway's Plan of Union. Cruelly torn between conflicting loyalties, Galloway fervently desired some compromise to settle the controversy. His plan, similar to the Albany Plan of 1754, although it also included a federative colonial council with a power to veto Acts of Parliament relating to the Colonies, might have been adopted had not ill-timed rumors of a British attack on Boston so strengthened the radicals that they gained control. The delegates then, on September 17, quickly adopted a series

[57] Cobbett and Wright, *Parliamentary History*, XVIII, 56.
[58] *Ibid.*, 33.

of resolutions denying obedience to the Acts of 1774 and recommending that public money be withheld from the provincial treasuries until government should be put on a constitutional basis, or until such time as Congress might direct. In mid-October had come the "Declaration of Rights," in which the Congress affirmed that since Americans could not from their circumstances be represented in Parliament, their own assemblies must and did hold the power of legislation within their own borders. Hitherto they had submitted in the common interest to the Laws of Trade and Navigation. They could not, however, accept that series of grievous laws running from the Revenue Act of 1764 to the Quebec Act. A few days later, Congress adopted an "Association" by which delegates bound their colonies in a strict nonimportation, nonexportation, and nonconsumption agreement. Local committees would enforce it. The petition to the King was adopted on October 26. Moderate and noble in expression, it was directed wholly against the ministers. To a King who had "the Signall distinction of reigning over freemen we apprehend the language of freemen cannot be displeasing. Your royal indignation, we hope will rather fall on those designing and dangerous men who daringly interposing themselves between your royal person and your faithful subjects" now make such a petition necessary. To British minds such sentiments meant open rebellion.

As soon as the transactions of the Congress became known in England, a cabinet was held. Rochford reported to Sandwich, who had been absent: "absurd as you are inclined to believe the Americans to be, [the proceedings of the Congress] exceed all Ideas of rebellion and even inconsistency." The inconsistency complained of was, of course, the anomaly of a petition to the King directed against those ministers whom the King himself had chosen, and who, moreover, commanded an overwhelming majority in Parliament.

Rochford was also plainly annoyed with Dartmouth who was becoming increasingly reluctant to form and direct co-

ercive measures against all the North American colonies:
"What surprises me," complained Rochford, "is that . . . Lord
Dartmouth does not come with some plan to Cabinet. . . . I have
been free enough to tell him to do it."[59] Still Dartmouth pro-
crastinated, and so it fell to North to draw up such a plan.
Dartmouth had, in fact, hit upon the idea of sending a royal
commission to America to examine there on the spot the
troubles and to negotiate a settlement. North liked the suggestion and on consultation found Mansfield in agreement.
When he approached the King, however, George declared he
was "not so fond of the sending Commissioners," for the colonists might take it as a sign of fear. Moreover, with the Bedfords and Suffolk watching his every move and with Dartmouth his only support, North was apprehensive that any suggestion smacking of compromise would be political suicide.
Thus, to Dartmouth's great disappointment, he felt obliged
to drop for the moment the plan for a conciliatory gesture.[60]

Dartmouth, foiled of his commission, now sought to lay
the storm by extracabinet means. This attempt would demonstrate his own sincerity in seeking an amicable settlement with
the Colonies and the irreconcilability of the antagonists' views.
At Dartmouth's instigation, David Barclay, a Member with
Old Whig connections, and Dr. John Fothergill, a well-known
philanthropist, both Quakers and friends of Franklin, approached that American in December, 1774. Although they
held no official powers and the Colonial Secretary never came
out from behind the screen, daily reports of their conversations
came to both Dartmouth and North.

Franklin, of course, possessed no authority save what his
own considerable prestige in America and Britain might give
him. Responding to a question by the two Quakers—how a

<hr />

[59] Hinchingbrooke Papers, Rochford to Sandwich, December 10, 1774;
also printed in Navy Record Society, LXIX, *Sandwich Papers*, I, 55–57.

[60] Fortescue, *Correspondence of George III*, III, No. 1563, the King
to North, December 15, 1774; RHMCR. *Dartmouth Papers*, II, 251, North
to Dartmouth, December, 1774.

peaceful settlement might be achieved—he brought forward certain proposals in a list of "Hints."[61]

1. All acts binding colonial trade should be reconsidered and then re-enacted by the colonial assemblies.

2. America should maintain her own military establishment, and there should be no requisitions during time of peace.

3. No British troops were to enter or to be quartered in any province, nor royal forts built within the Colonies without consent of the individual assemblies.

4. The tea duty, the Coercive Acts, and the Quebec Act were to be repealed, and Parliament should renounce internal legislation for America.

5. Colonial judges should hold office during good behavior. They and the governors should be paid by the assemblies.

6. In return, Franklin was willing to agree to reimbursement for the East India Company's losses at the hands of the Bostonians and to guarantee the British trade monopoly.

Such demands must have staggered both Dartmouth and North, for the talks were allowed to lapse. In February, 1775, however, Fothergill and Barclay resumed their conversations with Franklin. Meeting on the fourth, they presented him a list of counterproposals, which, they admitted, had come from certain ministers, obviously Dartmouth and North.[62]

1. The suggestion that Acts of Parliament should be re-enacted by the assemblies was completely unacceptable: it implied a deficiency in the power of Parliament. However, funds arising from the Acts of Trade might remain in the Colonies.

2. Customs officers would continue to be appointed from England.

[61] Sparks, *Franklin's Works*, V, 12–14; RHMCR. *Dartmouth Papers*, II, 264.

[62] Sparks, *Franklin's Works*, V, 56.

3. Castle William would be returned to Massachusetts, but the other "hint" concerning the troops and forts was inadmissible.

4. The Boston Port Act would be repealed. The Quebec Act would be amended by reducing the Canadian boundaries to their former limits.

5. The other Coercive Acts and especially that changing the charter of Massachusetts were absolutely necessary as "a standing example of the power of Parliament."

6. That Parliament should renounce the right of internal legislation for the Colonies was unthinkable.

Franklin found the counterproposals so unsatisfactory that he abruptly ended the conversations, declaring that "while Parliament claimed and exercised a power of altering our constitutions at pleasure, there could be no agreement." It was therefore with concern and regret that Fothergill reported to Dartmouth, on February 6, that Franklin and, through him, America had indicated an indisposition to peace and were not in a spirit of compromise.[63] Thus Dartmouth was again disappointed in his search for a peaceful settlement, and both parties continued to rush headlong toward war.

In the Opposition, Chatham and Rockingham clung to their separate ways. Both parties were in a weakened state, but the Old Whigs had gained a powerful supporter in Charles James Fox when he had been dismissed from government in February, 1774. The driving force within that party was still, however, Edmund Burke. Proclaiming that the new Parliament would be more responsive to Old Whig arguments and maintaining that public discontents with the ministry were mounting, Burke spurned Rockingham's suggestion of a secession from Parliament. Sounding a call to battle for the Old Whigs, he turned once more to the electors, particularly the

[63] *Ibid.*; RHMCR. *Dartmouth Papers*, II, 266, Fothergill to Dartmouth, February 6, 1775.

merchants, for support, dragging a reluctant Rockingham in his wake.

Before the new Parliament was many months old, however, Burke had perceived that the general election had by no means impaired the position of the ministry. More ominous for the Old Whigs, hoping against hope to repeat their performance of 1765, was a steady growth of anti-Americanism among the merchants. William Baker, Member for Hertfordshire and Burke's liaison with the London merchants, reported soon after the turn of 1774 that most of those trading to America had lately met in London and had shown themselves in chief part friends to the ministry's American system.[64] Although these London merchants were eventually brought to present a petition, Burke called it "cold and jejune." Even so, this mild document, setting forth the losses and dangers to British commerce likely to arise from any continuance of the American troubles, was a triumph for Baker.

Burke, disgusted with the London traders for their timidity, then turned to those of Bristol, taking the precaution of sending them a model petition. Adopted by the Society of Merchant Venturers of that city, it deplored the decrease of the American trade and, with it, that to Africa and the West Indies. Earlier saved from catastrophe by the repeal of the Stamp Act, but now threatened anew by the Townshend taxes in conjunction with the Coercive Acts, they prayed a return to "the former System of commercial Policy."[65]

In late January, petitions from Norwich, Glasgow, Birmingham, Dudley, Liverpool, Manchester, and Wolverhampton deplored the state of trade with America and asked redress. Yet, moderate in tone and few in number, these missives evidenced no very profound revulsion against American measures. It was soon obvious, even to Burke, that the Old

[64] Wentworth-Woodhouse, Burke Papers, Baker to Burke, December 26, 1774.
[65] Ibid., Bristol petition.

Whigs were not again to ride to power on a wave of merchant discontent.

Nor was union with Chatham possible. Chatham, through his associations with Franklin, Sayre, and other Americans, was turning increasingly radical. Convinced that the proceedings of the Continental Congress offered a fair basis for restoring harmony, he attributed the revival of American troubles to the Old Whigs' Declaratory Act. Of this persuasion he curtly informed Rockingham, adding that "the *no* right to tax, and the *right* to restrain their trade, &c. was a most clear proposition." Indeed, he told the Marquis, he proposed to move in the Lords for a reconsideration of the Declaratory Act.[66] With a few sentences, then, Chatham had destroyed all hope of a united Opposition. Both parties could take a little comfort from the thought that probably, even if united, they could have done nothing to alter the course of events.

Both, however, were to try, though separately. The proceedings of the Continental Congress had obliged Dartmouth to lay the American papers before his House on January 19. The next day, Chatham made a previously much-advertised motion, the nature of which he had communicated to no one, save that it was to be about America. In the form of an address to the King, it called for the immediate removal of Gage and his soldiers from Boston. Proclaiming that America owed obedience only in a limited degree to the Laws of Trade and Navigation, he termed the recent colonial resistance as "necessary as it was just." The Americans were justified in defending "to the last extremity" their sole right to tax themselves. Indeed, to maintain this principle was "the common cause of the Whigs on the other side of the Atlantic as on this." England would eventually have to back down: let her do so now "while we can, not when we must."[67] To Lyttelton's charge that should

[66] Albemarle, *Rockingham Memoirs*, II, 261–64, Rockingham to Burke, January 8, 1775.

[67] Cobbett and Wright, *Parliamentary History*, XVIII, 150 ff. The notes for the speech are in Chatham Papers, 74.

America be indulged, she would at once proceed against the Laws of Trade and Navigation, Chatham replied that in such case he would be the first to advocate force. This statement he would have occasion to remember.

Chatham was undismayed by his overwhelming defeat— the vote was sixty-eight to eighteen against him—indeed, he said, he had only "knocked at the Minister's door." Moreover, when Dartmouth gave notice that American affairs would be taken up on February 2, Chatham determined to anticipate this move by offering a plan of his own. Working in great haste, but making no attempt to communicate with Rockingham until the very eve of his new motion, he proceeded to draft his Provisional Act for Reconciliation with America. Franklin was several times called in to help, but his influence on the bill, according to his own laconic testimony, was negligible.

On February 1, then, Chatham presented his plan "for settling the troubles in America, and for asserting the Supreme Legislative authority and superintending power of Great Britain over the Colonies."[68] Embodied in the Provisional Act, this plan was essentially as follows:

1. It opened with a declaration that the Colonies "have been, are, and of Right ought to be Dependent upon the Imperial Crown of Great Britain, and subordinate unto the British Parliament."

2. Parliament had full power to bind the Colonies "in all matters touching the General Weal of the whole Dominion of the Imperial Crown of Great Britain." Most especially did this apply to "an indubitable and indispensable Right to make and ordain Laws for regulating Navigation and Trade," for "the deep policy of such prudent Acts" contributed to the welfare of the Royal Navy.

3. The Colonies could not justly appeal to the Declaration

[68] Cobbett and Wright, *Parliamentary History*, XVIII, 198–205. Chatham's rough draft and notes for the bill are in Chatham Papers, 74.

of Right as an argument against keeping British troops in North America. That declaration, in forbidding a standing army save by consent of Parliament, applied only to Great Britain; the King's right to send forces to any British dominion was indisputable.

4. The Colonies might rest assured, however, that while the stationing of troops was a matter beyond their competence, such forces, though legally posted, could never lawfully be employed to violate or destroy the rights of the people.

5. No tax for revenue could ever be levied on a colony but by the consent of that province expressed in an act of its own assembly.

6. The meeting of the second Continental Congress scheduled for May, 1775, was to be declared legal, so that it might consider "the making due Recognition of the Supreme Authority and superintending Power of Parliament." A declaration to this effect was to be a necessary prelude to the meeting of that body.

7. The Congress was further to consider making a free grant of a perpetual revenue to the King, subject to the disposition of Parliament. Congress was to be authorized to assign quotas of the total sum to the various colonies participating in the meeting. Such a provision was not to be an act of redress but of "affection" for the mother country.

8. The powers of the Courts of Admiralty and Vice-Admiralty were to be retracted to their traditional limits; trial by jury in all civil cases was to be guaranteed; capital cases were to be tried in the vicinage of the crime, and the accused was to have a jury of his peers.

9. All the grievous Acts whereof Americans had made complaint, including the Revenue Act of 1764, the Coercive Acts, and the Quebec Act, were to be declared suspended, and, from whatever day the Congress made due recognition of the supreme legislative and superintending power of Parliament, were to stand repealed.

10. Judges were to be appointed by the Crown and were to hold salaries from it, but their tenure was to be for good behavior only.

11. Charters were to be declared inviolable.

Chatham had persuaded himself that his bill, unlikely to be adopted in its totality, would be accepted as a basis for negotiation. While it was going through changes and amendments, America would have time to signify her attitude, and in an easy atmosphere of "give and take," a peaceable settlement might be found. Even had the bill been accepted by Parliament, however, it would not have been well received in America. Many of the grievances listed by the Congress in their petition, Chatham accepted as valid. He was willing to guarantee to the Colonies a sole exercise of the right of internal legislation. On the other hand, many American complaints he rejected or ignored. He sternly condemned the colonial argument against maintaining troops in America, a cardinal complaint of the colonists. Further, the Congress would never have allowed its "affection" to be legislated by Parliament.

The Bill, moreover, offended Parliament more than it did the Americans. It demanded a renunciation of even a theoretical right to tax for revenue, although it sought to soften this action by holding out a permanent colonial grant to the Crown. As a practical means of settling the Anglo-American problem, Chatham's effort was a failure. The bill is important, however, because it demonstrated that a great British statesman understood—albeit intuitively—that the only way Britain could maintain and keep an empire was by accepting a new imperial structure. Such a new fabric would contain areas of local autonomy not to be infringed by the supreme power of an imperial Parliament. Unfortunately, those areas of local autonomy, as laid down by Chatham, were too large to be approved in Great Britain and too small to satisfy American leaders. Both at home and in the Colonies, then, the bill was received with coolness or disapprobation, the Lords declining it by a division of sixty-one to thirty-two.[69]

Meantime, Dartmouth had not given up hope of the ministry's adopting some conciliatory measure. When he had first heard Chatham's bill, he had been anxious to have it lie on the table, and had given up the idea only after his brother ministers had taken an uncompromising stand against it. He was still eager, too, to send a royal commission to the Colonies. Barclay was dispatched to talk once more with Franklin, and Dartmouth himself continued to press his cabinet colleagues for some step of a conciliatory nature.

North himself had undertaken to form the ministry's plan for dealing with what was recognized in all but form as a rebellion in New England, an obligation which Dartmouth apparently had abdicated. On February 2, therefore, North moved in the Commons for an address declaring New England in rebellion and asking his Majesty speedily to reduce that area to obedience. Despite fierce opposition from Fox, Burke, and Governor Johnstone, the crucial division stood at 296–106, and the Lords quickly concurred in this official recognition of rebellion. An augmentation of the forces requested in the King's answer on the tenth was quickly granted. North followed by moving for a bill to restrain the trade of New England and to exclude her people from the Newfoundland fisheries. Permission followed by an overwhelming majority.

Suddenly, in the midst of a violent debate on this harsh bill, North arose and moved his Conciliatory Proposition. Dartmouth's persistent efforts in this direction had triumphed at a cabinet meeting on January 21, when the resolution embodying North's proposition was adopted. Perhaps Dartmouth's unremitting insistence had worn down the Bedfordites and Suffolk into acquiesence; perhaps they saw it as a means of overturning North. Whatever their reasoning, the cabinet "agreed,

---

[69] RHMCR. *Stopford-Sackville Papers*, II, 1, Suffolk to Germain, June 15, 1775; Add. MSS 35427, f. 21, Hutchinson to Hardwicke, June 17, 1775.

that an address be proposed to the two Houses of Parliament to declare that if the Colonies will make sufficient and permanent provision for the support of the civil government and administration of Justice and for the defence and protection of the said Colonies, and in time of war contribute extraordinary supplies, in a reasonable proportion to what is raised by Great Britain, we will in that case desist from the exercise of the power of taxation, and that whenever a proposition of this kind shall be made by any of the Colonies we will enter into the consideration of proper laws for that purpose, and in the meantime to entreat his Majesty to take the most effectual methods to enforce due obedience to the laws and authority of the supreme legislature of Great Britain."[70] Dartmouth was apparently the only member of the cabinet who expected any good result of this proposition. North was not sanguine about it, though he hoped it would unite the nation at home since it was "precisely the plan which ought to be adopted by Great Britain; even if all America were subdued." The King, too, was not optimistic, but neither he nor North overlooked the possibility that the Conciliatory Proposition might prove a wedge which would destroy colonial unity.[71]

Having a day earlier notified the leading members of Opposition, North moved his resolution on February 20. In his speech, he maintained that every part of the empire was bound to pay its share for the common defense. If, however, America would undertake to raise its quota by self-taxation, he was certain Parliament would suspend the exercise of its own right. His resolution was mainly in accordance with the cabinet's previous decision, but it further provided that the net produce of trade regulations be carried to the account of each individual colony.

[70] RHMCR. *Dartmouth Papers*, II, 372–73, cabinet minute, January 21, 1775.
[71] Fortescue, *Correspondence of George III*, III, No. 1595, the King to North, February 15, 1775; No. 1599, North to the King, February 19, 1775.

North's position was not a comfortable one. The House was in the greatest confusion. Taunted by Fox and the Opposition, he was also threatened by a revolt among his own supporters. Franklin later declared he saw the Bedfords counting votes to see if they could overturn him. In the end, King's Friend Sir Gilbert Elliot rallied the ministerial ranks, and the proposition carried on February 27 in a division of 274–88. Dartmouth had won his point.

Again, however, an attempt to win a peaceful settlement was to fail. American claims against Parliament had already gone beyond the question of taxation, and the entire doctrine of parliamentary supremacy was now at issue. As with Chatham's Provisional Bill, the importance of the Conciliatory Proposition is to be found in its implications rather than in its surface content. It represented the first glimmering of a retreat from that absolute and uncompromising statement of the supreme power of Parliament laid down in the Declaratory Act. It recognized, after the fulfillment of certain conditions by those bodies, a sphere of authority reserved to colonial assemblies. Into this sphere Parliament would bind itself not to intrude. Despite the reservations and conditions laid down, which were indeed to result in the Americans' refusal of the offer, the proposition did represent the first appearance of a federal tendency in British imperial politics.

Unfortunately, more than a glimmering of federalism was needed to prevent a revolution in America. The principle had already been stated and accepted there. Had it, however, been equally received in Great Britain, it would have meant the end of the British Empire as then understood by British politicians. More concessions would have been needed, and the difficulty with which Dartmouth and North finally brought forward the Conciliatory Proposition showed that until the pressure of events became much greater, Great Britain had gone as far as she could go.

Meantime, in debates on the Restraining Act, the ministry was riding roughshod over the feeble opposition of Old Whigs and Chathamites. The bill, amended to include New Jersey, Pennsylvania, Maryland, Virginia, and South Carolina, all of whom had acceded to the nonimportation and nonexportation association, passed the Lords by a huge majority, seventy-three to twenty-one. The Old Whigs, however, were determined to present their own plan for America. They had been annoyed with Chatham who had seized the Opposition initiative with his Provisional Bill. Rockingham had been strongly advised by his friends to take countermeasures and especially to disclaim any thought of an American revenue, which Chatham's plan had promised.

On March 22, therefore, after he had sought full consultation with Chatham, Burke presented the Old Whig's Plan of Conciliation.[72] Announcing that "the proposition is peace," he called for a reconsideration of the Restraining Act, "that most infamous bill for famishing the four provinces of New England," which had been returned to the Commons for concurrence with a Lords' amendment.

Burke argued that by adopting North's Conciliatory Proposition, the "ransom by auction," Parliament had admitted that conciliation might come before American submission and that America's complaint about the exercise of the right of taxation was not unjustifiable. The proposal for peace should therefore come from the mother country. Refusing to innovate as Chatham and North had done, he insisted that in a great empire, occasional friction between the component parts was to be expected. Outlying districts necessarily possessed certain privileges, but the very exercise of them was an acknowledgement of the supreme power at the center. Recognizing and rejecting the new element which had entered British imperial thinking with Chatham and North, Burke declared, "I put my foot in the tracks of our forefathers; where I can neither wander nor stumble." With Georgian obstinacy holding firm to the De-

[72] Cobbett and Wright, *Parliamentary History*, XVIII, 495 ff.

claratory Act, he called for a return to the system before 1763. To achieve that end, he wished to establish the legal competence of colonial assemblies to support their own governments and to give public aids in time of war. Further, the Coercive Acts were to be repealed, and the powers of the Admiralty Courts restricted.

Burke's speech demonstrated again his immense talent for intensifying the thought around him, but of the three solutions to the American problem offered that session, his alone contained no hint of a federal principle. Looking nostalgically to the past, Burke sought once more to ignore the ugly question of right, a question which, once raised, had made a return to the old system as impossible as a return to childhood. To have avoided a breakup of the first British Empire would have demanded a genius who could cast in a new mold both the imperial and the domestic political scheme of things. It was an impossible task.

While the ministry, Chatham, and the Old Whigs sought parliamentary solutions to the American troubles, the City Radicals were carrying on an unceasing propaganda war outside of Parliament. A court of the Common Council voted a strong petition to the Lords against the Restraining Act. The Bill of Rights Society donated £500 for the New England sufferers. The Livery of London sent a remonstrance and petition against the American measures. William Lee, late sheriff of London and still a member of the corporation, was discovered in seditious attempts to dissuade the soldiers en route to America from serving against their American brothers.[73] Sixty-one Quakers, including John Fothergill, petitioned the King for a negotiated union with the Colonies. Burke, in his correspondence with the New York Assembly, was also doing his utmost to discredit North's Conciliatory Proposition, stating the pious wish that the ministers had been in earnest for a

[73] RHMCR. *Dartmouth Papers*, II, 280–81, Lee to Josiah Quincey, March 17, 1775. American letters were being intercepted regularly.

conciliation. As the New Yorkers had refused to elect delegates to the second Continental Congress, Burke pointedly told them, "I find that Ministry place their best hopes of dissolving the union of the Colonies and breaking the present Spirit of resistance, wholly in your Province."[74] When, however, Parliament refused to receive New York's petition and remonstrance, framed independently of the Congress, Burke's interpretation of ministerial policy was accepted, and the radical party quickly forced an election of delegates to the Congress. New York's accession made American union complete. On May 29 arrived the startling news of a clash at Lexington and Concord. "The horrid Tragedy is commenced,"[75] Sayre exclaimed to Chatham, and it was generally agreed that war had come.

In America, the colonists flew to arms. Denying that they intended independence or entertained "desires incompatible with the honour and dignity of the King and the welfare of the whole empire,"[76] they were determined to rid themselves of the unbounded supremacy of a Parliament which to them appeared as tyrannical as any Stuart monarch. In England, the ministry and a large majority in Parliament were resolved to defend that supremacy, which they had inherited from the Glorious Revolution and which they had long considered their only safeguard against royal absolutism.

[74] Wentworth-Woodhouse, Burke Papers, Letterbook, Burke to the New York Assembly Committee of Correspondence, and to James Delancey, both of March 14, 1775.

[75] Chatham Papers, 55, Sayre to Chatham, May 29, 1775.

[76] RHMCR. Dartmouth Papers, I, 377–78, Dr. Joseph Warren to the Selectmen of Boston, May 13, 1775, copy.

CHAPTER SIX

CIVIL WAR

THE outbreak of hostilities in America took the British public by surprise. Their reaction was uncertain and slow to form. Only a few had expected the Americans to take up arms. But, for a moment, many hesitated to commit themselves to a civil war. John Wesley, leader of the Methodists, wrote to his coreligionist Dartmouth, "All my prejudices are against the Americans." Yet he could not avoid thinking "that an oppressed people asked for nothing more than their legal rights and that in the most modest and inoffensive manner which the nature of the thing would allow. But waiving this, waiving all considerations of right and wrong, I ask is it common sense to use force toward the Americans?"[1] The Dissenters, subject to varying degrees of legal disability in England, were the group most sympathetic to the American position; but politically disorganized and, for the most part, excluded from office, they had no way of bringing effective pressure to bear in the formation of official policy.

On the political scene, however, reaction was swift and vigorous. William Eden, Suffolk's undersecretary of state and an accomplished fisher in troubled waters, referred to the ministry as "tottering"; but Suffolk, henceforth a leader of the "war party," spurning all means but force, admonished him not to despond: "Now is the time for men of real Talent,

[1] RHMCR. *Dartmouth Papers*, I, 378–79, Wesley to Dartmouth, June 14, 1775.

Spirit, and Honour to appear gloriously." Already, as northern secretary, Suffolk was negotiating for twenty thousand Russian mercenaries. He would fail to buy their services, but at the time he believed they would "be charming visitors at New York and civilize that part of America wonderfully."[2] The King, too, favored quick, decisive measures, believing that "when once those rebels have felt a smart blow, they will submit." Charles Jenkinson, expressing an attitude now general among his colleagues, sharply told a friend—who had suggested sending peace commissioners—that the Americans had first to submit to the authority of Parliament. Only when they had thus earned their forgiveness would it be proper to tell them what terms they might have.

Immediately outside ministerial circles might be heard the same calls for prompt action to crush the rebellion. John Yorke feared only that the manufacturers might induce the government to adopt a conciliatory plan. Lord George Germain, soon to enter the ministry, was among the foremost in his demands for coercion; and out of the similarity of their American views, he struck up a confidential friendship with Suffolk. Hutchinson, still selling short the American fighting man and so engendering false optimism in official circles, warned that there could be no middle course between forcibly suppressing the rebellion and losing the Colonies.[3]

The situation of the Earl of Dartmouth, pious and a lover of peace, was tragic. Desperately he sought to delay the final plunge as long as possible. For the moment, he had North's co-operation. Both were hoping against hope that the second Continental Congress, which had met on May 10, might pro-

[2] Add. MSS 34412, f. 339; Stevens, *Facsimilies*, No. 851, Suffolk to Eden, June 20, 1775.

[3] Add. MSS 35375 ff. 145–46, John Yorke to Hardwicke, June 14, 1775. Add. MSS 35427, ff. 22–23, Hutchinson to Hardwicke, June 24, 1775. Hinchingbrooke Papers; Navy Record Society, LXIX, *Sandwich Papers*, I, 63, the King to Sandwich, July 1, 1775. Add. MSS 38306, f. 1, Letterbook, Jenkinson to Sir James Jay, July 17, 1775.

vide some ground for reconciliation. Nor, in their opinion, had the Conciliatory Proposition had its ultimate effect.[4] Sincerely desiring peace, they knew that the war party—Suffolk, Rochford, the Bedfords, and the rest of the King's Friends—expected vigorous action to defend Parliament's supremacy and to punish the colonists who had so boldly denied it. This group, as did Germain, believed that "it is come to that crisis which makes it necessary for Administration to adopt real offensive measures or to resign their offices and leave the conciliatory plan of meanness and submission to those who wish to be their successors upon such terms."[5]

North was not the man to resist such united demands for long, no matter what his personal views might have been. The news of the Battle of Bunker Hill was decisive. He capitulated to the war party, admitting that it was now necessary to treat the rebellion as a foreign war and the Americans as an alien foe.[6] Dartmouth, isolated in the cabinet, was soon reported to be declining cabinet meetings on American affairs and "letting it be understood in his own circle, that he is too old a *Whig* to approve of the Measures."[7] Pinning his hopes upon the Continental Congress, he struggled valiantly to delay the publication of the Proclamation of Rebellion until that body had been heard from. But the American Secretary had now to combat the wounded military pride of his colleagues. The Battle of Bunker Hill was accepted in London as a victory. Eden's laconic comment, however, indicated that it was such a one which gave no great cause for rejoicing: "If we have eight more such victories there will be nobody left to bring the news of them."[8] It was at once perceived that the fighting

[4] RHMCR. *Knox Papers, Various Collections*, 120–21, Dartmouth to Knox, August 6, 1775; 119, Dartmouth to Knox, July 3, 1775.
[5] RHMCR. *Stopford-Sackville Papers*, I, 135–36, Germain's letter of June 29, 1775.
[6] Fortescue, *Correspondence of George III*, III, No. 1682, North to the King, July 26, 1775.
[7] Add. MSS 35375, ff. 150–53, John Yorke to Hardwicke, July 29, 1775.

ability of the Americans had been underestimated; and the cabinet—except Dartmouth—agreed that "one decisive blow at land" was necessary. The government thus found itself committed to a land war.

Meantime, the Congress, immediately upon its assembling in May, had taken steps to organize colonial resistance, adopting the forces about Boston for its army and appointing Washington commander-in-chief. The moderate element, led by Dickinson and Jay, were able to carry one last petition to the King, the "Olive Branch." In it, the Congress stated that Anglo-American union had been broken by the ministry and its system of statutes and regulations pursued since 1763. They beseeched his Majesty to relieve America of her grievances and to direct some mode of reconciliation.

This petition, carried from America by Richard Penn, made a slow crossing, and it was not till August 21 that a copy reached Dartmouth's office. The Colonial Secretary, worn out with his struggle to delay publishing the Proclamation of Rebellion, had, moreover, gone to the country for a rest, so that he did not actually receive this document until the twenty-fourth. Appealing as it did to the King for aid against his own ministers, the Olive Branch could have had but slight effect, yet this delay was unfortunate; for the Proclamation of Rebellion was published on the twenty-third. The King and Suffolk had won. Dartmouth's last pitiful attempt to stave off war had failed.

Based on the declaration of 1745, the Proclamation of Rebellion called upon all good men to help suppress rebellion and to desist from any correspondence with the rebels. The nation thus stood committed to war, and there were immediate demonstrations that the people were rallying to the cause. In

[8] Add. MSS 34412, f. 340; Stevens, *Facsimilies*, No. 456, Eden to North, August, 1775. Howe referred to the battle as "most dreadful," and as attended with "fatal consequences"; 92 officers were killed or wounded, 160 rank and file killed, and 300 wounded. The rebels suffered 100 killed and 30 wounded. See Fortescue, *Correspondence of George III*, III, No. 1668.

September, Manchester, Lancaster, Liverpool, and Leicester, all strong manufacturing districts, presented loyal addresses. Bradford, Trowbridge, Milksham, and even Burke's Bristol joined in the cry. In October, the Irish House of Commons carried a resolution declaring their allegiance and loyalty to the Crown and expressing abhorrence of America's attempt to cast off her dependency. Affairs appeared in good train, then. A united nation, ignoring the arguments of Opposition, was firm in support of the ministry and looked for a speedy crushing of the rebellion. That events took no such course is due primarily to the fact that the head of the government was unfit to direct the struggle now beginning.

Frederick North, son of the Earl of Guilford and a courtesy lord, had shown no small ability as first lord of the Treasury. Of Old Whig background, he was of an amiable and conciliatory disposition, a master of parliamentary debate and procedure, and an excellent leader of the Commons. As head of a ministry and director of the course of empire, however, North was never able to establish an ascendency over his colleagues or to weld his cabinet into an effective whole. He had been called to his high office because George III saw in him those qualities he had hoped to find in Chatham in 1766. The two men could work together. For the first time the King found in the head of ministry not only one with whom he was to develop a deep personal attachment but also one who accepted him as an active political force. With North, the King's campaign to regain what he conceived to be his rightful place in British politics—as chief executive of the state, free of factions and parties trying to give him the law—was brought to a victorious conclusion. That he found in him, then, his ideal minister, is a symptom of his own mediocrity.

The fact that North had neither the strength of character nor the desire to "ape the Prime Minister"—as the King would some years later complain he did—spelled disaster for the empire, although it made him an agreeable working companion for George III. Constitutionally, the office of "Prime Minister" did not exist. This had not, however, prevented Walpole, Pelham, and Newcastle from establishing themselves as masters of the political field, or Pitt from exercising dictatorial power in a time of crisis. Inclined to vex himself and to fuss about trivialities, subject to periods of acute depression and melancholia, North was unable to rise to heights from which a comprehensive and statesmanlike view of the empire might have been possible. With no inkling of grand strategy, he had sought to solve a first-rate crisis with, at best, second-rate abilities. His personal tragedy was that he recognized his own lack of ability but did not possess the strength to refuse to serve when his sovereign called. Thus it was that he found himself driven into the leadership of a war naturally repugnant to him, and of whose outcome he was skeptical from the first.

North's pessimism in the summer of 1775 arose from several causes. He professed to fear that Opposition's attack in the coming session would be sustained and dangerous, and he was anxious about the reaction of the merchants to the Olive Branch. Furthermore, American propaganda was working its effect among the City Radicals, and the extent of seditious activity might well be great. A more fundamental reason for North's apprehension was his realization of his own inadequacies in dealing with a situation rapidly growing more complex. Immediate and grave decisions had to be made. General Burgoyne in America was violently impugning the abilities of his senior officer, Gage, and of Admiral Graves. William Howe and Henry Clinton, sent out to bolster Gage, were advising an evacuation of Boston for New York, while Burgoyne himself favored a withdrawal of the army from the Colonies altogether, leaving the Americans to fight among themselves.

Nor was the search for mercenaries proceeding with dispatch. By spring, 1776, an army of twenty thousand men had been promised the American commanders, and it had been assumed that Suffolk's negotiations with Russia would produce the required number of reinforcements. When the Czarina abruptly ended this hope—in a manner not devoid of humiliation to George III—North had to consider the extraordinary step of calling out the militia, although he admitted that "upon military matters I speak ignorantly, and therefore without effect."[9]

The manpower problem was somewhat relieved, though by no means solved, by a decision, illegal in the strict sense, to employ five regiments from the Irish establishment. The introduction of Hanoverian troops into Port Mahon and Gibraltar, although it deeply angered the Opposition, released additional contingents for American service. Yet despite these emergency measures, North's promise of an army of twenty thousand simply could not be fulfilled.

The state of the naval forces in American waters was equally deficient. There was growing a bitter criticism of the commander, Graves, for his supposed "delicacies" with the rebels. Incompetent as he was, however, it must be said that his force of twenty-seven ships, including only three ships of the line, frigates, sloops, and schooners, was much below the fifty vessels which were the estimated minimum for an effective naval force. Although reinforced with ten vessels in September and October, Graves' force remained well under the minimum.[10]

A third problem faced Lord North at home. His obvious hesitation to plunge into a war with the Colonies had caused much discontent among his cabinet colleagues. While North waited with growing and bitter disappointment for some salutary effect from the Conciliatory Proposition, the rest of the cabinet were pressing for extreme measures. Suffolk and Rochford were voluble in their demands. Germain, soon to join the

---

[9] Add. MSS 34412, ff. 343–44; Stevens, *Facsimilies*, No. 458, North to Eden, August 22, 1775.

[10] See Hinchingbrooke Papers; Navy Record Society, LXIX, *Sandwich Papers*, I, 66–67, Sandwich to Graves, July, 1775, 68–72, Sandwich to Graves, August, 1775, 64–66 and footnote, memorandum of Sir Hugh Palliser.

ministry, would agree with them. Gower, Thurlow, and their Bedford friends maintained an ominous silence, and North knew they were watching him narrowly, ready to overturn him at any false move. On the other hand, Dartmouth was sullen at cabinet. Barrington was openly opposing a land war and predicting gloomy consequences should his advice be ignored. Grafton, holding the privy seal but not one of the cabinet, was increasingly alienated by North's American measures. William Eden, already showing that amazing capacity for intrigue which he was to develop to so high a degree in the next decade, warned North that several of his ministers were "surly in their Language, sulky in their Conduct, and ill-disposed to your Administration."[11] North, then, sat at the center of an uneasy balance of power. Fully aware of his internal danger, he knew too that his colleagues, his King, and the nation at large expected vigorous action.

Events, however, now conspired to make him somewhat more secure. In response to pressure from the war party, Graves and Gage were recalled. And when Lord William Campbell, governor of South Carolina, suggested that two thousand men could subdue his province since the backsettlers were loyal, North eagerly adopted the idea. Without consulting with Secretary at War Barrington—an omission which caused that neglected minister's indignation to reach new heights—North recommended that the five Irish regiments, earlier destined for the army at Boston, should undertake a winter campaign against Charleston. The King quickly concurred and the war party was satisfied.

Secondly, when Parliament met on October 26, it soon became obvious that North's earlier fear of an effective Opposition attack had been chimerical. His ministry proved itself undisputed in control and backed by overwhelming majorities in both Houses.

[11] Stevens, *Facsimilies*, Nos. 853–54, Eden to North, September 13 and 17, 1775.

Furthermore, cabinet harmony was greatly increased when, early in the session, Grafton went over to the Opposition. His defection presented an ideal opportunity to provide a retreat for Dartmouth, now increasingly obnoxious to his colleagues and unhappy in his employment. The former American Secretary took the privy seal without a seat in the cabinet. Rochford was induced to retire. Bedfordite Weymouth became southern secretary. The fateful Lord George Germain, with his pathetic determination to redeem a soiled reputation by a brilliant military victory over the rebels, became secretary of state for the colonies. The team with which North would lose America had now been chosen.

Finally, any lingering doubt among the nation at large about the justice of stern measures was ended when in the autumn news arrived that the Americans had invaded Canada. No longer, in British minds, could the colonists maintain that they were merely repelling a wanton aggression. Rather, they had embarked upon a career of conquest. When North moved the land tax of 1776 to be four shillings, the country gentlemen supported it without a murmur.

Within the government there was a general optimism which transmitted itself to the nation. The ministry was firmly established at home. America's expedition against Canada was proving a fiasco, and the Congress, it was believed, was becoming unpopular with the colonists. Dartmouth's more vigorous successor was cheerfully predicting the end of the rebellion in one campaign and declaring that he would "establish his reputation as a minister by it."[12] The manpower problem appeared solved when in January, 1776, Britain received into her service some twenty-three thousand German mercenaries.

Feeling that he had proved himself to the war party, North turned his thought once more to an accommodation with America. Both he and Dartmouth had long favored sending

[12] RHMCR. *Carlisle Papers,* 306, George Selwyn to Carlisle, December 8, 1775; see also, 303, Gower to Carlisle, November 25, 1775.

royal commissioners to investigate the troubles on the spot and to negotiate a peaceable settlement. The idea had earlier been dropped in view of the opposition to the Conciliatory Proposition. In autumn, 1775, however, conditions had changed, and North, believing that commissioners could now be sent without the appearance of his being forced to the measure, determined to espouse the plan once more.

Indeed, steps had been taken even before the meeting of Parliament. By October 10, William Eden, to whom North had turned for assistance in forming the Peace Commission—much to the jealousy of John Pownall, undersecretary of state for America—had made sufficient progress to write to Lord George Germain. Germain was not yet in office, and North and Eden now offered him the commission. Eden explained that with the removal of Gage and Graves and with the prospect of a large force, both naval and military, an early end of the war seemed assured. North believed it might be hastened by giving a commissioner power to go to the Colonies to settle everything in dispute.

Eden continued that North had resolved never to bring forward such a plan until military and naval preparations were sufficient to show that he was not being compelled. That time had now arrived. The first minister had consulted his principal friends in both Houses and had assured them that the plan was not one of "wavering." Most of them had agreed in general with the projected commission, although, Eden admitted, a few had proved "rather rigid in their ideas" for uncompromising and forceful measures.

The commissioner would be empowered to supersede governors, to call assemblies, and to settle a form of taxation on easy terms in accordance with the Conciliatory Proposition. He would grant pardons, open ports, and make "corrections" in some of the colonial governments.[13]

[13] RHMCR. *Stopford-Sackville Papers*, II, 10–12, Eden to Germain, October 3 and 21, 1775.

Germain's refusal of the offer meant a temporary postponement of the plan. Meantime, a new question was raised. How
was an Act of Parliament embodying the commission to be
framed? Consulting with Lord Mansfield, who had long
favored sending commissioners, Eden concluded it would be
impossible to draw an act which would be for the purpose of
qualifying and diminishing the power of Parliament. They
then hit upon the idea of allowing the Crown to take the initiative in drawing up the commission. Parliament would simply
give approbation through a joint address. This point, though
it appears to be a minor one, was in reality of great importance. Deny it as they would, those engaged in forming the
commission knew that they were retreating from the concept
of absolute parliamentary supremacy. North, Eden, and Mansfield believed, moreover, that it was an act of necessity; and
the great lawyer openly expressed his fear that "neither our
Force nor the Exertion of it will be equal to the Magnitude
and Exigency of Affairs."[14]

The delay occasioned by Germain's refusal and the consultations with Mansfield caused Eden to be unprepared for
North to appoint a commissioner until February, 1776. A
short time before, Lord Howe, brother of Sir William, had
been named naval commander-in-chief in American waters.
As Howe had previously expressed his willingness to undertake a commission for restoring peace and had actually talked
of such a scheme with his friend Benjamin Franklin, Eden proposed that he now be appointed though joined with a civilian
colleague. Eden himself coveted the second post. Only Howe's
refusal to serve with Eden or with any one else prevented his
little intrigue from succeeding. Indeed, it was with great difficulty that Howe was finally induced to accept his own brother,
Sir William, as a fellow commissioner.[15]

14 Add. MSS 34412, ff. 369–70, Eden to North, November, 1775.
15 Add. MSS 34413, f. 17; Stevens, *Facsimilies*, No. 465, Germain
to Eden, February 18, 1776.

The beginnings of the Howe Peace Commission had thus not been auspicious. Worse was the settling of the powers of the commissioners. This brought North into a headlong conflict with the war party which nearly overturned his administration. The war party, while not objecting to a commission as such, were utterly determined to prevent even the shadow of a retreat from the principle of parliamentary supremacy. They believed—and North agreed with them—that indispensable conditions for peace were the laying down of arms by the rebels, the dissolution of Congress, and the restoration of legal governments. These acts North was prepared to accept as an adequate submission to Parliament's authority. The remainder of the cabinet, led by Germain who had but recently become American secretary, insisted however on a full and specific declaration of submission by the reconstituted colonial assemblies. Else there could be no treaty with the Americans. Germain, indeed, announced his intention of resigning if overruled on this point.

The Bedford group watched silently as battle lines were drawn, ready to seize any opportunity to strengthen their own position. The old Grenvillites Suffolk and Wedderburn openly assured Germain of their support. Suffolk wrote to the American Secretary, urging that he give up all thought of retiring even if North should succeed in vetoing his demand for colonial declarations of submission. Believing the point to be of little importance, Suffolk assured Germain, "If Lord North can ever insist upon anything derogatory to the authority of Parliament, I shall be against him. If he can mean to make a *paix plâtrée*, I shall be against him. If to get out of the war at any rate can be his object, he will find a very different intention mine."[16]

Wedderburn, too, wrote hastily to Germain, begging him not to resign, and his argument was more sinister. The imme-

[16] RHMCR. *Stopford-Sackville Papers*, II, 23–24, Suffolk to Germain, March 7 and 27, 1776.

diate effect of Germain's retreat, he contended, would be the abandonment of all coercive measures.[17] Thus encouraged, Germain stood fast for the declaration. North, as usual when forced with resolute opposition, was desperately seeking a compromise. However, he now found himself caught midway between two irreconcilable extremes—Germain on the one hand, and Dartmouth, supported by Germain's own undersecretary, William Knox, on the other.[18] Both of the latter were violently opposed to including any mention of Germain's declaration either in the commission or in the instructions to the commissioners. Avoiding a decision himself, North submitted the question to his cabinet. The result was a foregone conclusion, and John Pownall, who was drawing up the instructions, was directed to include the demand for a declaration.

Wrangling within the ministry had, however, by no means ended. Germain, fundamentally opposed to appeasement, as he regarded a negotiated settlement of the conflict, now insisted that the declaration of submission by the reconstituted assemblies should be previous to any treaty whatsoever with the Colonies. Infuriated at what he considered the hamstringing of the commission, Dartmouth declared he would "speak out" against Germain and resign his post. North, fearing to lose the only minister he could trust, announced that if Germain continued to press his point, he himself would retire. Germain countered with the statement that rather than permit North to resign he would do so himself. A breakup of at least a part of North's government thus appeared inevitable.

The showdown was to be in the cabinet meeting of March 18. In a last minute bid to stave off an open break with Germain—and probably his own overthrow as well—North proposed on the seventeenth that he and the American Secretary allow the venerable Mansfield to arbitrate their dispute. Mans-

[17] *Ibid.*, 24–25, Alexander Wedderburn to Germain, March 7, 1776.

[18] RHMCR. *Dartmouth Papers*, II, 416, Knox to Dartmouth, March, 1776. See also RHMCR. *Knox Papers, Various Collections*, Knox's account, "The First Commissioners of the American Colonies."

field's proposal, accepted by both parties was a compromise: instead of the commissioners demanding the declaration, they were to await proposals from the Colonies. Any province, however, refusing to satisfy them on this point of submission was to be denied the King's peace; and no treaty would be begun with that colony until they had received further instructions.

This cabinet crisis over, a new one immediately took its place. Lord Howe, the commissioner designate, complained that the terms of the commission were too narrow, and began to demand discretionary power. As late as March 26, he declared that he would not accept the commission as it then stood. Germain reassured the Admiral upon most of his doubts, but Howe did not subside until he had offended the King and most of the ministers.[19]

These ill-natured bickerings prevented the commission and instructions from reaching final form until May. Precious months, during which America was steadily moving toward independence, had thus been wasted. In its final form, the commission stated that its purpose was to restore quiet on the basis of a mutual confidence and to induce submission to a lawful authority. To achieve these ends, the commissioners were instructed:

1. To proclaim free pardon for all, within certain time limits and excepting certain ringleaders.

2. To demand as a preliminary condition—before any colony should be declared at peace—a dissolution of all usurping revolutionary assemblies and of the Congress.

3. To demand that legitimate officers of government be allowed to resume their functions.

4. To require that armed forces acting under the Congress or under any revolutionary authority be disbanded and that colonial forts be delivered up to royal troops.

[19] RHMCR. *Stopford-Sackville Papers*, II, 25–27, Lord Howe to Germain, March 26 and April 1, 1776; see also 28–30, Alexander Wedderburn to Germain, April 24, 1776.

5. To summon legal assemblies, and upon their application, to relieve the provinces of restrictions upon their trade.

6. To declare a colony at peace, providing its application should indicate a true desire to return to duty.

7. To enter into treaty with those colonies so declared at peace.

8. To insist that loyalists be compensated, the damages to be adjudged by the Superior Court in each colony.

9. To implement North's Conciliatory Proposition. It was to be clearly understood, however, that monies raised under it were to be paid to a royal receiver, and Parliament was to be the last judge of the adequacy of the sum raised.

10. To leave to the treating province the mode of raising the money, although duties on the produce of British manufacturers or on colonial goods used by those manufacturers were not to be taxed.

11. To grant the tenure of judges during good behavior should that be requested.

12. To constitute colonial councils as separate and independent branches of the provincial legislatures.

13. To promise due examination by Parliament of American grievances, although any discussion of the Quebec Act was to be forbidden.

14. Any subject arising not covered by the instructions was to be referred to the home government, and all agreements were to be subject to its ratification.

Additional instructions covered the colonies of Rhode Island and Connecticut whose elective governorships had long been regarded as a grave weakness in the colonial system. Those provinces were to be required to repeal their laws restraining the subject's right of appeal to the Privy Council in civil cases. All laws impeaching the royal or parliamentary authority were to be abolished. Both colonies would have to accept royal government, or at least such alteration of their charters as would restrain the elected governor from entering office until royal approbation had been expressed. Until Rhode Island and Connecticut should agree to these demands, the commissioners were not to treat with them unless their refusal to do so should endanger a treaty with other colonies. In that case, both were to be declared at peace on the same terms as the rest.[20]

It is unlikely the American would have accepted such offers even before the outbreak of hostilities. After all the only major concession was a reaffirmation of North's Conciliatory Proposition, and this the Colonies had already contemptuously refused. The commission allowed of no colonial rights against the supreme power of Parliament and promised no more than a consideration of grievances after due submission had been made. The terms thus held out were those a victorious and reasonably benevolent mother country might have granted to discouraged and chastised rebels. As such, they were totally inadequate to achieve a restoration of peace.

In June, Lord Howe, arriving in America, proceeded to proclaim himself and his brother peace commissioners, and to call upon the rebels to return to their duty. No response came from the Congress, and the battle for New York followed. It was not, indeed, until September that a meeting was arranged between the commissioners and a committee of Congress. Meantime, the Declaration of Independence had been signed. At the conference on Staten Island, September 11, Lord Howe was careful not to admit the Congressional committee as a representation from a legal body. It was obvious from the first, moreover, that no agreement was possible, for neither party could nor would compromise on the great point of independence. The conferences broke off abruptly and, seeing the futility of looking to Congress for a solution, the commissioners had to content themselves with a declaration to all

[20] Add. MSS 34413, ff. 45–53, orders and instructions to the Commissioners, and additional instructions, May 6, 1776.

well-affected subjects, inviting conferences on the best means of restoring tranquillity. The feeble response to this invitation demonstrated the abject failure of the commission.

The period of optimism after the repulse of the Americans in Canada was not of long duration. Barrington rendered himself increasingly unpopular with the King and the ministers by his constant gloomy prognostications. Sandwich was profoundly disturbed by the steady arrival of news, from December, 1775, onward, that France and Spain were giving the rebels munitions and war stores and that France was stepping up her naval program. His efforts to keep pace with France were persistently blocked by both North and the King who were anxious at once to spare expense and to avoid offending France. On the other hand, out of Germain's bitter criticism of Sandwich for the lack of naval force in America was generated an ill will which in the troublesome times to come, was to assume the proportions of an open feud.[21]

How unfounded now seemed the fair hopes of autumn, 1775! Sir William Howe had evacuated Boston in March, 1776. It had been a tactical withdrawal, but the rebels had been elated at their first major success. Ministerial gloom increased in August when it was learned that the expedition against Charleston had miscarried due to a failure to co-ordinate measures with the western Carolina loyalists. Tension in the cabinet increased with the failure of the Howe Peace Commission.

Furthermore, in December, 1776, Franklin arrived in Paris

21 Add. MSS 29475, f. 5, Germain to Eden, April 9, 1776. See also RHMCR. *Knox Papers, Various Collections*, 130–32, Germain to Knox, June 13, 15, 24, and July 1, 1777. Two points were at issue between the two ministers: the appointment of naval commanders which Germain tried to make a matter of joint cabinet decision; and Germain's insistence that Sandwich delegate authority to the West Indian governors to issue letters of marque. Sandwich violently resisted. Ships with letters of marque, because of the rich prizes they took, were constant temptations to sailors of the Royal Navy to desert. Furthermore, such privately owned ships were not over nice about their victims, and Sandwich feared embroilments with France and Spain. Germain was unsuccessful in his meddling, but not until the two ministers had become openly hostile.

as commissioner from the Congress. Other American agents, bent on securing aid from Britain's enemies, were soon busy throughout the continent. Industriously they spread the story that should Britain fail to recover the Colonies, she would recoup her losses by an attack on the foreign West Indies. This view Vergennes and the French government secretly accept-ed.[22] It soon became obvious that French naval preparations were increasing ominously. Sandwich, well aware of this steady build-up, was frantic. Though Lord Howe had demanded re-inforcements, Sandwich steadfastly resisted his calls. He was trying to convince North and the King that vessels sent to the Colonies had to be replaced with newly commissioned ships in home waters. Both, however, rejected his pressing argu-ments. George III was particularly adamant. Convinced that the rebels would treat before winter, 1777, he wished to avoid what seemed an unnecessary expense. He believed, moreover, that "any farther demonstrations than absolute necessity re-quires would undoubtedly be highly imprudent as it would revive the jealousy of our Neighbours."[23]

Similarly, the King was offended with Germain's constant "harping" on his scheme to raise new corps of highlanders. These, George had learned from various military leaders, could not be available for service until 1778. By that time, he imagined, the rebellion would be crushed. Eager to avoid what seemed to be an enormous expense, wantonly incurred, the King directed North to "crush the plan in the Bud."[24] His ill-timed zeal for economy and his reluctance to offend France,

[22] Stevens, *Facsimilies*, No. 897. Vergennes read a secret paper to the French King in cabinet on August 31, 1776, in which this view was set forth. It referred to Britain's guardships as "an imposing scarecrow" and maintained that the American rebellion offered France a unique opportunity to attack her old enemy.

[23] Add. MSS 37833, f. 163, draft; Fortescue, *Correspondence of George III*, III, No. 1974, John Robinson to the King, March 14, 1777. See also Hinchingbrooke Papers; Navy Record Society, LXIX, *Sandwich Papers*, I, 159–62, Sandwich to Lord Howe, October 17, 1776.

[24] Add. MSS 37833, f. 165, 170, the King to John Robinson, March 14 and 15, 1777.

with North's willingness to accept his arguments rather than those of Sandwich and Germain, would be responsible for Britain's deplorably unready state in the coming war with France.

At first, it appeared that George III's optimism was not wholly unfounded. True, Howe had retired from Boston, and from his new base of operations, Halifax, he had reported that until the rebel armies should be defeated, there was not the least prospect of reaching an accommodation with America, or even of drawing a respectable number of loyalists to open support of the Crown.[25] (A final quietus had thus been put to Barrington's periodic and grumpy demands for a solely naval war.) Howe had then proceeded to deal hard blows to the rebel power in the summer of 1776. By the end of his campaign, the Peace Commission had failed, but New York had been wrested from Washington, and the American army driven across the Jerseys into Pennsylvania. The King and the ministers were elated. Jubilantly, Germain confided to Eden, "It is clear that the Rebels will never face the King's Troops." To him Washington's withdrawal seemed proof that the rebellion was nearly finished. High in praise of Sir William Howe, only on one score did Germain criticize the General. The pardon which he and his brother had proclaimed for repentant rebels, he feared, might so depress the loyalists that they would hesitate to declare for the mother country.[26]

It was therefore with some reason that the King and his ministry looked to an early victory. Washington's pitiful and

---

[25] RHMCR. *Stopford-Sackville Papers*, II, 30–31, Sir William Howe to Germain, April 26, 1776.

[26] Add. MSS 34413, ff. 147–48, Germain to Eden, January 1, 1777. See also RHMCR. *Knox Papers, Various Collections*, 128, Germain to Knox, December 31, 1776, for more criticism of the commissioners. See, however, RHMCR. *Dartmouth Papers*, II, 431–32, Ambrose Serle to Dartmouth, January 1, 1777. Serle, serving with the British army in New York, was in charge of issuing pardons to repentant rebels. The proclamation had had the greatest effect, he wrote, with hundreds of pardons having been issued, the general sentiment in New York being that the rebellion was broken.

beaten army would dissolve under the hardships of a rigorous winter. The rebel governments, suffering from an inflated paper economy and from the ravages of war, would submit. Indeed, the American forces in their Pennsylvania retreat were in desperate circumstances. Had Howe plunged after them, instead of ending his campaign in December, he might well have ended the rebellion then and there. And yet Washington's force, however weakened, remained intact, a rallying point for the rebels. Their assemblies continued to function, and the control of the Congress was unshaken. John Yorke marvelled that "there is something which supports and keeps them together which the Ministers have not yet discovered."[27]

During the Christmas season, a time when all good professional soldiers should have been in winter quarters, that mysterious "something" carried Washington and his army across the Delaware for their amazing foray against the Hessians at Trenton. When in February news of this exploit arrived in Britain, it killed the hope that the rebel army would dissolve during the winter. Indeed, General Howe informed the ministers, this little success had so restored their morale that another campaign would be necessary.[28] To insure the end of the rebellion in 1777 he needed more troops, twenty thousand more.

This request was a signal for bitter outbursts on the part of the King and Germain against both Howe and his brother. George III well knew that such mammoth reinforcements were impracticable, and that, indeed, the General's requisition was fantastic. His shock betrayed itself in severe criticism of the Howe brothers for what he supposed to be their leniency toward the rebels. "Regaining their affection is an idle idea," he thought: the Americans could be defeated by that force already under the Howes' command if only the two command-

---

[27] Add. MSS 35375, ff. 185–86, Yorke to Hardwicke.

[28] RHMCR. *Stopford-Sackville Papers*, II, 53–55, Howe to Germain, December 31, 1776.

ers would exert themselves.[29] As Howe's exorbitant request had also angered Germain, the General ultimately got only twenty-five hundred more men. He then felt so restricted that he warned the home government to give up all hope of ending the rebellion in 1777.[30] Germain, however, was not dependent wholly on Howe's efforts.

General John Burgoyne, a Member of Parliament, earlier sent to Boston with Howe and Clinton, had returned to England in the winter of 1776–77, filled with his own thoughts on how to crush the rebellion. He immediately converted Germain to the idea of a descent with a British army from Canada. It was not actually a new idea. Howe's first plan had also been to isolate New England. He had proposed attacking Boston and simultaneously moving a column up the Hudson to Albany to join a force coming down from Canada. By the latter part of December, 1776, however, Howe had decided that the Canadian army could not reach Albany until September, 1777, at the earliest. Wishing to avoid a summer of inactivity, and believing Pennsylvania to be loyal at heart, he notified Germain that Philadelphia would be his prime target during the summer of 1777. Burgoyne and Germain, however, believing that Howe could take Philadelphia and then return to form a junction with the Canadian army at Albany by early autumn, continued work on their own plan. Their miscalculation was a fatal one, and they must bear the odium of it. North, who had broken his arm in September, 1776, and was recuperating from a persistent fever at his country place, had long been unable to meet the cabinet. Had he done so, he might have ex-

[29] Add. MSS 37833, f. 137, the King to John Robinson, March 5, 1777. Fortescue, *Correspondence of George III*, III, No. 2072, the King to North, October 28, 1777. Criticism of the Howes' supposed leniency was growing steadily. See Hinchingbrooke Papers, Sandwich to Lord Howe, March 10, 1777, urging the Admiral to more vigorous action against the Americans.

[30] RHMCR. *Stopford-Sackville Papers*, II, 56–57, Germain to Sir William Howe, January 14, 1777; 63–65, Howe to Germain, April 2, 1777.

ercised a co-ordinating influence in the formation of plans for this dual offensive.

Orders for the descent from Canada went out to General Sir Guy Carleton, governor of Canada, on March 26, about three weeks after Germain had sent Howe the royal assent for his expedition against Philadelphia. Giving way to characteristic spite—Carleton had testified against Germain at the latter's court martial after the Battle of Minden—the American Secretary induced the King to agree that the command of the expedition should be given, not to Carleton, the senior officer, but to Burgoyne. That General then proceeded to Canada, carrying orders minutely detailing the campaign he was about to undertake. Germain was taking no chances. Credit for crushing the rebellion was a prize he did not intend to give to another.

A tragedy of conflicting plans, ambiguous orders, and bad luck unfolded itself. Before he left New York in July, Howe received a letter from Burgoyne stating that his army was before Ticonderoga and was in full health and spirits. Thus made secure in a belief that Burgoyne was capable of fending for himself, Howe embarked for Philadelphia. Because of an extremely tedious passage—he arrived at the Head of Elk only on August 30—he was obliged to write Germain that co-operation with Burgoyne would now be impossible. He was disappointed too, he said, at the small number of loyalists who had come over to his standard. The situation was thought by no means critical, however. Early in August had come the comfortable report that Burgoyne's progress was without opposition and that Ticonderoga had fallen. The King and the ministry were in a fever of anticipation awaiting glorious news. On September 25, dispatches arrived from Burgoyne, and with them a cloud no bigger than a man's hand appeared on the horizon. His progress, the General wrote, had been as rapid as possible through the northern wilderness, but he had heard nothing from Howe. Of ten messengers sent to New York not one had returned.[31] Germain knew what Burgoyne did not: that the Canadian army would be disappointed of a junction with Howe's. Far from being alarmed, however, Germain merely reflected that it would be the greater honor for Burgoyne to reach Albany without assistance from New York.[32]

This general optimism grew on apace. William Knox predicted to his friend Governor Henry Ellis that an extraordinary *Gazette* would soon proclaim a great victory. William Eden was certain that the campaign then under way would see the end of the rebellion. Henry Dundas, the future Lord Melville, at his house in Ayrshire could scarcely wait for every post. John Robinson urged North to delay the opening of Parliament until the good news had arrived. There were, of course, some ominous undertones. "It has for many months been clear to me," Eden wrote North, "that if we cannot reduce the colonies by the force now employed under Howe and Burgoyne, we cannot send and support a force capable to reduce them." Dundas, too, though hoping for "some splendid business done this campaign," confided to Eden that if the present effort should not defeat the rebels, he would have "a very desperate opinion of the business." Old and ailing Henry Ellis replied to Knox's exuberant predictions with a quotation from Voltaire: *"le probable n'arrive presque jamais!"*[33] North, the King, the ministry, and the nation, however, confidently awaited good news.

Assuming that the conflict was practically over, North turned to the problem of the disposition of the "conquered" Colonies. Never fully trusting any cabinet colleague except

---

[31] Fortescue, *Correspondence of George III*, III, No. 2061, Germain to the King, September 25, 1777.

[32] RHMCR. *Knox Papers, Various Collections*, 139, Germain to Knox, September 29, 1777.

[33] *Ibid.*, 135, Ellis to Knox, August 13, 1777. Add. MSS 29475, ff. 11–12, Dundas to Eden, August 30, 1777. RHMCR. *Abergavenny Papers*, 17, Eden to North, August 25, 1777.

Dartmouth—and he was no longer in the cabinet—North found his confidants among the undersecretaries and subministers. Eden had been a moving force in the formation of the Peace Commission. North's own secretary to the Treasury, John Robinson, had been called upon to discharge the balance of the First Minister's duties during the latter's illness. Now it was to Charles Jenkinson, a lord of the Treasury, that he turned for advice, much to Eden's jealousy. North was frankly at a loss as to how to proceed, believing only that—whether any or all of the revolted provinces returned to their duty—Canada should henceforth be the main support of British authority in North America.[34] He was therefore anxious to receive suggestions for the future of the rebellious Colonies.

North conferred on several occasions with Jenkinson and with the latter's brother-in-law Cornwall, who was also a member of the Treasury Board. In June, 1777, just as he was about to depart for a vacation in France, Jenkinson wrote to North, summarizing the points raised in their conversations. His views are of interest because they represent those prevailing among British politicians. They serve to indicate that the American conflict had not as yet produced any radical change in British imperial thinking. Reaction to the American war was, as yet, primarily conservative. The vision of a new imperial relationship would be vouchsafed only when distress and defeat should prepare men for it.

Jenkinson contended that it was impossible ever to end the war by a negotiated treaty. While it had been wise to hold out such a prospect at the beginning of hostilities, nothing now could be done but "to state to the Americans in plain and explicit Terms, the Conditions on which alone you will allow them to resume a share in their own Government, and in the mean time to Govern them by Powers vested in the Crown." Jenkinson elaborated his analysis in a letter from Aix-la-Cha-

[34] RHMCR. *Abergavenny Papers*, 14–17, North to Carleton, August 3 and 26, 1777.

pelle in July. He then proposed that the Laws of Navigation should be tightened. The Colonies, he maintained, might be allowed to enjoy their own coasting trade, but all other trade should be carried on in ships belonging to subjects resident in England, Ireland, or in the colony producing that article of trade. Such a provision would serve to increase British naval strength and carrying trade. At the same time, it would restrain the growth of that branch of commerce in New England where, before the outbreak of hostilities, they had proved themselves formidable rivals to the mother country. Furthermore, such restrictions would diminish the colonial capacity for producing a naval force. The now existing American navy had already inflicted grievous losses on British shipping, and it should not be allowed to happen again.[35]

While Jenkinson indicated for the mother country the role of a stern parent, North was falling into melancholy. As the summer waned and September turned into October, the First Minister grew more apprehensive that the campaign would prove indecisive.[36] In early October, news of the capture of Philadelphia served to reassure the doubters, and for a time, London was tumultuous with joy. At the end of the month, however, Germain and the ministry learned of the affray at Bennington. The American Secretary immediately concluded that Burgoyne's campaign was "totally ruined"; but surely the General had withdrawn to Ticonderoga! Germain was seriously alarmed, however, at Burgoyne's apparent assumption that he possessed no discretionary authority, and that his orders were so positive that he had to press on to Albany at all costs.[37]

Parliament was to meet on November 18. Before that time, tension among the ministers had become almost unbearable. The drafting of the King's speech for the opening of the new

[35] Add. MSS 38306, f. 71, Letterbook, Jenkinson to North, June 26, 1777; ff. 72–74, Jenkinson to North, July 9, 1777.

[36] Add. MSS 34414, ff. 209–10, North to Eden, October 4, 1777.

[37] RHMCR. *Knox Papers, Various Collections*, 140, Germain to Knox, October 31, 1777.

session proved a difficult problem. On the ninth Eden sent
North a sketch for the speech "on the Supposition of goodish
News," and advised that, should such news not arrive before
the eighteenth, the Parliament be prorogued for ten days.
Eden had outlined a firm conciliatory message. More liberal
than Jenkinson, he would have had the King promise the
Americans that whenever they should return to their duty,
they would be given proof of Parliament's benevolent care
for them.[38] Both Eden and Jenkinson believed, however, in
the supreme power of Parliament. They might agree to the
puny qualification of it embodied in the Howe Peace Commission, but the time for a negotiated treaty was past. But what
would be their attitude and that of the ministry in the face of
new and catastrophic intelligence from Saratoga?

America, since the lingering death of Jacobitism, was the
first fully developed "issue" in British politics. It was not to
be a biding one, but the divisive force which it engendered was
to remain, and new issues and principles springing from it
would bring Britain to the threshold of her modern party system. The American problem in British politics had resulted
in the consolidation of a new conservatism, the seedbed of a new
Tory party. But it was also preparing, about the Old Whigs
as a nucleus, the emergence of a new Whig party.

It would be a mistake to call the Opposition "pro-American," except in a very limited sense. Yet the Americans and the
Opposition shared much common ground: a belief that King
and ministers had somehow—mysteriously though corruptly—
come to dominate the political scene free of any constitutional
check. Both groups detected in the reign of George III an
insidious attempt to re-create old Stuart despotism. The American reaction had been the formulation there of the concept
of a federal empire. That solution, however, was viewed in the
mother country as the very step which would render the Crown
independent of Parliament. When, therefore, that solution

[38] Add. MSS 34414, ff. 337–39, Eden to North, November 9, 1777.

had been rejected by Britain, whose own political development rendered it impossible, the colonists proceeded to declare themselves independent. That same political development within the mother country, which saw the King as an active agent in British politics, meant for the Opposition—Old Whigs, Radicals, and Chathamites alike—that the American struggle was but one of several symptoms of a basic political maladjustment. In fact, however, the King and the North Ministry had merely placed themselves at the head of a system created by the Old Whigs themselves under the first two Georges. Those claiming descent from the Walpole and Pelham Whigs had, perforce, to find a new basis whereon to stand and to create myths to explain both their origin and their long exclusion from office. Both Old Whigs and Americans, the first because of their long sojourn in the wilderness, and the second because they could not reconcile their federal idea with the traditional concept of empire, were passing beyond the eighteenth-century framework.

During these years of the American war, a twofold impact upon the Opposition became evident. First, among their shattered and divided ranks were men for whom military defeat and national disgrace were not necessary prerequisites for glimpsing a new vision of empire. In their gradual acceptance of the Americans' federal idea, they were groping toward the only way by which Britain, as a free country, could build and keep an empire. Secondly, seeing the American issue in a broader context, the Old Whigs and those acting with them set themselves upon a path leading to an abridgement of the powers of the Crown and to parliamentary reform. Success would come to their descendants but not, indeed, until the nineteenth-century, long after the American Colonies had been irretrievably lost.

There is a subtle relationship between the American federal idea, the Opposition's growing acceptance of it, and the attack on the "overweening" influence of the Crown. The

Americans, Lord Mansfield had stated during debates on colonial petitions, sought, with their argument that the Colonies were bound to the mother country only through the person of the King, to reduce the monarch to a figurehead or "cipher." He was right. Before a federal empire—or a commonwealth of nations—would become possible, the King would have to retreat from a role of active participation in politics, would have to rise above the domestic scene where modern, well-organized parties in which he had no active part dominated. He would have to become a symbol wherein all portions of the empire might find union in equality. During the American war, and largely because of it, the Old Whigs and their friends began that domestic battle which would result in so salubrious an end.

The arrival, in June, 1775, of reports of the outbreak of hostilities caught the Opposition scattered throughout the kingdom, for Parliament was in recess. Chatham was so ill that Lady Chatham kept the news from him. Rockingham threw up his hands at the impotence of his own party, exclaiming that politics must be left "to take their own Time and their own Turns." Lord Edgcumbe, formerly an Old Whig, had already put his parliamentary seats at North's command, and most Old Whigs felt reluctant to engage against measures to put down open rebellion. Only the eccentric Duke of Manchester called for an immediate halt to the war, but his plan, whatever it may have been, was negatived by Rockingham. Even Burke was convinced that the Americans would have to suffer heavy blows.[39]

Burke, as so often before, was for action, and he became the driving force in his own party. War had begun, but Parliament had not yet committed itself. Again and again, he urged the necessity of an immediate consultation among Old Whig

[39] Chatham Papers, 10, Lady Chatham to William Pitt, July 16, 1775. Wentworth-Woodhouse, Burke Papers, Rockingham to Burke, June 23, 1775; Lord John Cavendish to Rockingham, August 2, 1775.

leaders: "I protest to God," he wrote to Rockingham, "I think that your reputation, your duty, and the duty and honour of us all . . . demand at this time one honest, hearty effort, in order to avert the heavy calamities that are impending." Should that last effort fail, Burke believed the Old Whigs would be justified in leaving the people and the ministry to their fate. But to that last effort they were clearly obligated. He was not so sanguine as to believe that his party could carry the nation against the war, but by factious conduct, he proposed to impede that war in every possible way. Acting under a set plan, the Old Whigs, he believed, could "clog a war in such a manner, as to make it not very easy to proceed."[40]

Rockingham expressed initial agreement with Burke, and in September wrote to his lieutenant that he would be in London for general consultations ten days or two weeks before the opening of Parliament. His plan at that moment was to resist the loyal address, and further, to induce all parts of the Opposition to join in a remonstrance to the King. In it they would warn him that the royal power could subvert the authority of Parliament, and that American measures were part of "a *System,* which somehow are thought more particularly patronized by his Majesty." Having thus placed themselves on record, the Old Whigs would then absent themselves from Parliament whenever American affairs were under discussion.[41]

Reassured by Rockingham that some plan would be adopted before the opening of Parliament, Burke turned to his own constituency, the city of Bristol. What he found was not encouraging. Formerly the most pro-American city of the kingdom, Bristol was now undergoing a profound change. Burke's colleague, the American Henry Cruger, had reacted to the outbreak of hostilities in a disconcerting manner, lashing out

[40] William, Fitzwilliam, and Bourke, *Burke Correspondence,* II, 33–34, Burke to Rockingham; 39–41, Burke to Rockingham, August 4, 1775; 46–57, Burke to Rockingham, August 23, 1775.

[41] Wentworth-Woodhouse, Burke Papers, Rockingham to Burke, September 11, 1775.

at his erstwhile fellow-countrymen for their violence and folly. After a canvass of the city, Burke estimated that only a fourth of the corporation was with the Old Whigs. Another fourth would act with them in a limited way. The other half were Tories, but they, too, were divided. The Bristol Quakers, a strong mercantile group, were still Burke's friends, but their London brothers had gone over to the Court. Furthermore, the Bristol merchants tended to view the present crisis as merely another alarm, and to feel that all would in the end be well. The rest of the merchants of the kingdom, upon whose support the Old Whigs had ridden to power in 1765, had already abandoned them. Considering America lost, they looked to the ministry for an indemnity. Government contracts had begun to overcome their initial opposition to war. This in conjunction with the great increase of northern European commerce made the American trade seem of secondary importance.

Burke nevertheless fell energetically to work. At his instigation, a secret committee of correspondence was created among his merchant supporters in Bristol. Although he at first predicted that this example would be followed in twenty or thirty other places—a number which was never achieved—his most sanguine opinion before he had been long at his task was that he and his party were strong enough in Bristol to prevent their enemies hurting them.[42]

A second and greater disappointment was in store for him. After a September meeting of several of his friends in Yorkshire, Rockingham informed Burke that he had changed his mind: he now believed that it would be futile to call a general meeting of Old Whigs before the opening of Parliament. "The generality of the people of England," the Marquis wrote, "are now led away by the misrepresentations and arts of the ministry, the court, and their abettors; so that the violent measures toward America are fairly adopted and countenanced by a ma-

---

[42] William, Fitzwilliam, and Bourke, *Burke Correspondence*, II, 57–66, Burke to Rockingham, September 14, 1775.

jority of individuals of all ranks, professions, or occupations, in this country." Opposition could do nothing to alter events, and Rockingham was convinced that only national disaster and disgrace could change the situation.[43]

Burke was nearly beside himself at what he considered a palpable rationalization and excuse for inactivity at this time of supreme crisis. Abandoned by Rockingham, he turned to the young Duke of Richmond. As that nobleman was possessed of large estates in Ireland, Burke suggested that he join other Old Whigs with Irish interests and induce the Irish Commons to express their disapprobation of the American war. They should also be persuaded to refuse extraordinary grants and supplies for troops to be used outside their kingdom, thereby helping to prevent the mother country's "enslaving all its dependencies." Should that be done, Burke was convinced, the ministry would hesitate to take "a contest with the whole empire upon their hands at once."[44] When Richmond failed to respond to this desperate plan, the disappointed Burke realized that his party, believing that only disaster would awaken the public, had overruled him.

A new snub awaited him. Despite their utmost efforts, his friends had been easily overwhelmed when Bristol adopted a loyal address to the King expressing their support of the government in its struggle with the American rebels.[45] In London, Burke and his party, working through the radical Members for the City—Oliver, Bull, Sawbridge, and Hayley—suffered an even greater rebuff.[46] Even before the meeting of

---

[43] Wentworth-Woodhouse, Burke Papers, Rockingham to Burke, September 24, 1775.

[44] William, Fitzwilliam, and Bourke, *Burke Correspondence*, II, 71–76, Burke to Richmond, September 26, 1775.

[45] Wentworth-Woodhouse, Burke Papers, Paul Farr to Burke, September 30, October 7 and 14, 1775; Richard Champion to Burke, September 26, 1775.

[46] *Ibid.*, Sir William Baker to Burke, October 4, 5, 1775. See also RHMCR. *Dartmouth Papers*, II, 392, William Molleson, a London merchant, to Dartmouth, October 11, 1775.

Parliament, then, it was obvious that the Old Whigs would have no chance of rallying the merchant interests of the kingdom to their support.

Old Whig contact with the London Radicals did nothing to improve their odor with the public. With the outbreak of hostilities, Wilkes and his group had become objects of great suspicion. It was known that large numbers of foreign officers and engineers, mostly French, were in London awaiting passage to America and that they were being received and aided by some of the Radicals.[47] An open appeal had been made by the revolutionary provincial congress of New York for support among this very group. By autumn, inflammatory and seditious fly sheets had begun to circulate. The ministry, who had been intercepting suspected correspondence for months, was, moreover, aware of attempts to debauch the soldiery.

Firm and decisive ministerial action against potential firebrands was to prevent any violent revolutionary or radical activity. Even the horrible Gordon Riots of 1780, having no direct connection with the American war, would be reactionary rather than radical in character. That radical parson of Brentford, Horne Tooke, upon his expulsion from the quarreling Society of the Supporters of the Bill of Rights, had formed the Society for Constitutional Information. In June, 1775, his group voted £100 "for the relief of the widows, and orphans, and aged parents, of our American fellow-subjects, murdered by the King's troops at Lexington and Concord." Rebellion had already been acknowledged by Parliament, and as soon as the Proclamation of Rebellion was made, Tooke was arrested and convicted of libel. In November, 1777, he was fined and sen-

[47] RHMCR. *Dartmouth Papers*, II, 349, John Pownall to Dartmouth, August 5, 1775. Pownall estimated that there were two hundred such officers in London at the time. For the extent of seditious activity among the Radicals, see RHMCR. *Dartmouth Papers*, II, 376, an anonymous officer of the East India Company to Dartmouth, September 9, 1775; 376–77, circular letter of Thomas Joel, September 4, 1775; Charles Simpson, Town Clerk of Litchfield, to Dartmouth, September 9, 1775; Sergeant John Osbaldeston to Dartmouth; see also 427–28.

tenced to a year in prison. It is noteworthy that his incarceration was unattended by that public clamor that had been raised at Wilke's imprisonment.

Radical ardor was further damped when, in autumn of 1775, a former sheriff of London, the American Stephen Sayre, was briefly committed to the Tower, charged on very flimsy evidence with plotting to seize the King's person at the opening of Parliament. Upon his release, he left the country and allied himself with his fellow Americans on the continent. Held in abhorrence by the great majority of men, the activity of the Radicals served to increase the nation's support of the ministry and to discredit all groups, however respectable, who opposed the American war.

Parliament met on October 26. As yet no effort had been made to secure Old Whig-Chathamite co-operation. Chatham was still sick, although reports of his recovery were circulating, and Burke grudgingly admitted that it would be wise to concert measures with him and with his friends. Even so, the first approach came from the Chathamites. On the twenty-eighth, Dr. Joseph Priestly, close friend and confidant of Shelburne, wrote to Savile seeking to present a comprehensive statement of Shelburne's views. The Earl, he said, was prepared to act with, or even under, Rockingham if only definite, distinct proposals were adopted. Not mincing words, he told Savile that the Americans would have more confidence in Shelburne than in Rockingham, whose Declaratory Act the colonists would never accept. It is clear, then, that in case a coalition of the two parties should achieve office, Shelburne counted on having the direction of American affairs.

Priestly was frankly despairing, however, of any chance to treat with the Americans. The chief interest of his letter lies in its indication that Shelburne was already looking beyond the American struggle. The war he saw as only one of several symptoms of a fundamental illness in the State. The object of future opposition, Shelburne believed, should be to achieve an abridgement of the power of the Crown, especially in respect to the disposal of revenue. Already, then, he was moving toward that "platform" of economy and reform which was to make possible his future coalition with the Old Whigs.[48]

Despite Savile's cautious reply, the debates of November indicated that substantial union had been achieved. Grafton's accession was a heartening sign, and when Burke was drawing up his bill for composing the troubles in America, he was in close communication with Camden, Shelburne, and other Chathamite leaders. No one indeed was so sanguine as to believe that North's ministry could be overturned. When, for instance, Richmond moved in the House of Lords in November that the Olive Branch afforded grounds for reconciliation with America, the combined Opposition could vote only thirty-two against eighty-six. They were, however, seeking to "go on the record." During the debates of October and November, their attitude toward the war was clearly delineated: America had been driven to resist because of Britain's unjust demand for a revenue. She did not aim at independence. The mother country had falsely assumed that she did and now sought to coerce her by force. Such an attempt was doomed to failure. Underlying their whole argument was the theme that the struggle must be brought to an immediate end: if it continued, France could not be expected to remain neutral. From an independent member of Opposition, former colonial Governor Johnstone, came a more creative analysis. In a brilliant speech he presented the first clear statement yet heard in Parliament of the principle of a federalistic empire. Johnstone maintained that it was ignorant to deny as the ministry did that two independent legislatures could not coexist within the same political community. A free government always contained many clashing jurisdictions: "The supremacy of the legislative authority of Great Britain! This I call unintelligible jargon; instead of running

[48] RHMCR. *Savile-Foljambe Papers,* 149, Priestly to Savile, October 28, 1775; 150, Savile to Priestly, October 29, 1775.

the different privileges belonging to the various parts of the empire into one common mass of power, gentlemen should consider that the very first principles of good government in this wide-extended dominion, consist in sub-dividing the empire into many parts, and giving to each individual an immediate interest, that the community to which he belongs should be well regulated."[49] His pronouncement indicated that a new idea was at work in imperial thinking, one which the government was eventually to accept under the harsh necessity of military defeat.

Johnstone, in his vision of a federal empire was far ahead of the rest of Opposition. Nonetheless, there were signs that the Old Whigs were feeling their way toward that solution. On November 16, Burke brought forward his bill for quieting America. Marking a fundamental change in Old Whig thinking and a limited acceptance of Johnstone's thesis, the bill signified Old Whig willingness to repudiate the right to tax America for revenue. Paradoxically, Burke proposed to achieve this object without actually repealing the Declaratory Act, for which his party had been responsible. He was still unwilling to admit that they had been wrong. Charles James Fox had earlier called for a repeal of all acts concerning America passed since 1763. In his own argument, however, Burke disagreed, maintaining that a repeal of the Declaratory Act would constitute a denial of the legislative power of Parliament, while a repeal of all the Acts of Trade since 1763 would destroy the whole system of British-American commerce. It is difficult to reconcile his attitude toward Fox's proposal with the new thesis enunciated in his bill: that sovereignty was an idea capable of great complexity and infinite modifications according to the temper of those governed and to the circumstances of the time. The power of taxation, although inherent in the supreme power of society taken as an aggregate, did not necessarily reside in any particular organ of that society. What he now pro-

[49] Cobbett and Wright, *Parliamentary History*, XVIII, 740–57.

Courtesy Library of Congress

EDMUND BURKE

posed was passage of a new act denying to Parliament the right to lay any tax upon America except for the regulation of commerce. Even in that case, the produce was to be remitted to the Colonies. A general congress was to be authorized whenever required by the colonists. The Coercive Acts would be repealed, and a general amnesty granted.[50]

Although the Old Whigs still clung to their Declaratory Act, believing that consistency demanded it, this proposal was a step forward for them. Once more, however, they found themselves on middle ground and satisfying no one but themselves. The ministry was hostile because of the proposed infringement of Parliament's supremacy. Governor Johnstone, on the other hand, attacked Burke's plan just as bitterly, branding it as only "part of a system." The Old Whigs knew their motion would be defeated—the House subsequently divided in favor of the previous question by 210 to 105—but they had gone on the record.

Despite the Opposition's positive achievement in pointing out the way to a federal empire, their attacks were clearly without influence in Parliament. Indeed, their numbers were steadily diminishing. In late November, on a rash motion of the City Radicals, they divided only 10 against 163. When, on December 1, North brought in his Prohibitory Bill, which forbade commerce with the rebels, the Opposition did not dare bring the debate to a division. A week later, when David Hartley moved to address the King asking an immediate cessation of military operations because of the colonial submission made in the Olive Branch, his motion was defeated by 21–123. Opposition could do no better in the Lords. Nothing apparently could alter the prevailing view that America must somehow be compelled to acknowledge the legislative supremacy of Parliament. Only after that would she be allowed to resume her privileges and rights.

Outside Parliament, Burke's campaign to build a network

[50] *Ibid.*, 963–92.

of local committees of correspondence and to win petitions against the ministry's American measures was meeting with no more success than Opposition had had in Parliament. Committees patterned after that of Bristol were set up in London and a few other places. The committee in Westbury, Wiltshire, sent Burke a petition deploring "the present unnatural and destructive contest with our American brethren."[51] But it was soon obvious that the movement had by no means achieved the magnitude necessary to exert any influence on Parliament. Indeed, public opinion in Bristol was running so strongly against Burke and his friends there that according to one of them, Paul Farr, "the stream runs too strong against us for us to stem it; if we can escape drowning, it is all we have to expect." With the Prohibitory Act, all pretense of merchant resistance even in Bristol collapsed. The merchants, perceiving that further attempts to halt the headlong rush to war were futile, now sought merely to salvage what they could from their American investments and to compensate themselves in other areas of trade.[52]

Their cause rejected by Parliament and public alike, their faith in the people and contact with them lost, the Old Whigs had now to pin their hopes on the defeat of British arms. The country was thus presented with the strange spectacle of a party claiming the name of patriot while desperately wishing her defeat and disgrace. "I look to the moment of the determination of the operations of the Campaign," wrote Rockingham to Burke. "Men's minds in this country are hung up, in the Suspense of Expectation; the End of the Campaign is the *Set-*

[51] William, Fitzwilliam, and Bourke, *Burke Correspondence*, II, 84–85, Rockingham to Burke, November 2, 1775. See also Wentworth-Woodhouse, Burke Papers, Lord Craven to Burke, November, 1775, concerning maneuvers in the city of Abingdon and the county of Berkshire; the Committee of Correspondence of Westbury, Wiltshire, to Burke, November 21, 1775.

[52] Wentworth-Woodhouse, Burke Papers, Paul Farr to Burke, October, 1775, and public letter from Nathaniel Wraxall, Paul Farr, Richard Champion, and others to Burke, December 12, 1775.

tling Day." When that day arrived, the people would look to the Old Whigs for leadership, for that party had incessantly warned them against the American war.[53]

In August, 1776, arrived the report that America had declared herself independent. While Chatham from his sickbed let it be known that he still abided by his Provisional Bill and would never agree to colonial independence, the Old Whigs vainly tried to ignore the American declaration. They still professed to believe that a negotiated peace was possible if only Britain would make the concessions outlined in Burke's bill. By October, it was known that Sir William Howe had been successful at New York. While Fox declared he was "far from being dismayed by the terrible news," Rockingham was despondent: the ministers were exultant, and "the Publick like a silly echo can only repeat the Sounds it hears . . . while the still voice of Reason is lost, as it were, in Vacuum."[54]

Parliament met on October 31, and although Old Whigs and Chathamites worked closely together, the number of their humiliating defeats continued growing. After a final attempt early in November when Lord John Cavendish moved to revise all laws wherein America thought herself aggrieved, the great majority of Old Whigs withdrew from Parliament. Fox was the most notable exception. Until future events should give them fresh ground whereon to make a stand, the Old Whigs knew that further opposition could only discredit them. "We are not only patriots *out of place*, but patriots out of the opinion *of the public*," wrote Savile to Rockingham. The successes of British arms, he maintained, had converted ninety-nine in every hundred to the ministry's support.[55] When North brought in his bill suspending habeas corpus for those suspected of high treason in America and on the high seas, only Fox and the Chathamites Dunning and Barré were present to

[53] *Ibid.*, Rockingham to Burke, July 12, 1776.
[54] *Ibid.*, Rockingham to Burke, October 22, 1776.
[55] Albemarle, *Rockingham Memoirs*, II, 304–307, Savile to Rockingham, January 15, 1777.

resist it. In the House of Lords, only one peer—Lord Abingdon—signed a dissent against it.

Outside Parliament, after a winter of quiet, Burke once more took up the cudgel. In April, 1777, in his famous letter to the sheriffs of Bristol, he indicated that the Old Whigs were moving toward an acceptance of American independence. The ministers, he charged, had proceeded on a false premise: that the recovery of America depended upon her unconditional submission. Such was no longer to be expected. Nothing could now restore the old system. Justifying his party's opposition to the war, he asserted it was desirable for the Americans to believe there was "a formed American party" in England. Better for them to carry many points, "even some of them not quite reasonable," with the help of a British party than to be driven to seek foreign aid. Now agreeing with Fox, Burke called for a repeal of all acts concerning America passed since 1763. He believed the Americans would not then continue to insist upon independence. Even if they did, however, he preferred American independence without war to independence with it.[56]

In April, 1777, the King had to ask a grant of £600,000 so he could pay the arrears on the civil list. The Old Whigs, perceiving that their absence from Parliament had been attended with as little success as their presence, returned to assume a role they were to fill throughout the remainder of their existence: that of champions of economic reform as a means of abridging the overweening powers of the Crown. In both Houses, they now demanded particulars of the civil list. Failing to win their point, they charged that the debt had been incurred for the corrupt purpose of gaining unconstitutional influence. That influence had now become so strong, they declared, that any group could be called to lead government however independent of or contrary to the opinion and approbation of the electors.

At the end of the session, on May 30, Chatham appeared

[56] Edmund Burke, *Works*, III, 160 ff.

in the Lords to move for a cessation of hostilities.[57] It would be impossible, he solemnly warned, to conquer "the map of America." He scoffed at the ministry's "spring hopes and vernal promises" that the struggle would be won with the present campaign. Instead, he predicted, "at last will come your equinoctial disappointment." Adding his opinion that France would soon come openly to the aid of the Americans, he joined in full agreement with Burke's and Fox's earlier demands for a repeal of all American acts passed since 1763. However, with the defeat of Chatham's motion in a division of ninety to twenty-eight, Opposition once again lapsed into lethargy. All eyes—the ministry's and Opposition's alike—were now fixed upon the course of military operations. The former were confident of victory; the latter hoped desperately for defeat.

The summer of 1777 was indeed one of anxiety for both ministers and Opposition. As autumn came, and still no news from Howe or Burgoyne, Rockingham thought he detected "some dawn of Light breaking in upon the Minds of the Public," although he was convinced that if "what is called *good News*" should arrive from America, the public would suffer a "relapse" and again be hopeful.[58] The report of the capture of Philadelphia was as great a blow to the Old Whigs as was the loss of that city to the Americans. "The wild tumult of joy . . . in the minds of all sorts of people, indicates nothing right in their character and disposition," Burke told Rockingham. Governor Johnstone's brother William Pulteney, who had now thrown in his lot with the Old Whigs, expressed his agreement with Burke, Savile, and Portland that the victory made a settled plan for Opposition impossible. That would be practicable only after the country had suffered military disaster.[59]

[57] Cobbett and Wright, *Parliamentary History*, XIX, 316–51.

[58] Wentworth-Woodhouse, Burke Papers, Rockingham to Burke, October 20, 1777.

[59] William, Fitzwilliam, and Bourke, *Burke Correspondence*, II, 198–

Hope lay, perhaps, in the long delay of news from Burgoyne. In late November, a general meeting of the Opposition determined to move in both Houses a consideration of the state of the nation. Chatham had not been present, but Rockingham had sent to him asking his sentiments, and despite the usual verbiage, his answer was clear. Chatham was for "right forward" action, and he agreed that union was necessary.[60]

A few days later, on December 3, came the thunderbolt of Saratoga. Rockingham immediately penned a one-line note: "My dear Burke, My Heart is at Ease."[61] That military defeat which the Old Whigs had predicted, indeed had longed for, had come at last. They now had, they thought, a fair field on which to stand.

201, Burke to Rockingham, November 5, 1777. Wentworth-Woodhouse, Burke Papers, Pulteney to Burke, November 6, 1777.

[60] Albemarle, *Rockingham Memoirs*, II, 324–25, Chatham to Rockingham, November 27, 1777.

[61] Wentworth-Woodhouse, Burke Papers, Rockingham to Burke, December 3, 1777.

CHAPTER SEVEN

AGONY AND REVELATION

IN THE summer of 1777, days of golden hope, the North Ministry seemed the darling of good fortune. Burgoyne's expedition was proceeding well. Howe, at Brandywine, had administered a severe defeat to Washington. A dissolution of the rebel army seemed imminent. Philadelphia was captured. France, grown more conciliatory, had forced American privateers who had carried British captures into French ports to disgorge their prizes. The stocks had risen.

In such an atmosphere North searched for a means of ending the civil war. "I am very melancholy," he admitted to Eden; "my idea of American affairs is, that, if our success is as great as the most sanguine politician wishes or believes, the best use we can make of it is to get out of the dispute as soon as, possible." Consulting with Eden on drafting the King's speech which would open the autumn session, he asked: "How shall we mention America? Shall we be very stout? or shall we take advantage of the flourishing state of our affairs to get out of this d——d war, and hold a moderate language?"[1] While Lord North thus debated with himself and with his friends, news was speeding across the Atlantic which would make all his doubts academic.

Early in the evening of December 2, Captain Moutray of the "Warwick" arrived from American waters carrying dispatches for Sandwich. At nine that same evening, the Admiralty Lord sent urgently to the King: Burgoyne with all his

[1] Add. MSS 34414, ff. 309–10, North to Eden, November 4, 1777.

army had surrendered to Gates at Saratoga some two months earlier. The shock was staggering. Next morning, Germain, agonized at the new development, wrote of the appalling news to Eden. Declaring he could think of nothing but America, he asked what Eden knew of North's reaction, whether the First Minister had slept, and, above all, if he had "thought of any Expedient for Extricating this Country out of its distress."[2] Secretary at War Barrington could not "write or talk about the dreadful catastrophe of Burgoyne's army, and I wish I could think of any other thing." The Duke of Marlborough, Eden's patron and a loyal supporter of the ministry, hoped "they will not think of sending more troops; for I suppose, they may as well think of subduing the moon, as America by force of arms."[3] While a troubled monarch tried to sooth his panic-stricken First Minister by calling the surrender a "misfortune . . . not without remedy," North knew that "some material change of system" was now indicated: peace, desirable before, was now imperative.[4] To achieve it, to salvage some part of the American connection, and to avoid a war with France, greater concessions must be made: greater than had hitherto been dreamed of in ministerial circles.

Burgoyne's surrender was followed by four major developments, much interrelated: a spate of "unofficial" negotiations with the American commissioners in Paris; the near-fall of the North Ministry; a concerted effort to change the mode of war in America; and the Carlisle Peace Commission.

Only two days after the catastrophic intelligence, Paul Wentworth, former colonial agent and now British secret agent, was dispatched to Paris there to seek out the American commissioners Franklin, Silas Deane and Arthur Lee. It was a measure of the influence Eden had achieved with North that

---

[2] *Ibid.*, f. 394, Germain to Eden, December 3, 1777.

[3] *Ibid.*, f. 517, Marlborough to Eden, December, 1777. RHMCR. *Lothian Papers*, 325, Barrington to Buckinghamshire, December, 1777.

[4] Fortescue, *Correspondence of George III*, III, No. 2094, the King to North, December 4, 1777; No. 2095, North to the King, December 4, 1777.

Wentworth worked under his immediate supervision in an area which appertained, strictly speaking, to the southern, not the northern, secretary of state. Behind Eden, however, stood North himself, fully supporting this attempt to achieve an accommodation through extracabinet and unofficial negotiations.

Before Wentworth departed for Paris, Eden wrote him a letter—to which North must have been privy—intended ultimately for perusal by the American commissioners. He admitted that Great Britain appeared far from her object, if that were reduction of the Colonies to obedience. He warned, however, that defeat and disgrace would but reanimate the nation should America persist in her demand for an unqualified independence. Nonetheless, "the Language, Sentiments and Expectations of the Country on the original pretensions of the War are certainly moderated." Should the Colonies desire "to revert to their old Connection on new grounds," he saw a good prospect for ending the war to the satisfaction of both sides. The Americans might insist that they already possessed a *de facto* independence. But surely they could not wish a final settlement which would leave them prey to anarchy and confusion. A "qualified controul" should rest somewhere; and surely—here Eden betrayed Britain's deep-seated fear of French intervention—the Americans could not wish it to rest in the hands of France, a nation wholly alien to the common blood, language, and constitution of Great Britain and America. If such were their sentiments, Eden urged the American commissioners to state frankly and fully what they considered acceptable grounds of an accommodation and the proper mode of negotiating it.

Eden then posed a list of questions to serve as a basis of negotiation with the commissioners:

1. Should Great Britain desist from taxing the colonists, would they bear the expense of their own governments?

2. Should colonial charters be restored intact, would the Colonists replace all property seized or confiscated, and the colonists pay their quitrents?

3. Should Great Britain consent to the Colonies undertaking their own military protection, would they bear that charge?

4. Should American ports be reopened and bounties revived, would the Americans place their trade on "some ground analogous to the Act of Navigation"? (It is significant that Eden made no mention of the Laws of Trade.)

5. Would both countries exchange mutual guarantees of possessions and restore common citizenship?

Eden professed to be cordially disposed, when he had the answers to these questions in his hands, "to turn such knowledge to the most immediate, the most benevolent, and the most important purposes."[5]

North and Eden, well aware of the probable reaction of France to the American victory over Burgoyne, knew they had reason to hurry. On December 6, the French King wrote *"Approuvé"* on Vergennes' paper expressing willingness to entertain propositions from the American commissioners looking toward an alliance. This was the same day Eden gave Wentworth his instructions, arranging to correspond with him in cypher through the British ambassador's messenger.

Wentworth left for Paris on December 10. He had close contacts with the commissioners, being a friend of the secretary, Edwards, and an acquaintance of Franklin's private secretary, the double-traitor Bancroft. Upon his arrival, Wentworth got in touch with Deane and arranged a meeting. On the fifteenth, they dined together, and had a long conversation, pledging themselves to secrecy and to "the Confidence of Private Gentlemen wishing well to both countries." Both were

[5] Stevens, *Facsimilies*, No. 483, Eden to Wentworth, December 5, 1777, draft.

Freemasons, and Wentworth asked the American to join him in building a "Temple of Peace and Concord." It soon appeared that Deane was jealous of Franklin and rather hostile to France, but, he assured the emissary, independence had struck such deep roots with the American people that they would never give it up.

The conference continued the next day. Deane, assuring Wentworth that America's prospects were growing better by the hour, put forward three propositions. The authority and conservatism with which he spoke would seem to indicate that he had conferred with his colleagues in the meantime. Deane now proposed: a cessation of all hostilities; an evacuation of the United States by British forces; and the appointment of British commissioners to treat with Congress for a basis of future Anglo-American relations. It was his opinion that "the Materials of the old House should be removed out of Sight, and the new Fabrick raised on new ground and foundations." Wentworth objected to this statement, asserting that some of the old material should be retained, namely, "the King's Authority and Rights." Should that be added to Deane's propositions, he thought peace might be obtainable.

All questions were now laid aside, however, to permit a discussion of the nature of a future union between the two countries. Deane thought it should be a commercial one, but refused to accept any system of Navigation Acts. Wentworth approached the question from another angle. Britain might lend America one million pounds at 7½ per cent interest, and another three million pounds at 5 per cent so as to place her economy on a sound footing and to sink the enormous quantity of paper money issued to finance the war. Security would be furnished by farmers willing to mortgage their land in exchange for individual loans. The only condition to be imposed upon them would be the cultivation of one-fourth of an acre of an assigned commodity, the increase of which was to be sent to England. An agricultural officer in each colony would teach the inhabitants the cultivation of African and Asian products. A loan bank would be established in each province. Deane liked this variation of the mercantile theme, and another meeting was arranged.[6]

At this point, Franklin's secretary, Edward Bancroft, received a letter from London, unsigned, but obviously from a person of some authority, probably William Pulteney, a Member of Parliament and a brother of Governor Johnstone.[7] Independent of party affiliation although agreeing with the Old Whigs in American questions, Pulteney had asked Germain, as early as December 6, if he might go to Paris to ascertain Franklin's terms.[8] Because of great secrecy surrounding the North-Eden project, Germain was unaware that Wentworth had already been sent. Thus he did not reject Pulteney's idea, though he pointed out the difficulties it involved. Pulteney wrote again on the ninth, urging speed to forestall a Franco-American treaty, and saying he believed he could convert Franklin to terms short of independence.[9] We may assume then that Germain acquiesced, and that Bancroft's anonymous letter came from Pulteney.

The letter informed the secretary that the government intended, immediately after the recess, to make parliamentary offers designed to end the war. The author had been asked by a person of high rank to request of Bancroft some general intimation concerning terms which would be likely to satisfy the Congress and the American people. Peace, he hoped, would be obtained on "terms a little short of absolute Independency," terms which would save the honor of the Crown by leaving the King "a nominal sovereignty" and the exercise of "some small regal Prerogatives, particularly that of Putting America into a State of War and Peace with Great Britain."

[6] Add. MSS 34414, ff. 433–42, Wentworth to Eden, private dispatch, December 17, 1777.

[7] Stevens, *Facsimilies*, No. 1787, under date of December 19, 1777.

[8] RHMCR. *Stopford-Sackville Papers*, II, 81–82, Pulteney to Germain, December 6, 1777.

[9] *Ibid.*, II, 82–83.

Wentworth's mission and Pulteney's anonymous letter gave the American commissioners a strong hand. They could—and did—now play Britain against France. When Deane informed his colleagues of his conversations with Wentworth, the Americans at once notified the French Court urging that France take a decided part, since attractive offers were expected from Britain. It should have been obvious to Wentworth that the commissioners had no thought of an agreement short of independence. Though he suspected that he was being used, he was not sure. Inept at conveying his thoughts in writing, he produced rambling and verbose reports resulting chiefly in confusion at home: "I was above two hours reading Wentworth's dispatches last night," North told Eden. "I do not know what to think of them, and can not pretend to judge whether there is, or is not any wish of peace in 51 [code designation for Deane]."[10]

In Paris, the astute Franklin had now assumed direction of the interviews with Wentworth. Deane, pleading illness, had avoided another meeting, but the commission secretary, Edwards, had met him and had informed him on behalf of the commissioners that an acknowledgement of America's independence was a first requisite. Afterwards, an alliance would be possible. Edwards warned, however, that speed was of the utmost consequence. The ominous meaning of his statement—that a Franco-American alliance was in preparation—could not be misunderstood. Indeed, a subsequent meeting with Edwards on the twenty-seventh convinced Wentworth that France and Spain would, within six weeks, recognize American independence and attack Great Britain.[11]

Wentworth's intelligence in turn persuaded North that a Bourbon war was near. When he sought to urge this view upon the King, however, George III, obstinately and with great lack

[10] Add. MSS 34414, ff. 461–62, North to Eden, December 23, 1777.
[11] Ibid., ff. 463–66, Wentworth to Eden, December 25, 1777; ff. 468–72, Wentworth to Eden, December 28, 1777.

of foresight, refused to see it. Wentworth, he said, was "an avowed stockjobber" trying to make a "killing." He would depress the public stocks and then capitalize on a restored market when the war rumors had proved unfounded. North, taking his cue from his royal master, thereupon allowed his initial anxiety to subside.

Meantime, the tempo of international intrigue increased. Thornton, an agent from the American commissioners, tried to arrange a meeting with North in London, but North refused to receive him, thereby probably missing firsthand and authentic information about the projected Franco-American treaties.[12] In Paris, Franklin met Wentworth, talked much at random, and remarked that Eden's letter was a "very interesting sensible letter—pity it did not come a little sooner." Obviously, Franklin and his colleagues had no serious thought that Wentworth, having no power to recognize American independence, could negotiate peace. On January 9, therefore, Edwards warned Wentworth for the last time that an acknowledgement of independence was a *sine qua non* and that it must come at once to forestall an American treaty with France. The substance of the projected agreement was actually communicated to the British agent.

Franklin himself sent word by the dull, but well-meaning Moravian James Hutton that recognition of independence was immediately necessary. David Hartley, too, was in touch with Franklin, begging him not to throw America into the arms of France, and recommending North's plan of peace. William Strahan, to whom Franklin had first made his "Hints," joined in the steady stream of English politicians who sought to persuade Franklin to make peace on the basis of the Conciliatory Acts. The fact that neither Franklin nor the other commissioners had power to negotiate with Britain did not discourage

---

[12] Add. MSS 34415, f. 24, copy, Samuel Wharton to M. Maisonville, January 2, 1778. Thornton was a friend of Wharton, and was concealed at the house of a relative of David Hartley during his stay in London.

the thought that should Franklin—with his immense prestige —be brought to agree to British propositions, Congress would accept them too. Even after the existence of the Franco-American treaties was known in Britain—they were signed in early February—unofficial efforts continued. In March, Pulteney went over to Paris (under the name of Williams), with full approbation of King and ministry, to try to draw Franklin into negotiations based on North's plan. In April, Hartley arrived and asked Franklin for an interview. Although Franklin saw his old friend, he kept his new ally Vergennes fully informed, and he steadfastly refused to become involved in unofficial negotiations.[13] The British approaches to the American commissioners, in their futility, clearly indicated that a Bourbon war was inevitable. That George III and Lord North failed to accept this betrays a shocking want of capacity. One fact North did comprehend, however: no treaty negotiations could begin with the American commissioners without a prior recognition of American independence. North and his colleagues therefore knew that the only course remaining was to make propositions directly to the Congress and the American people.

The attitude of the American commissioners was, however, only one of North's problems. In the hectic days following the receipt of the news of Burgoyne's surrender, the First Minister had to face an apparently inevitable collapse of his ministry. Eden, rising rapidly in influence with North—eventually the First Minister would unwittingly earn Eden's wrath and be reduced to begging abjectly that he remain in office—considered the administration as falling. Only a coalition, Eden believed, with at least one of the Opposition groups could save

---

[13] RHMCR. *Stopford-Sackville Papers*, II, 91–92, Hutton to Germain, January 25, 1778. Sparks, *Franklin's Works*, VIII, 237–38, Hartley to Franklin, February 20, 1778; 268–70, Franklin to Vergennes, April 24, 1778. Franklin also reported to Vergennes a conversation with Chapman, a Member of the Irish House of Commons who, Franklin supposed, had come from Shelburne. See also Stevens, *Facsimilies*, No. 1893, Strahan to Franklin, March 13, 1778.

it.[14] Within the cabinet, tensions approached the breaking point. Criticism of Germain was becoming bitter. Never able to work long in harmony with any military commander, Germain, convinced that Sir William Howe had sabotaged the Canadian army's offensive, was treating the General so coldly that Howe was demanding to be recalled. Germain had already resolved to throw Burgoyne to the wolves should that be necessary to save his own skin, and had determined to cover himself by a parliamentary inquiry into the surrender. When he raised the matter at a cabinet meeting, however, he found to his chagrin that his colleagues were divided—and evenly. Suffolk, Sandwich, and North supported him. Chancellor Bathurst, so offended with Germain that he was rapidly losing his habitual timidity, Dartmouth, and the two Bedfordites Gower and Weymouth were against him. In the face of such prodigious opposition to what he thought would be a matter of routine, Germain was forced to drop his proposal, although not without bitterness.[15]

Personal ambitions were further disrupting the ministry. Suffolk aspired to the Garter, an honor which the King resolutely denied him. Thurlow and Wedderburn, the law officers, earlier promised promotion by North, chose the present crisis to press their claims. North, unable to impose any effective control upon his squabbling colleagues, wrote despondingly to the King, "Let the resolutions taken by Administration be what they will, if a question is moved suddenly in both Houses at one time, it will always be very possible that the Ministers in the two Houses may think differently about it."[16] In the face of grave danger, both from France and from the coming Oppo-

---

[14] Hinchingbrooke Papers, Eden to Sandwich, December 27, 1777; printed in Navy Record Society, LXIX, *Sandwich Papers*, I, 314–15.

[15] RHMCR. *Stopford-Sackville Papers*, II, 88–90, Germain's memo; Fortescue, *Correspondence of George III*, III, No. 2126, North to the King, December 26, 1777.

[16] Fortescue, *Correspondence of George III*, IV, No. 2163, North to the King, January 14, 1778.

sition attack in Parliament, it was clear that a ministerial crisis was building up.

Early in February, Germain wrote to Howe that his resignation had been accepted and that Clinton would succeed him as commander-in-chief. The letter was so cold that Bathurst, whose reaction to Burgoyne's surrender had been to declare "for peace on any terms," curtly told Germain and Suffolk that he considered Howe's retirement as attended with "fatal consequences." He had then asked North to request the King's permission to withdraw his name from the list of his Majesty's confidential servants.[17] North, immediately concluding that his ministry had collapsed, told the King that he should think of a new ministerial arrangement, pointing out Chatham as the person in Opposition likely to be of most service to the King and least extravagant in his demands. Indeed, North revealed, approaches had already been made to Chatham. However the great man, lamenting in true Chathamesque style, feared that it was too late to save the country. He would undertake to form a government only with a direct mandate from the King and full power to re-form the whole ministry.[18]

The King, to whom Chatham's pronouncement conjured up visions of a sovereign in chains, determined then to prevent North's capitulation by inducing Bathurst to remain in office. Suffolk implored the Chancellor not further to embarrass the King's affairs, "which, God knows, are already sufficiently embarrassed." Germain himself offered him an humble apology and undertook to write to Howe again in a more friendly manner. The offended minister was thus placated, but while expressing esteem for most of his colleagues, he conspicuously excluded Germain.[19] And although both North and the King

[17] RHMCR. *Bathurst Papers*, 16–17. See also RHMCR. *Stopford-Sackville Papers*, II, 93, Bathurst to Germain and Suffolk, February 16, 1778; RHMCR. *Dartmouth Papers*, II, 457, Bathurst to Dartmouth, February 13, 1778.

[18] Fortescue, *Correspondence of George III*, IV, No. 2193, North to the King, February 16, 1778.

[19] RHMCR. *Bathurst Papers*, 17, Gower to Bathurst, February 18, 1778.

were hoping that the American Secretary would take the initiative and resign, he resentfully clung to office.

One danger, which North viewed with deadly fear, did not, however, materialize. The Opposition was never able to generate enough power to overturn him. As soon as news of Burgoyne's surrender had arrived, Rockingham had written to Chatham. The Marquis, Richmond, and Manchester had then called on Shelburne. Sawbridge, radical Member for London, conferred with Old Whig leaders, and it appeared that at least some of his fellows would make common cause with a united Opposition.

The storm soon broke about the ministers' heads. On December 5, David Hartley moved a series of resolutions against the further prosecution of the American war and asked "a perpetual federal alliance" with America, based on "a compact of trade."[20] In the debates that followed, the ministers argued that Burgoyne's defeat furnished only the more reason for continuing the war. The Old Whigs, in reply, gave indications that they were moving steadily toward accepting American independence as the only means of making peace with America and avoiding war with France. The great question in all minds was how would the country gentlemen react? It soon became evident that despite mutterings, they remained staunch in their support of the ministry. In point of numbers, the Opposition was forced to conclude, there had been no improvement in its condition. In the critical division of December 10, for instance, on the ministry's motion for an adjournment until January 20, which the combined Opposition had fought tooth and nail, they were able to vote only 68 against 155.

Events during the recess further demonstrated a public attachment to the ministry. A stream of loyal addresses poured in from Manchester, Liverpool, London, and several other cities. Widespread public subscriptions and private raising of

[20] See Cobbett and Wright, *Parliamentary History*, XIX, 549–60, for the debates at this time.

troops for the royal service indicated that the country had perceived the French menace however willfully blind might be the
King and his First Minister. Burke had reverted to his favorite scheme of petitioning, only to find that his friend Paul Farr,
although promising to do what he could in Bristol, was not at
all hopeful. So great was the "langour or timidity or prudence
or caution or what ever else you may please to call it of the
Whigs in this City," said Farr, that the slightest effort would
require more spirit than was apt to be found.[21]

Chatham was being widely mentioned as the probable
leader in the approaching war with France. The nation appeared to be uniting in a patriotic fervor it had never known
during the American war. At this critical moment, then, a sustained and united Opposition assault led by the popular Chatham might have brought down North's wavering ministry.
Suddenly, however, Chatham blasted all such hopes. Late in
January, he wrote to Rockingham that as the Old Whigs had
apparently resolved to accept American independence, he could
not possibly co-operate with them. Rockingham was aghast,
answering that no matter what were their differing views on independence, the two parties could surely work together in demanding an inquiry into "the causes, mismanagements, distressed state, and impending ruin of this country." But the
irascible old man, nearing the end of his long and eventful
life, but still hoping to be called to form yet another ministry,
now refused to be ruled by broader considerations. He would
not be drawn into even limited co-operation with persons who
differed with him so much on the fundamentals of an American settlement.[22] The Old Whigs would never forgive him.
Their maledictions would follow him to his grave. Thus they
had lost Chatham. They had also lost the City Radicals who

[21] Wentworth-Woodhouse, Burke Papers, Farr to Burke, January 31,
1778.
[22] Taylor and Pringle, *Chatham Correspondence*, IV, 489–91, Rockingham to Chatham, January 26, 1778; 492, Chatham to Rockingham,
January 27, 1778.

had "betrayed" their allies shortly before the recess by bitterly attacking the Declaratory Act. They were alone once more.

Alone but not voiceless. The spring session saw them rise to new heights of invective and, in their hatred of the ministry, sink to grave depths of indiscretion. Striving to bring down North and his colleagues, to restore peace with America, and to avoid war with France, they publicly unmasked Britain's military weakness and naval unreadiness.[23] Early in February, young Richmond announced in the Lords that the current establishment of Britain, Ireland, Gibraltar, and Minorca amounted to five thousand troops less than was usual even in time of peace. A few days later, the Old Whig peers introduced testimony in the Upper House showing that 559 ships, valued at £1,800,634, had been lost in the war. Moreover, marine insurance had doubled. Such information could only confirm France in her opinion that the old enemy was ripe for defeat. The government was further belabored for employing Indians in the American conflict. All requests for funds, to meet whatever extraordinary expenditures, were opposed with great violence. When in February North introduced his Conciliatory Bills, the Old Whig attitude, after an initial acceptance, was one of carping criticism, while they claimed the credit for whatever good might be in them. When the Old Whig Admiral Keppel was named to command the home fleet, instead of acting with dispatch to meet the growing French menace, he felt obliged to make conditions. Demanding an audience of the King, he refused to take ships under his command except those he himself reported manned and ready—a vicious blow at Sandwich. When Governor Johnstone was given a naval command, the Old Whigs threw a score of taunts at the ministry.

Old Whig violence was now having one grave effect in that it had begun to raise doubts among the country gentlemen.

[23] See Cobbett and Wright, *Parliamentary History*, XIX, 614 ff., for debates.

When North opened his budget, on March 6, the House was truculent. There was a manifest air of revolt. Opposition was actually able, with the support of the rural gentry, to carry in committee a motion to tax by one-fourth the income of all place-men and pensioners, with a few exceptions, holding incomes above £200 a year. The move was defeated in the House in a very close division of 147 to 141. A motion by Fox to inquire into the defenseless state of the nation—as if that had not been done all too well by his colleagues in the Lords—was defeated by the previous question, but only after North had assured the Commons that "Versailles had checked her ardour" for war. This statement, patently untrue to the most casual observer, is a measure of the First Minister's desperation.

In direct contradiction to North's comfortable assurance to the House on the sixth, Secretary of State Weymouth received from the French ambassador, exactly one week later, a formal declaration that there now existed a commercial treaty between the French court and the Americans. Furthermore, the French King was determined to protect his trade. Such language made war inevitable. Four days afterwards, on March 17, North presented a royal message informing Parliament of the declaration. The immediate result was a decision by the Old Whigs to espouse, openly and formally, the cause of American independence. They were convinced that only by such action could a French war be avoided. This, in turn, brought them into open and violent conflict with the Chathamites.

Shelburne had already taken sharp issue with the Old Whigs. Addressing himself to the ministry, during debates in the Lords over the French ambassador's declaration, he told them that a French war was not now to be avoided. He had then called upon them to put their house in order, to "relieve the people of the burden of corruption," and to "drop scandalous exertion of undue influence." A more formal and dramatic break was to come on April 7, when Richmond moved

in the Lords for an evacuation of America and an acknowledgement of that country's independence. It was a challenge which
Chatham, sick as he was, could not let pass. Having dragged
himself to the House for the last time, he directed his feeble,
often incoherent, argument against a recognition of independence. The strain of the debate and its awful implication, the
dismemberment of an empire which he, more than any man,
had created, were too much for him. When he sought to rise
a second time to answer Richmond, his weakened frame gave
way; he swooned and was borne from the House a dying man.

Never again would he cross the Old Whigs; and it was with
satisfaction that Burke, with malice rising from a thwarted
soul, wrote to his friend Champion of Chatham's "apoplectick
fit after he had spat his last Venom."[24] When the debate resumed, however—it had been adjourned until the eighth as a
compliment to Chatham—Shelburne held the banner of his
fallen chief. Declaring solidly against independence, he
made a thinly disguised bid for coalition: "Combine and con-
nect every party and description of men. Leave a way open
for every man to enter, and every man will enter and co-operate
in the support of government." To Richmond's demand to
know how he would regain America without an acknowledgement of her independence, Shelburne was vague. Declaring
he would "leave the Americans to themselves," he expressed a
conviction that they would soon send commissioners to offer
terms. A natural necessity would force them back into an alliance with Britain; and he refused to believe they could be so
heedless of their own welfare as to continue long in close alliance with France.[25] The Chathamite pendulum had now swung
as far to the left as it was to go. Although the division on Richmond's motion revealed a surprisingly wide acceptance of his
view—the Old Whigs and their supporters dividing thirty-

---

[24] Wentworth-Woodhouse, Burke Papers, Burke to Champion, April 11,
1778. The printed version in William, Fitzwilliam, and Bourke, *Burke
Correspondence*, II, 210–11, deletes this disgusting passage.

[25] Cobbett and Wright, *Parliamentary History*, XIX, 1031–58.

three to fifty—a united Opposition was nonetheless impossible.

In the Commons, too, Old Whigs moved for American independence. Fox spoke powerfully for it on April 10, and for the first time tied it to the cause of internal reform. Maintaining that should his motion pass, Britain would be spared a war with France, he charged that American dependence actually profited no one but the ministers and their hangers-on. For them it had a sinister significance: the power of the executive, growing for some years, already threatened the Constitution. A dependent America would give such advantage to the Crown that it would achieve what the Stuarts had never done: a perpetual control of the British Parliament.

Though Fox's motion failed, there were signs that Old Whig emphasis upon economic reform was drawing an increasing number of country gentlemen to their support. In April, one of them, Sir Philip Jennings Clerke, won leave, against the opposition of the ministry, to bring in a bill disabling contractors. North by the greatest effort was able to recover his position, but the primary fact could not be submerged. The country gentlemen, many of them Old Tories, had on two separate occasions—the Contractors' Bill and the tax on placemen's salaries—affirmed their independence of court control. Because of the high taxes and ill success in the American war, they were becoming restive under a King and ministry who, unconsciously, were laying the foundation of a new Tory party. The cry for reform and economy in government would, in the next few years, unite with the continuing misfortunes of the American war to cause the fall of the North Ministry.

Saratoga had not destroyed the ministry because the King was strong enough to prevent North's resignation; and the Opposition, caught between a rising tide of patriotism—produced by the approaching French war—and their own disunion, were too weak to force it.

The King was determined, at all events and at all costs, to retain North as first minister. Time and again, North pressed to resign; time and again, the King refused to allow it. He had no objection to North's making offers for a coalition to some Opposition group, but only with the specific understanding that any contemplated change would leave North at the head of the ministry.

North felt as the *coup de grâce* to his ministry the French Ambassador's declaration of March 13. Dismayed, and greatly fearing the effect of this development on raising the national loan, an integral part of his budget, he confessed to Eden that "the Ministry seems to be overturned."[26] The harassed First Minister immediately presented to the King the outline of a new ministry which Eden had drawn up for him. While it proposed that North should continue at the Treasury, that man, now declaring himself broken in mind and body, begged leave to resign. In general, Eden had envisaged a coalition with Shelburne, who would be a secretary of state, though not in charge of American affairs. Sir Joseph Yorke, ambassador at the Hague, would be Shelburne's colleague; and Amherst would be commander-in-chief. Shelburne's friends Dunning and Barré would become attorney general and secretary at war respectively, and Fox, treasurer of the navy. Germain would be retired at once—with a peerage—since, Eden maintained, the most pressing need of change was in the American Department which would be given to Yorke or possibly to Amherst. So urgent was the change that North declared to his royal master, "The present ministry cannot continue a fortnight."[27]

There followed the most pathetic episode in the history of the friendship between North and his sovereign. Desperately pressing to be allowed to resign for his country's welfare and his own health, North was kept in office against his will by a King fearing "capture." To achieve his purpose, George III

[26] Add. MSS 29475, f. 15, North to Eden, March 13, 1778.
[27] Add. MSS 34415, f. 1, Eden's outline of a new ministerial arrangement. See also Fortescue, *Correspondence of George III*, IV, No. 2219, North to the King, March 15, 1778.

used every appeal to his minister's loyalty, affection, and self-interest. The King believed that it required no more than an interior cabinet reshuffle, based on Thurlow's succeeding Bathurst as chancellor, to give the ministry the required stability. Therefore, he obstinately refused to see any leader of Opposition. Their demands of immediate access to the King and their threats of a complete sweep were altogether unacceptable. Fighting for his "system" and for his own position at the center of politics, the King, in rising hysteria, vehemently declared "no advantage to the country nor personal danger" could ever force him to call Opposition to his assistance. He would rather abdicate his crown than wear it with "the ignominy of possessing it under their shackles." Nor would he open the door to "a set of men who certainly would make me a slave for the remainder of my days." Rather than call Opposition, he would "see any form of Government introduced into this Island"; and "whilst any ten men in the kingdom will stand by me I will not give myself up into bondage."[28] Never was North's weakness and indecision more evident; never had his loyalty and love of the King been so severely tested. He would not, however, have had the moral strength to continue his campaign to be allowed to resign—in the face of such plain spoken sentiment—had he not been encouraged by William Eden. (The Undersecretary was counting strongly on replacing Yorke as ambassador at the Hague.) Sincere in his devotion to the King, bound to him by ties of affection—and there was also the £20,000 which the King had paid on North's personal debts—the First Minister gave way. The fatal collapse of Chatham in April, 1778, ended all thought of a coalition. All was to remain the same, and George III determined to ride out the storm with a first minister who had become the mere sum of the forces operating upon him.

North's agony thus continued. In April, the French Tou-

[28] Fortescue, *Correspondence of George III*, IV, Nos. 2221, 2224, 2226, 2230–32, all from the King to North.

lon fleet under D'Estaing sailed for an unknown destination, widely believed to be America. The cabinet was thrown into a paroxysm of anxiety. The Commons watched narrowly as the King and Sandwich repaired to Portsmouth to hurry a fleet under Byron in pursuit. While there, Sandwich received urgent reports from John Robinson in London of "more real ill humour" in Parliament than he had yet seen.[29] The ministry had been hard run on the Contractor's Bill, and new Irish bills holding out some small relief to Irish trade had upset country gentlemen and British manufacturers alike. Wedderburn, Barrington, and Germain were agitating for promotion or threatening to resign. Suffolk, in bad health, nearly died in June.

Feeling the confidence of the Commons slipping from him, and troubled by a factious cabinet, North told the King once more at the beginning of May that a new ministerial arrangement was indicated. With almost inexpressible pathos, he wrote of the violent parliamentary attacks against him because of delays in the sailing of Byron's fleet. He declared from his anguished heart that his personal disgrace was certain whether he remained in office or resigned. A more important matter, however, was "to prevent the ruin and disgrace of the Country," which would be the result of his continuing in the cabinet, "where I never could nor can decide between different opinions."[30] In the face of such confessions, it was a moral crime for the King to hold North in office, yet he did so because his system was at stake. Ever convinced that his was the right way, he extorted from his wretched Minister a promise to remain in place so long as the King desired.

Saratoga did not, then, mean the fall of North's administration because the King was strong enough—and weak enough —to prevent it. It did, however, make a French war inevitable; and it further implied the necessity of a basic change in the

[29] Navy Record Society, LXIX, *Sandwich Papers*, II, 44–45, Robinson to Sandwich, May 5, 1778.

[30] Fortescue, *Correspondence of George III*, IV, No. 2322, North to the King, May 1, 1778; No. 2329, North to the King.

mode of conducting war in America. Henceforth, that war was to be merged into the larger framework of a traditional Anglo-French struggle.

A most surprising change had meanwhile occurred in the thinking of Lord George Germain. Thoroughly deflated and on the defensive since Burgoyne's surrender, he declared it necessary to make the American war primarily a naval one: a few seacoast posts should be held by the army whose activity would be confined to attacks along the seaboard in support of naval operations. The King, too, believing that Wentworth's expedition had proved that America would not treat but on the basis of independence—and there was not, he maintained, "a Man either bold or mad enough to presume to treat for the Mother Country on such a basis"—also agreed that a change was needed. General Amherst, examined at a cabinet called to deliberate upon a new mode of war, added the weight of his authority. It was impossible, he said, to reduce the Colonies by land without thirty thousand more troops in America. Such a reinforcement was admittedly impossible. The American war had, therefore, to become a secondary consideration: future operations would be chiefly of a naval character.[31]

In very secret orders of March 8 Germain informed the new commander, Sir Henry Clinton, of the cabinet's decision: despite "the just ground there is to expect that the new Commission to negotiate will supersede the necessity of another campaign," he wrote, yet it was imperative there be no slackening of preparations for the new mode of war. If Washington could not be forced to a general action early in the present campaign, all idea of offensive inland operations must be abandoned. The troops that could be spared from the defense of posts already held were to attack American ports from New York to Nova Scotia and to destroy as much American shipping as possible.

[31] Add. MSS 34414, f. 394, Germain to Eden, December 3, 1777. RHMCR. *Stopford-Sackville Papers*, II, 84–85, Germain to Sir William Howe, December 11, 1777; 93–94, Germain to Sir William Howe, February 18, 1778.

Should it not be feasible to carry out this plan and still retain Philadelphia, that place was to be evacuated. Clinton would receive five thousand reinforcements, and with their aid attacks upon the southern provinces should be launched in the autumn. Should that plan prove successful, "the Northern Colonies might then be left to their own Feelings and distress to bring them back."[32] The idea of at least a partial loss of the rebel provinces had begun to operate in British thinking.

The decision that henceforth the American war should be mainly naval, made without regard to grim reality, rendered Sandwich's position well-nigh impossible. Early in December, he warned his colleagues that Britain possessed only forty-two ships of the line, and that the country could not hope to make necessary detachments to America and remain on a par with Bourbon in European waters. Sandwich and two members of the Admiralty Board, Lord Mulgrave and Sir Hugh Palliser, constantly pressed throughout December for permission to undertake emergency building and preparations. North, however, anxiously watching Wentworth in Paris, deep in the preparation of his Conciliatory Plan, and hoping vainly that the King would allow him to resign, let the precious weeks slip by with no decision taken. Again, at the beginning of March, Sandwich protested to North against the shocking delay in approving naval appropriations and told the cabinet that should war come with France, he would probably have to withdraw ten or twelve frigates from American waters. But, again, North, while expressing a general agreement, hesitated. He was too heavily engaged with the budget and the Conciliatory Plan to enter into details with Sandwich. It is plain that George III's insistence upon retaining him was having a most disastrous effect on Britain's preparation to meet the coming onslaught of France. It was not, indeed, until March 16, three days after the French ambassador's declaration, that the Ad-

[32] RHMCR. *Stopford-Sackville Papers*, II, 94–99, most secret orders of March 8, 1778.

miralty was allowed to order the Navy Board to put extra workmen in all naval yards where building, repairing, or fitting was under way. Nor were naval builders now to wait the regulation time for seasoning of wood.[33] Where all had before been hesitation, now all was haste.

As soon as France had recognized American independence, vessels of the young nation began to operate from the ports of her ally with new and unhindered freedom. American privateers, already active enough to cause alarm to the merchants, now doubled their effectiveness. There were severe inroads on British shipping; large coastal areas in England and Ireland were held under constant alarm by audacious attacks, which could not be prevented because of the lack of frigates. From various maritime parts of the kingdom came urgent requests for naval protection and adequate coastal defenses. The supply of seamen had become so critically low and the want of frigates so great, however, that Sandwich admitted to the Lord Lieutenant of Ireland, Lord Buckinghamshire, that means were simply not available to mount effectual measures against these privateers.[34]

A counterstroke was necessary. But where? An expedition against the French West Indies had been suggested in December. As Amherst fully approved the design, it was adopted by the cabinet on March 18. On the twenty-first, therefore, Germain dispatched to Clinton a new set of most secret orders —so secret that the Carlisle Peace Commissioners, still in England, were not informed of them.[35] The General was ordered

---

[33] Hinchingbrooke Papers, Sandwich to North, December 7, 1777; Sandwich's paper of December 8, 1777. Printed in Navy Record Society, LXIX, *Sandwich Papers*, I, 327–35; 363, the Admiralty's order to the Navy Board.

[34] Fortescue, *Correspondence of George III*, IV, No. 2391, the King to North, July 12, 1778. Hinchingbrooke Papers, North to Sandwich, May 10 and July 12, 1778. RHMCR. *Lothian Papers*, 330, Sandwich to Buckinghamshire, May 4, 1778.

[35] RHMCR. *Dartmouth Papers*, II, 461–62, most secret orders of March 21, 1778.

to detach five thousand troops immediately, to name a commander for them, and to embark this force for an attack against St. Lucia. It was essential, the orders stated, that the scheme be executed without delay. An additional three thousand men should be dispatched to St. Augustine and Pensacola for the defense of those ports. Philadelphia would be evacuated, and Clinton would retire to New York to await the outcome of the Carlisle Peace Commission. Should New York prove impossible to hold with his depleted army, he would evacuate the port, leave enough troops with the garrison in Rhode Island to hold that place, proceed to new headquarters at Halifax, and send any surplus troops to General Haldimand in Canada. This redisposition of Clinton's force of some fourteen thousand troops was tantamount to official recognition that land conquest of the Colonies was impossible.

Indeed, the St. Lucia expedition, and Sandwich's insistence that Britain strengthen her naval force in European waters, further meant an abandonment of even the idea of a large-scale naval war against America. In consequence of a report to the cabinet by Sandwich on March 15, thirty-three of the seventy ships in American waters were recalled to England or were ordered sent on the St. Lucia expedition.[36] A few days later, Sandwich told his colleagues that a suspension of all naval and military operations in America might become necessary.

The magnitude of the King's folly and of North's procrastination in the face of Sandwich's repeated warnings came home fully to the cabinet when in April, D'Estaing took command of the Toulon fleet and sailed for America. Both King and cabinet demanded that the French admiral be halted at the Straits of Gibraltar, but a force adequate to stop him was simply not available. Should Keppel's home fleet be sent out, the English and Irish coasts would lie naked, and the Brest fleet could then attack at will.[37]

[36] Hinchingbrooke Papers, Sandwich's paper of March 15, 1778, "State of the Force in North America." Printed in Navy Record Society, LXIX, *Sandwich Papers*, I, 362.

The situation was even blacker than first appears. Almost half of Lord Howe's fleet had been recalled from American waters or ordered sent to St. Lucia. Should D'Estaing's objective be in European waters, Howe's ships would be urgently needed at home. On the other hand, should the Frenchman be destined for America, as seemed more probable, the force there, even if Howe had not already sailed for home, would be inadequate to meet him. Moreover, D'Estaing's arrival in America would bear directly upon the plans for the British expedition against St. Lucia. But how? The blundering incompetencies of George III and Lord North had robbed Britain of the initiative.

Indeed, calamity seemed to stare the country in the face. Sandwich believed it impossible to carry on the war in America. Weymouth felt that peace was highly desirable. Germain expressed himself happy at no bad news from America, since he had long ago given up expectations of good news from that country. The King himself, although suspecting that Franklin in the Paris talks sought only to delay the departure of the Peace Commission, so desired to end the American war that he was willing to keep open the channel of intercourse with that "invidious man." Even George III had begun to think of the Colonies as "abandoned." Barrington declared that there was no general in the country fit to direct the army in case of invasion. North himself believed an accommodation with America urgently necessary. If that could be achieved, Britain could avoid a French war, the expense of which, he predicted, would ruin her. As so often before, he warned his sovereign that peace with America and a change of ministry could alone save the country.[38] He was fervently hoping for the success of the Carlisle Peace Commission.

[37] Hinchingbrooke Papers, Sandwich's paper of April 6, 1778; printed in Fortescue, *Correspondence of George III*, IV, No. 2275.

[38] Navy Record Society, LXIX, *Sandwich Papers*, II, 292–94, Sandwich to Rear Admiral Gambier, commander at Halifax, April 13, 1778. Fortescue, *Correspondence of George III*, IV, No. 2246, North to the King, March 25,

The impact of the American problem on British imperial thinking reached its climax in this effort to end the war. North had thought tentatively of making peace even before the news of Saratoga had arrived. This surrender and the fear of French intervention were the prime movers behind the Peace Commission. Nonetheless, the Acts of Parliament creating it— there were no more hairsplitting questions about the propriety of acts for the admitted purpose of qualifying the powers of Parliament—the commission itself, and the instructions for it marked an acceptance by British political leaders of the federal principle in crude and unfinished form. Out of the stresses and the strains of the American war, a new concept of empire had emerged. Grenville's classic idea of a supreme center and subordinate parts had vanished.

The history of the Carlisle Peace Commission must begin with a letter from Eden to Lord North. On December 7, 1777, during a time of wildest confusion among ministerial circles, Eden sent North an analysis of the disastrous state of his government. He wrote "with the feelings of a man who has just seen some dreadfull Calamity or is this moment awakened from a feverish dream." He begged North to put aside his intention to resign, and to stand firm in the present crisis. He should, however, adopt a positive plan of action immediately or within three days at the most. Eden then outlined his own proposals. It would be wise, he thought, to desist from any internal operations in America. Should it be deemed necessary to hold any posts at all, they should be chosen from among New York, Long Island, Staten Island, perhaps Rhode Island, and those along the Canadian border. Halifax, New York, and St. Augustine should be strengthened, but Pennsylvania evacuated. The Howes should be recalled, their Peace Commission cancelled, and a purely naval war begun.

1778; No. 2247, North to the King; No. 2248, Weymouth to the King, March 25, 1778; No. 2251, the King to North, March 26, 1778. See also RHMCR. *Knox Papers, Various Collections,* 143, Germain to Knox, April 19, 1778.

Courtesy New York Public Library

WILLIAM EDEN (later Lord Auckland)

By far his most important point, however, was Eden's assertion that it was now highly expedient to bring into Parliament and before the public some plan for pacification. This should be done, he urged, immediately after the Christmas recess. The ministry could at that time lead an inquiry into the state of the nation, and "at a proper stage," produce a bill repealing every existing Act of Parliament touching America either by indulgence, restraint, or regulation. Commissioners should then be appointed to prepare the way for a new, comprehensive, and final act of legislation for the regulation of the Colonies.

That negotiation with the Colonies had become absolutely necessary should now be openly admitted. Eden well knew that by doing so North would open himself to severe criticism, and that his enemies would taunt him with his earlier declaration, at the time of his Conciliatory Proposition, that he would never agree to more drastic terms. To this, Eden advised, North should reply honestly and openly as he himself had answered Fox on that score: " 'I asked fifty guineas for my grey Horse last year, but He has since broken his Knees and I should be glad to get twenty.' "[39]

Thus stimulated, North roused himself from despair to begin a series of feverish conferences lasting through the Christmas recess. Eden, Jenkinson, Wentworth, the law officers Thurlow and Wedderburn—all subministers—North could not trust his cabinet colleagues—were consulted. Under the strain of formulating in great haste a pacific plan which would be acceptable to Parliament and to at least some of the colonists, North drove himself without pity. By late January, though near physical and mental collapse, he had at least a plan. It was to repeal the tea duty and the act regulating the charter of Massachusetts, and to create a commission to negotiate with the Colonies on every other point in dispute.[40]

[39] Add. MSS 34414, ff. 395-98, Eden to North, December 7, 1777.
[40] Fortescue, *Correspondence of George III*, IV, No. 2179, North to the King, January 29, 1778.

The King, while believing that a complete but temporary evacuation of the Colonies might become necessary—in order the more effectively to attack French and Spanish New World possessions should a Bourbon war break out—urged caution upon North in bringing forth a plan of conciliation. Germain, grumbling because he was not being consulted by North, strengthened the King's reticence,[41] but North, firmly supported by the undersecretaries and subministers, who agreed that a commission with the most extensive powers was necessary, could not be swerved from his path.[42]

To Eden, North assigned the task of perfecting the details of his plan; and, working immediately under the First Minister, Eden sketched out a draft of a conciliatory act. His close friend, Wedderburn, now completely won over to conciliation, also produced a draft bill.[43] On the basis of these two, Attorney General Thurlow drew up a third draft of a bill enabling the King to appoint commissioners. Meantime, North had begun to have qualms about an outright repeal of the tea duty and the Massachusetts Regulating Act. Eden, deciding that such unpleasant action was, after all, both needless and insufficient, then suggested a second bill renouncing completely the right of taxation. North accepting the suggestion, Eden, aided by John Hatsell, Clerk of the Commons and an expert on parliamentary procedure, drafted the bill. Stating that the right of taxation was given up "in the just and reasonable Expectation" that in return the Colonies would contribute to the cost of the common defense, the bill was sent to North on February 7, the day after the Franco-American treaties had been secretly signed in Paris.[44] While this event was unknown in London,

---

[41] *Ibid.*, No. 2182, the King to North, January 31, 1778.

[42] Stevens, *Facsimilies*, No. 344, William Fraser's report.

[43] *Ibid.*, No. 346, Eden's memorandum, "Measures for an Accommodation with America," January, 1778; No. 348, Eden's "Heads of Address on the American War."

[44] Add. MSS 34415, ff. 191–92; Stevens, *Facsimilies*, No. 355, Eden's paper on the Taxation Act. See also Add. MSS 34415, ff. 187–88; Stevens,

it was suspected that such an agreement was in the offing. It was thus with a sense of urgency that Eden, Wedderburn, and the King himself pressed North to get the bills quickly through Parliament.[45]

Throughout these proceedings, North had told his colleagues nothing of the plan. He had not so much as held a cabinet on the subject. Germain's conduct was becoming threatening, and having heard from some source that the tea duty and the Regulating Act were to be repealed, he took a heated protest to Eden. By that time, of course, North and Eden had decided in favor of renouncing taxation instead of repealing the two acts. Eden, in a friendly though somewhat patronizing vein, was therefore able to assure the American Secretary that the acts were not to be repealed since it was now proposed to give up the right completely. Mollified by Eden's letter and aware of the necessity for a treaty, Germain replied, "You go rather beyond my idea in putting so much Confidence in their [colonial] Generosity, but if that step will not revolt our friends, it is the most manly method of proceeding. The appointing Commissioners with the most ample powers must make part of the plan."[46] The most likely chief of intracabinet resistance to the Conciliatory Plan had thus been neutralized.

North presented the entire scheme at a full cabinet on February 11. He met with no opposition; and on the twelfth, stating that he "expected to be roasted," he brought his proposals before the Commons.[47] In his speech, long and comprehensive, although he labored under obvious and severe

Facsimilies, No. 360; Add. MSS 34415, ff. 110–11, Eden's draft of the Taxation Act.

[45] Add. MSS 34415, f. 133. Stevens, *Facsimilies*, No. 371, Wedderburn to Eden, February, 1778; No. 356, Wedderburn to Eden, February, 1778; No. 369, Eden to North, February 7, 1778. See also Fortescue, *Correspondence of George III*, IV, No. 2190, the King to North, February 9, 1778.

[46] RHMCR. *Stopford-Sackville Papers*, I, 139, Germain to General Irwin, February 3, 1778. Add. MSS 34415, f. 113; Stevens, *Facsimilies*, No. 370, Germain to Eden, February 10, 1778.

[47] Add. MSS 35375, ff. 204–205, John Yorke to Hardwicke. North's speech is in Cobbett and Wright, *Parliamentary History*, XIX, 762–67.

handicaps, he had not the courage to accept Eden's advice and make a frank plea of necessity. Rather, he sought to brazen it out, claiming even the virtue of consistency. Never had he thought an American revenue practicable or possible. He had merely inherited the tea duty which he had been unable to get rid of. All he had ever wished was a reasonable self-imposed American contribution to imperial expenses. Always disposed to peace, he had been shocked when the Coercive Acts had produced effects quite unintended. He was, therefore, prepared to give them up in the interest of a general settlement.

His earlier Conciliatory Proposition, he maintained, had been just. It had, however, been misrepresented by the radicals in America and by the Opposition at home. The Howe Commission had also been criticized because of its limited power. Both of those objections would now be met by new acts creating a commission with the most extensive powers, and by instructions to the commissioners to seek from the colonists a promise of voluntary contributions. This latter, however, was not to be a *sine qua non*. Should no such contributions be forthcoming, however, Americans were not to complain if in some future hour of need Britain refused her aid and assistance.

All acts grievous to America would be adjusted, North declared, but it would be better to leave this in the hands of the commissioners, for the Americans would consider every concession made in Parliament to be a part of the basis of the treaty. They would accordingly accumulate new claims. He then outlined the proposed powers of the commission, declaring that he had not offered his propositions earlier because he had always thought the moment of victory the time for concessions. On news of Saratoga, he had thought to raise more troops to prosecute the war but had then decided that, even after the greatest victory, the terms now presented were substantially those he would have offered. Denying, then, that the concessions were forced, and maintaining that Britain could at need carry on the war much longer, he offered this conciliatory plan to prevent further and useless bloodshed.

Melancholy silence greeted North's speech, and the debate was short. Fox declared the terms outlined "ample and satisfactory," indeed, the same as those in Burke's bill three years before. The country gentlemen appeared stunned. North, assaulted with a question originally raised by Fox, was forced to admit that very likely a Franco-American treaty had been signed. In deep gloom, therefore, the resolutions were agreed to without division, and leave was given to bring in the bills. In two days time, by a ship dispatched for that specific purpose, Germain forwarded copies of the bills to the commanders-in-chief in America.

While affairs went on in Parliament, Eden turned to selecting the commissioners. Probably he himself coveted a place on the commission from the first. He had hoped to succeed Sir Joseph Yorke as ambassador at the Hague, but had seen that scheme fail because of the King's obstinate refusal to treat with the Opposition. For the moment, however, he satisfied himself with coyly remarking to North that he had been mentioned as a likely commissioner by some of his friends, at the same time suggesting Governor Johnstone as a suitable candidate. Eden also undertook to approach Richard Jackson who at the time was solicitor to the Board of Trade. In doing so, he once more hinted that he himself might be on the commission. Jackson replied that while he was not hopeful, he would accept if named, for he truly believed that a continuation of the American war meant ruin to the empire. One stipulation he made, however: that the instructions be full and precise, a demand directly opposed to Eden's and Wedderburn's plan to make the powers as broad and as discretionary as possible.[48]

Eden's design to become a commissioner soon became obvious. On March 1, his superior, Suffolk, sent his blessings to

[48] Add. MSS 34415, ff. 151–52; Stevens, *Facsimilies*, No. 378, Jackson to Eden, February 28, 1778.

Eden's aspirations. Two days later, Eden drafted letters to Germain and Sandwich declaring his readiness to sacrifice himself in any service thought useful to the public.[49] He had both a talent and inclination to serve his country in a diplomatic post, but a stronger motive now urged him on to a place in the commission. To Wedderburn he confided that he was by no means happy to be going to America. Should he not do so, however, he foresaw "on the coolest reflection that I shall return very suddenly to the utmost obscurity; for I *know* that the present Government is not equal to its difficulties; and it will neither suit my Pride nor my Principles to struggle on with them from present Bad to certain worse."[50] Eden's expedition to America was thus to be a flight from fury, and a means of divorcing his own political fate from that of the North Ministry. Nor would he be content to be a mere member of the commission. He would be the "efficient Commissioner." His hand is seen constantly at work in arranging the commission to his own satisfaction, a task he had completed by early March. In a paper setting forth the desired qualifications for members of the commission, he had stated they should be Members of Parliament from both Houses, men of ability, and "particularly conversant" with the dispute and with Britain's commercial interests. They should be of conciliatory manners and untainted by opposition to "the honourable species of accomodation." At least one should be from the moderate part of Opposition.[51] As men thus qualified, he had selected the young Earl of Carlisle, the twenty-nine-year-old son-in-law of Gower; Richard Jackson; and himself. These three, with the

---

[49] Add. MSS 34415, ff. 235–37; Stevens, *Facsimilies*, No. 385, Eden to Sandwich and Germain, drafts. See also RHMCR. *Stopford-Sackville Papers*, II, 44, Eden to Germain. Further, Stevens, *Facsimilies*, No. 384, Suffolk to Eden, March 1, 1778.

[50] Stevens, *Facsimilies*, No. 386, Eden to Wedderburn, early March, 1778.

[51] Add. MSS 34415, f. 158; Stevens, *Facsimilies*, No. 374, Eden's paper setting forth the desired qualifications for the commissioners.

commanders-in-chief in America, would form the commission.

Even in the drafting of their instructions—Wedderburn was in charge of that task—Eden gave his "Hints." As points upon which he feared negotiations might break off, Eden named: independence; an American attempt to charge Britain with the expense of the war; an attempt to undermine the British right to regulate commerce; or an impeachment of the King's prerogative in naming military officers and governors.[52] Accepting Eden's ideas, Wedderburn was duly guided by them in his work.

Eden took a grandiose view of the role he was about to assume. At last, he felt himself rising from the lowly position of undersecretary of state. He would bear in his hands a part, and he intended it to be a major part, of the dignity and honor of the British nation. Pomp and panoply were necessary to this viceregal expedition. Captain Elliott of the "Trident," which would convey the commissioners to America, would have to have, Eden insisted, a commodore's pennant. The commissioners themselves would require full ambassadorial rank and salary. They would be privy councilors. Such was Eden's tacky pomposity that when Lord Cornwallis was ordered to repair to America at the earliest possible moment, and Lord Sandwich proposed to give him passage on the "Trident," his passion knew no bounds. Inducing Carlisle, a callow and inexperienced youth, to join him, Eden wrote a stinging complaint to Germain: Sandwich had used the commissioners badly; he had repeatedly assured them that the ship was to be reserved to the commissioners exclusively. This petty display of egotism was not rendered the more palatable by the fact that Eden had already demanded and received permission to take Mrs. Eden junketing with him to America. That lady, moreover, would occupy two cabins aboard the crowded ship, one for herself, and one for four female servants. With great justice, the King dryly remarked, "Parade is not the object of the mission,

[52] Stevens, *Facsimilies*, No. 379, Eden's "Hints."

but business."[53] George III, furthermore, resolutely refused to make the commissioners privy councilors. Sir Henry Clinton did not hold that rank. If the other commissioners were to have it, Clinton would come last in the commission instead of second, and the King refused to acquiesce in so unmerited a slight to a valiant commander.

Richard Jackson had never been wholly satisfied with the instructions since they were not, as he had wished, full and precise. For him, the declaration of the French ambassador on March 13 was decisive. At a stormy session on the night of March 29–30, he told Eden, Thurlow, and Wedderburn that it was "idle and ruinous" to go to war with France. To forestall such an event American independence must be recognized at once. Unless the commission had authority to do so, it would assuredly fail. He himself wanted no part of it.

Eden was shocked at Jackson's withdrawal. North clearly expected the commission to leave for America by April 12, and with the time for departure so near, Eden professed himself on the verge of resigning in disgust and despair. He desisted, however, only because he knew that should he throw up the commission, government would be "instantly and completely check-mated." Hurriedly, he and Wedderburn consulted about a successor for Jackson. Governor Johnstone, his brother Pulteney, and Andrew Stuart were suggested. Eden preferred Pulteney, but he was still in Paris vainly trying to draw Franklin into negotiation. Wedderburn, who thought Jackson's resignation good riddance, thereupon approached Johnstone. The Governor accepted, but this last minute crisis had proved depressing, although Eden could not help boasting to his brother Morton of the success of "my own private negociation."[54]

All seemed in good train when suddenly Johnstone, who

[53] Hinchingbrooke Papers, Eden to Sandwich, March 8, 1778. Fortescue, *Correspondence of George III*, IV, Nos. 2201, 2270.

[54] RHMCR. *Carlisle Papers*, 322, Eden's memorandum. See Stevens, *Facsimilies*, No. 427, Wedderburn to Eden; No. 416, Wedderburn to Eden; No. 432, Eden to Morton Eden, April 9, 1778.

had declared in Commons irrevocably against independence, developed personal scruples. He was much upset by accounts of a conversation in which North had declared his belief that the commission would fail and that only a recognition of independence would bring peace. Because of his respect for Chatham, Johnstone, and a few of his own friends, however—North was quoted as saying—he could not yet propose such a step.[55] Eden again grew furious, promising Johnstone to bring the First Minister to a firm stand against independence.

North presumably gave Eden satisfaction on this point, and after a final correction in the commission—Sir William Howe's name had been inserted instead of Clinton's—Germain sent the commissioners their instructions on April 12. They were ordered to embark at once for America.

British public reaction to the Conciliatory Plan was calm with no excesses of either optimism or pessimism. Thurlow, in a farewell letter to Eden, wrote that a more important mission had never been entrusted to any hands. Although he had entertained serious doubts, he now refused to view the commission as "Quixotism." Samuel Martin, a merchant of Whitehaven with interests in the American trade, told Sandwich that the offers would certainly be rejected by the Americans. Moreover this view had been supported by Franklin himself who, when David Hartley had sent him copies of the Conciliatory

[55] The conversation was between North and Temple, probably John Temple, formerly a member of the Customs Board at Boston. Temple had married an American and was then in England. North arranged to send him back to America at about the same time, but not on the same ship, as the commissioners. He was to "exert his utmost influence in assisting the commissioners now going out to bring about a reconciliation or reunion" between Britain and her Colonies. Probably Temple's primary task was to seek to corrupt American politicians. Temple and a Dr. Berkenhaut took passage to America a short time after the commissioners had sailed. There is evidence that the two men proceeded to Philadelphia, where presumably they contacted loyalists. There is no further report of Temple's expedition which was apparently unsuccessful. See Add. MSS 34415, f. 334; Stevens, *Facsimilies*, No. 424, a copy of Temple's note to North, and North's explanatory note. See also Stevens, *Facsimilies*, No. 426, Wedderburn to Eden.

Bills, had blasted them as "little arts and schemes for amusing and dividing us." The commission was also bitter news to the many American loyalists both at home and in refuge in England. North's plan they viewed as almost a death blow to their hopes of regaining their lost property. Indeed one former New York merchant took his own life on hearing of North's speech.[56] As the commissioners boarded the "Trident" at St. Helen's in the morning of April 16, Eden sat down to write a last letter to his brother Morton: "I am given to speculation upon most occasions, but in this it fails me totally: some cool-headed sensible men are very sanguine . . . ; others of the same description are equally positive that we shall totally fail. I only know that I am in neither extreme either of Confidence or Despondency."[57] Uncertain of the reception they would be accorded in America, the commissioners set forth into the unknown.

They would fail to restore peace to a shattered empire. To emphasize their failure, however, is to overlook a consideration of the greatest importance. They carried with them in embryo a new colonial system which indicated that British imperial thinking had gone—or been driven—far along the path to a modern commonwealth of nations. The Taxation Act had already renounced forever Grenville's touchstone of parliamentary supremacy, the right to tax for revenue. The tea tax was repealed. By their instructions, the commissioners, together or individually, could treat with Congress "as if it were a legal body," or indeed with any assembly or groups of individuals, civil or military.[58] They were to accept the claim of independence "during the time of Treaty, and for the pur-

[56] Stevens, *Facsimilies*, No. 356, Sir Grey Cooper to Eden, March 8, 1778, No. 394; Add. MSS 34415, f. 252, Thurlow to Eden, March 7, 1778. Hinchingbrooke Papers, Samuel Martin to Sandwich, March, 1778. For the loyalists' view, see Add. MSS 35427, ff. 136–37, Hutchinson to Hardwicke, August 3, 1778; Add. MSS 38210. ff. 60–61, Henry Cruger to Jenkinson, May 3, 1778, in which Cruger includes extracts of American loyalists' letters.
[57] Stevens, *Facsimilies*, No. 446, Eden to Morton Eden, April 16, 1778.
[58] RHMCR. *Carlisle Papers*, 322–33.

pose of Treaty," although such a document was to be referred to Parliament for its approbation. All acts concerning America passed since 1763 could be suspended. In the case of the Declaratory Act, it would be superseded by a mutual declaration, to be made at the conclusion of the treaty, of the respective rights of Britain and America.

More specific concessions were also to be made:

1. The mother country, without consent of the assemblies, would keep no standing army in the Colonies in time of peace.

2. The Colonies would maintain, at their own charge, their own military force, either regular or militia.

3. No charter would ever be changed save with the consent and at the request of the individual assembly.

4. The home government would assist in securing the debts of Congress, and in sinking those great quantities of depreciated paper currency issued by it. For this purpose, an American Bank was authorized.

5. Americans would be given preference in the most considerable colonial offices in the appointment of the Crown. Indeed, if the Americans asked it, all civil offices might be made elective.

6. If judges were to continue as royal appointees, and if independent provision should be made for them by the Colonies, they would hold office during good behavior and not, as hitherto, during pleasure.

7. Crown offices deemed unnecessary by the Americans would be suppressed.

8. Any future customs service would be composed of Americans.

9. Parliament was prepared to consider an American representation in the House of Commons.

10. Should the Americans insist, they might retain Congress as a permanent institution so long as it did not infringe the sovereignty of Parliament.

What was this new "sovereignty of Parliament"? First and foremost, Parliament was to retain a power to regulate the trade of the empire. Even on this fundamental point, however, America was to be indulged, although if she expanded her foreign trade, certain duties would be levied. Further, all articles not of British manufacture or not sent to America from Great Britain were to be taxed. Nor were the Americans to maintain ships of war unless employed and commissioned by the King. The command of American forts and fortifications would be vested in the governors, although such places would be garrisoned by American troops. Military forces maintained by the Colonies would be commanded in the King's name. Provincial officers would hold commissions from him. There would be no independent coinage. American debts to British merchants would be acknowledged. The loyalists would be restored to their estates, and all prisoners of war would be released.

Even at the conclusion of a treaty embodying these conditions and concessions, no formal revocation of the Declaration of Independence would be necessary, since a treaty would be sufficient to render it null and void. Full pardon, amnesty, and indemnity would be extended, and all other matters of controversy raised during the treaty period would be referred to the home government.

Secret and additional instructions were also given to the commissioners.[59] Should the Americans demand the recognition of their independence as a prerequisite to any treaty, their claim was not to be rejected, but referred home. In the meantime, a cessation of hostilities should be arranged. During the armistice, British troops would continue to occupy New York, Long and Staten Islands, Rhode Island, Connecticut and any other place where the inhabitants would receive them. During this period, the Restraining Act directed against colonial trade would be suspended. No trade, however, was to be

[59] RHMCR. *Stopford-Sackville Papers,* II, 105–106.

carried on between any part of the British dominions and the Colonies except that in British or Irish ships. Colonial ships and commodities would be deemed alien in all parts of the empire except at New York, Rhode Island, and Beaufort, in Port Royal Island. In those places, colonial ships would be allowed to enter without hindrance during the period of the armistice. All inhabitants of the Colonies were to have freedom of movement and disposal of property. American debts to British merchants could be repaid in paper money at a reasonable rate of exchange.

No hindrance was to be given either to British or American vessels, or to those of nations at peace with Great Britain going in or coming out of American ports during the cessation of hostilities. Ships of war and privateers were to be required to depart forthwith. Finally, Massachusetts would have to renounce all claims to the Kennebec River and to the territory north and east of its westernmost boundary.

On one other point, North gave his advice in a letter written to Eden on April 23. Warning him that America would try to get Canada as a fourteenth state, he asked him to exercise care in his negotiations that this should not happen. So long as Canada remained in British hands, he asserted, the Americans, with this constant threat upon their flank, would have a powerful incentive to remain on good terms with Britain. Alarmed at reports of an attempted sabotage of the "Trident" before she left port, he declared himself as most solicitous for the success of the commission: "God Grant that it may succeed and that you may in the course of the year give us the comfortable news of a peace with America upon honourable terms!"[60]

In great anxiety, British politicians awaited the results of this proposal embodying the ultimate concessions they could bring themselves to offer. Further military disaster would in-

[60] Add. MSS 34415, ff. 398–99. Stevens, *Facsimilies*, No. 447, North to Eden, April 23, 1778.

deed force them finally to recognize independence itself; and the empire would be shattered. But that does not detract from the fact that the Carlisle Peace Commission, by envisaging a new imperial relationship, was a bold and statesmanlike attempt to preserve it. Unfortunately for the empire, it came too late.

En route to America, Carlisle, Eden, and Johnstone occupied their time drafting an initial letter to the Congress. With them aboard the "Trident," besides Mrs. Eden and the unwelcome Lord Cornwallis, were Dr. Adam Fergurson, secretary to the commission, Carlisle's personal secretary Lewes, and Anthony Storer, a Member of Parliament and mutual friend without an official position. On May 27, the vessel overtook a British man-of-war, and the commissioners learned that both commanders-in-chief, Lord Howe and Sir Henry Clinton, were at Philadelphia. After due consultation, the commissioners ordered the "Trident" to change her destination from New York to the Pennsylvania capital, since immediate communication with Howe and Clinton was deemed necessary. It was an ill-fated decision. Germain's most secret orders of March 21, which called for the evacuation of Philadelphia and the attack on St. Lucia, had never been communicated to the commissioners. Although the need of secrecy is obvious, since there had been no formal declaration of war against France and an element of surprise in the assault on St. Lucia was of great importance, this omission was a blunder of major proportions. Failure to tell the commissioners of the proposed operation offered a perfect excuse for their subsequent failure; and North earned the vindictive spite of William Eden, whereby that harassed First Minister's last years in office were rendered a hell on earth.

The "Trident" arrived off Reeds Island at the mouth of the Delaware on June 5. There the commissioners were astounded to learn that an evacuation of Philadelphia had not only been ordered, but was actually about to be executed. They were more than thunderstruck when they met Sir Henry Clinton in Philadelphia on the seventh, and learned from him that the move had been ordered by dispatches from Germain bearing a date more than three weeks prior to their own departure from England. They had counted heavily upon the presence of a respectable British force as an inducement to the Congress to treat with them. This advantage the orders of the twenty-first had quite cast away, providing, as they did, not only for the abandonment of Philadelphia but also for the dismemberment of Clinton's army.

In Eden cold and calculating anger succeeded the first violent flare-up of rage. He would exonerate Suffolk and Carlisle's father-in-law, Gower, from complicity in the "deception" which had been practiced upon him. Neither minister had been present in cabinet when the orders had been adopted; indeed both had been ill for some time thereafter. As for the rest of the cabinet, "I consider the silence however of the other Ministers as a Species of Perfidy, which I shall resent no otherwise than by managing a delay in the intended Evacuation sufficient to enable us to state our Proposals fully to the Congress and to gain an Answer from them before this weak story becomes public: In the course of that delay there may be some fortunate Change of Men or Measures in England or of both." Should this "decided trial" at negotiation fail, he was determined to return to England and throw up the commission.[61]

Eden and his colleagues were convinced that the orders of March 21 had dissipated any chance of success they might have had, but a second unpleasant shock was in store for them. To reduce their chances even further, the commissioners learned that France had moved all too swiftly since the surrender at Saratoga. Simeon Deane, brother of Silas Deane, had arrived not long before them with the news of the Franco-American treaty. Indeed, Congress had already resolved against the Conciliatory Acts and in favor of the treaty. Furthermore when

[61] Stevens, *Facsimilies*, No. 496, Eden's minutes, June 5 and 8, 1778.

they approached him on the subject, Clinton resolutely refused to delay the evacuation of Philadelphia, stating that his orders left him no such discretionary power.

Already discouraged, then, but working in great haste, the commissioners—except Lord Howe who had declined acting because of his imminent departure for England—drew up and dispatched their first letter to President Henry Laurens and to the members of the Congress.[62] Included with it were copies of their commission and of the Conciliatory Acts. Their one wish, they wrote, was to "reestablish on the Basis of equal Freedom and mutual Safety the tranquillity of this once happy Empire." Further, they would concur in every just arrangement for a cessation of hostilities. They would agree to work for the restoration and freedom of trade. They were ready to promise the prohibition of any military forces in the states of North America without the consent of the Congress or of the individual assemblies. They were prepared to aid in the discharge of America's debt and in re-establishing the credit of her paper money. To perpetuate an Anglo-American union, they would propose a reciprocal deputation of agents, colonial representatives to sit in Parliament, and British agents to sit in the assemblies. In order to effect a general and mutually satisfactory settlement, they were eager to meet representatives from Congress. The commissioners wished, in short, to build such a system "so that the British states throughout North America acting with us in Peace and War under one Common Sovereign, may have the Irrevocable Enjoyment of every Privilege, that is short of a total Separation of Interests." The benevolent and conciliatory tone of their letter was somewhat marred by a reference to the "invidious Interposition" of France. That country, they charged, had made her treaty with America only after the Conciliatory Plan had become known. They now appealed strongly to ties of language, blood, and religion in an attempt to draw America away from the French

[62] *Ibid.*, No. 1104, June 9, 1778.

alliance. To gloss over the impending evacuation of Philadelphia, they wrote that their instructions, as well as their desire to remove themselves from the scene of war, might cause them to retire to New York. They were willing, however, to meet representatives of Congress whenever and wherever the Americans should wish.

Pouring out all their concessions at the beginning, they kept back nothing for negotiation. They had no alternative, however, because Philadelphia would soon be evacuated. After that, it was all too probable, the Americans would be so elated that they would admit of no terms but independence. Their chance for success was, at best, a small one, and it was without great hope that the commissioners dispatched their letter. Even before the Congress had answered, Carlisle, young and homesick, had begun to think their business practically finished.[63]

The evacuation of the Pennsylvania capital was set for June 18. Shortly before that time, Eden, seething with anger, penned the commissioners' first report to Germain. It was their united opinion, including the commanders-in-chief, Eden stated, that America could have been separated from her French alliance and reunited with Britain on the basis of the terms held out by the commission had vigorous military measures been pursued for one more campaign. As matters now stood, however, all was doubtful. Johnstone appended a violent postscript to Eden's report, denouncing the evacuation as a "fatal, ill concerted and Ill advised Retreat, highly dishonorable to his Majesty's Arms and most prejudicial to the Interest of his Dominions."[64]

On the eve of the withdrawal the commissioners again boarded the "Trident," and set sail for New York. Eden spent the voyage in composing a bitter letter to his friend Wedderburn. In it he interpreted the orders of March 21 as a total

[63] RHMCR. *Carlisle Papers*, 341, Carlisle to Lady Carlisle, June 14, 1778.

[64] Stevens, *Facsimilies*, No. 1107, Eden to Germain, with a postscript by Johnstone, June, 1778.

abdication of the idea of coercing the Americans. For years, he went on, he had been trusted with "the most sacred secrets of their unfortunate Government." The only one which had ever been kept from him was the one which had sacrificed his private happiness and public character. The ministers had deliberately connived to make the commission "a mixture of ridicule, Nullity and Embarrassements." No favorable response was to be expected from Congress. They had laid the basis for an appeal to the people, but this, too, would probably be unsuccessful, for the contraction of the war in America was tantamount to a recognition of independence. In great despondency, he wrote that it was "impossible to see even what I have seen of this magnificent Country and not to go nearly mad at the long Train of Misconduct and Mischances by which we have lost it."[65]

The commissioners felt most keenly for the loyalists of Philadelphia, more than four thousand of whom had taken an oath of allegiance during the British occupation. The evacuation now informed them, in effect, that Great Britain could not protect her friends from their implacable enemies. In fact, Clinton actually advised the loyalists who could not or would not flee the town to make what peace they could with the Congress. The French treaty and the withdrawal from Philadelphia were decisive, the commissioners believed, making impossible any counterrevolution. Had Britain only pursued vigorous measures for a short time, they moaned, she would have been able to retain "such a dominion though greatly, very greatly abridged," which would have been satisfactory in light of the misfortunes of the war.[66]

The commissioners arrived in New York on July 3. Awaiting them was Laurens' reply for the Congress then sitting at Yorktown. He wrote coldly that only an earnest desire to pre-

[65] *Ibid.*, No. 500, Eden to Wedderburn, June 18, 1778.
[66] RHMCR. *Carlisle Papers*, 344–48, Carlisle to Lady Carlisle, June 21, 1778.

vent further bloodshed could have induced the Congress to read the commissioners' letter which contained such insults to their ally, the French king, or to consider propositions so inconsistent with the honor of an independent nation. The Conciliatory Acts, the commission, and the commissioners' letter supposed them in a state of dependence which was inadmissible. Congress was, however, inclined to peace, and would discuss a treaty of peace and commerce with Great Britain as soon as the British King demonstrated his good faith either by an acknowledgement of independence or by the withdrawal of his fleet and army.[67]

News of the sharp action at Monmouth Courthouse in the Jersies on June 29, between Clinton's retiring force and Washington's army, lifted the spirits of the commissioners for a time. At first, it was thought that the British victory had been decisive, but in fact the extreme heat had prevented a pursuit of the rebels, and it soon became clear that their main force remained unbroken. On July 5, therefore, the commissioners wrote again to Germain stating that in view of the British evacuation and the French treaty, Congress could not be expected to treat upon reasonable terms. Further, as long as Washington kept the field, they could not expect any province to declare for the mother country. From the answer from Congress it was evident to them, at least, that only a "decided exertion" of royal arms would bring even a part of America to accept their offers. This being the case, they asked permission to return to England at their own discretion.[68]

The commissioners then proceeded to make their appeal to the public. Under a proclamation of July 9, they published all pertinent correspondence and called upon all Americans to form opinions independently of the Congress. On the eleventh, in a public letter to Laurens they asserted that as

[67] Stevens, *Facsimilies*, No. 1110, Laurens to the commissioners, June 17, 1778.
[68] *Ibid.*, No. 1116, the commissioners to Germain, July 7, 1778.

far as independence meant "the entire Privilege of the people of North America to dispose of their Property and to Govern themselves without any reference to Great Britain, beyond what is necessary to preserve that union of Force in which our mutual Safety and Advantage consists," they considered that they had already complied with the demand of Congress for a recognition of independence. A withdrawal of British forces was, however, impossible, since it was now necessary both to protect the loyalists and to counter the French intervention. Tactlessly, they proceeded to question the authority of Congress to enter into the French treaty since the Colonies had not yet ratified the Articles of Confederation.[69]

This second approach to the Congress met with even less success than the first. Congress promptly published a resolution that since the commissioners had not accepted either of the alternatives, they would make no answer to this new communication.

A new development now completed the checkmate of the commission. Admiral D'Estaing, who had left Toulon the middle of April, arrived off Philadelphia shortly after it had been abandoned by Clinton. Finding the British fleet gone to New York, he followed and proceeded to blockade that port with Howe caught inside the bar of the harbor with his inferior force. Howe, impatiently awaiting the arrival of Byron's fleet, was saved only by D'Estaing's undue caution and his fear that the draft of his large ships would not allow him to cross the bar.

The immediate result was to cause the commissioners to abandon all hope that even their appeal to the people could have any success. The French fleet had landed the French minister at Philadelphia, and the jubilation at this open recognition of American independence convinced the commissioners that all American affection for the mother country had died.[70]

[69] *Ibid.*, No. 1119.
[70] RHMCR. *Carlisle Papers*, 356–57, Carlisle to Lady Carlisle, July 21, 1778.

In the end, D'Estaing's expedition wrought no material damage to the British fleet. Although Byron's force had become separated on its Atlantic crossing, depriving Howe of needed reinforcements, Howe nonetheless engaged the Frenchman off Rhode Island in August and after an inconclusive encounter, sailed for England in late September. Byron arrived on October 1, made one attempt to find D'Estaing, but had his fleet again scattered by a storm.

Besides bolstering American morale the arrival of the French fleet and its maneuvers off the American coast had another important effect. It immobilized throughout the summer the British expedition against St. Lucia, permitting it to act neither in America nor in the West Indies. It is futile to speculate on what a strong British military force, acting under a vigorous leader, might have accomplished in America during this important summer. For Eden the arrival of the French fleet was a blessing in disguise. It had forced "a Pause in our Course to Destruction."[71] He now implored the home government to modify the orders of March 21 so that the St. Lucia task force could act in the North American theater. Neither Germain nor his colleagues, however, would allow an alteration of plans, continuing to demand that the expedition sail at the earliest possible moment. The ministers, conceding the dubiety of their cause in America, were now intent upon making France pay the price of her intervention. It thus occurred that, unable to sail while D'Estaing hovered off the coast, the St. Lucia expedition remained a dead weight all summer—an inexcusable waste.

By autumn, then, the commissioners knew that they had failed. Supplies in New York were running perilously low. The Cork supply fleet, long overdue, was feared taken by D'Estaing; if so, Clinton was determined to evacuate New

[71] Stevens, *Facsimilies*, No. 508; Add. MSS 34414, ff. 441-47, Eden's minutes, July 29, 1778.

York.[72] Scorned by the Congress and the assemblies, the commissioners found themselves no longer negotiators but supplicants. Having no thought of requesting powers to recognize independence, they had no hope of drawing the Congress into negotiations.

One other matter remained to be settled with the Congress. On his surrender at Saratoga, General Burgoyne had entered into a convention with the victorious General Gates: his army was to be sent home on promise that it would not be used again in the American war. Yet Burgoyne's soldiers—a force which would be of the utmost value in fighting the French in Europe —still languished in American prison camps. The commissioners determined therefore to make a remonstrance and requisition to Congress demanding compliance with the convention— the notorious breach of which was a stain on the honor of Congress. Even in this, however, the commissioners failed, Congress replying through its Secretary, with much heat and a discreditable evasion, that they made no answer to impertinent communications.

What remaining dignity the commission may have possessed was destroyed by Governor Johnstone who had already laid the commission open to ridicule by a well-meaning but undignified attempt to open a private correspondence with Laurens. The Governor now became involved in an attempt to corrupt Joseph Reed and Robert Morris, both members of Congress, hinting at honors and emoluments for those who would help to restore Anglo-American unity. The affair became

[72] Stevens, *Facsimilies*, No. 519, Eden to Wedderburn, September 6, 1778. The Cork supply fleet finally arrived when Clinton was down to five weeks' provisions. The handling of the fleet demonstrated the widespread mismanagement and inefficiency of the trans-Atlantic supply system. The fleet was ordered to sail from England by dispatches bearing the date of March 21, but the orders were not issued until two months later. Even then, however, the fleet was directed to proceed to Philadelphia, although that port had been evacuated by Germain's secret orders of March 21. The fleet actually anchored at the mouth of the Delaware and waited for three days for pilots when it was accidentally discovered that the city was in the hands of the Americans.

public, and Congress, expressing its high indignation, resolved to have no more communication with the hapless commissioner. Johnstone at once announced his withdrawal from the commission and soon returned to England. Both Carlisle and Eden were thus confirmed in their conviction that "lingering" in America could be attended only with bad consequences.[73] They discarded as futile an idea they were entertaining at the time— that of making one last appeal to Congress for a truce on the basis of *uti possidetis,* the question of reciprocal rights to lie dormant during that time.[74] On September 5, therefore, they informed Germain that the American demand for a recognition of independence or the withdrawal of British forces, and the public reception of the French minister by the Congress made further approaches impossible.[75]

Eden and Carlisle were, however, by no means convinced that the struggle in the former Colonies should be given up, although Lord Howe, before his departure for England, had expressed such an opinion. This view, Eden combatted with all his might. Every letter home, now, sought to persuade his superiors to retain North America as the center of war. An evacuation of America or a recognition of independence would not bring peace. American demands would then soar to possession of the entire continent. It was necessary to "beat them, or at least persevere in the defensive system."[76] D'Estaing, Eden and Carlisle believed, had failed materially to alter the local situation. On the other hand, the recent predatory raid led by General Grey on Bedford, Connecticut, had had a small but gratifying success. If such a plan were systematically adopted—a plan of violence and destruction—there would still be

[73] RHMCR. *Carlisle Papers,* 360–61, Carlisle's minutes, August 21, 1778.

[74] *Ibid.,* 363–64, Carlisle's memorandum.

[75] Stevens, *Facsimilies,* No. 1144, Carlisle and Eden to Germain, September 5, 1778.

[76] *Ibid.,* No. 519, Eden to Wedderburn, September 6, 1778; No. 522, Eden to Wedderburn, September, 1778.

hope, not, perhaps, for a restoration of America to the empire, but for a larger British cause. French intervention, they reasoned, had fundamentally changed the nature of the American war. The question had ceased to be one of whether America could be coerced back into the empire, and had become one of whether she would become an accession of strength to an ancient enemy, an event which might well mean Britain's ruin.

Hitherto, reasons of humanity had forbidden a system based on a "mass of private calamities." But what might formerly have been inhuman and impolitic had now become absolutely necessary. Should America insist upon allying herself with Britain's strongest foe, it would be incumbent upon the erstwhile mother country to render her "as wretch'd and as miserable as we can." Now that America had refused Britain's most generous offer, she should be so reduced and exhausted that it would be long before France could benefit from her alliance.[77] It is to the credit of Clinton that he refused to lead such a war, and of the ministry that they refused to adopt it.

On October 3, the commissioners signed their last proclamation to the American people. In this final appeal, they announced that they would shortly leave America. They had held out the most honorable terms, but their offers had been rejected. It was, therefore, only fair to warn the Americans of the dreadful calamities that their obstinacy would bring upon them. Seeking to create a division between the people and Congress, they denied the right of Congress to reject their offers without referring them to the assemblies. It was equally "deceitful" for Congress to allude to "pretended foreign treaties" which had never been ratified by the people through their assemblies. The continuation of the war the commissioners laid solely at the door of the Congress.

They then made the assemblies the same offers which Congress had refused. All groups were invited to return to their duty. American soldiers were asked to give up the struggle

[77] *Ibid.*, No. 529; Add. MSS 34416, ff. 33–34, Carlisle's minute.

since no grievance remained, and to join in against the common and hereditary enemy, France. To the clergy went a warning against the danger of associating with papists. To those who persisted in demanding independence, however, it was solemnly declared that the "laws of self-preservation" would oblige Great Britain to use every means to make America's accession to France of as little value as possible. The proclamation was to continue in effect for forty days.

After this impotent gesture, the two disheartened commissioners turned their thoughts toward home. Their final acts in North America were to suspend the Prohibitory Act for the port of New York and to open it for limited shipping. Finally, they set up a procedure—which would be used only once, in the case of Georgia—whereby reconquered provinces could pass quickly from military occupation to civil government. On November 27, therefore, Carlisle and Eden embarked for England leaving behind them "an unsuccessful, embarrassing, and distressing Task."[78]

The Carlisle Commission had failed, and the first British Empire was dead. The dispatch of the commission represented the end of an historical process, which had begun with the first impact of the American problem on British politics. It had begun with the Peace of 1763 and with George Grenville whose concept of an empire in the classic sense, as "supreme center and subordinate parts," had first brought this problem into view. From this position the home government was soon forced to retreat. The Old Whigs under Rockingham had sought, by an appeasement of British merchant interests, which coincided for the moment with the colonial demand for a repeal of the Stamp Act, to bring quiet to the empire. They had succeeded but temporarily. Even so, their success was not really a reversal of Grenville's idea. Indeed, with their Declaratory Act, they gave his view of empire official sanction in the most

[78] Stevens, *Facsimiles*, No. 1213, Carlisle and Eden to Germain, November 15, 1778.

positive manner. With the disastrous Chatham Ministry following the Old Whigs, it seemed for a moment that the stream of imperial development would be diverted into more modern channels. Chatham and Shelburne denied the right of the British legislature to tax the Colonies for revenue. Had this view been implemented, the Colonies might well have been satisfied with this small abridgement of parliamentary supremacy. Unfortunately, the physical and mental collapse of Chatham allowed Townshend to bring forward a scheme even more offensive to the Americans than that of Grenville. That Townshend made his taxes of the "external" description carried no weight with the colonists. They were still taxes for a revenue wherewith a colonial civil list would be established. Having denied the validity of such taxes, they soon found themselves forced to extend that denial to trade regulations, and at last to parliamentary supremacy altogether.

North's Conciliatory Proposition, a step down from the high horse of unlimited parliamentary supremacy although it was thoroughly inadequate to the circumstances then existing in the Colonies, had set the government on the road to the Carlisle Peace Commission. Had a settlement been reached on the basis of the instructions to this body, a federal empire, albeit in crude and embryonic form, would have been created. Secure in their charters and holding a sole right of internal legislation, the Colonies would have enjoyed "home rule": they would have been, in effect, sovereign states within a sovereign union.

The offer, however, had come too late. The Americans, now committed to independence, had gained a powerful ally in France. A resurgence of hope, touched by desperation, drove the North Ministry onto the final scene of their tragedy. Clinton was reinforced. His armies conquered Savannah and Charleston; and for a time, Cornwallis threatened to roll up the American southern flank—for by then all hope or desire to retake New England had vanished.[79] In the end, however,

French intervention proved decisive. French troops and a superior French navy turned the scale and brought the final capitulation at Yorktown.

Why had the British government waited so long—too long indeed—to make the offers finally held out in the Carlisle Peace Commission? The answer must involve the King who had fought so desperately to regain a position lost by his two Hanoverian predecessors. His task had been simple because the Old Whigs had built up an elaborate machinery of patronage and political control. He had, then, only to displace them and to assume their old position. One fundamental reason for his easy victory lies in the splintered condition of the Whig party at the time of his accession. Another, however, was that American unrest created, strengthened, and made vocal a new conservatism—the origin of a new Tory party—centered around the King. A state of affairs in direct contradiction to the only permanent solution of the tangled problem of Anglo-American relations—the federal principle—was thus created. In the Carlisle Commission was a valiant effort, stimulated by defeat and by the fear of French intervention, to achieve a kind of federal settlement, but no real basis for its realization existed in the eighteenth century. It could only be achieved when the King should relinquish his central and active position in politics and assume a place impartial and above domestic affairs, a symbol of union in whom all members of the British Empire might find a common head. Only when the King had

[79] Add. MSS 38383, ff. 2–3, a paper by Charles Jenkinson, who was questioning the wisdom of continuing the war due to Britain's unhealthy economy. Jenkinson held that Britain should make a frontier of the Hudson River, abandoning New England completely. He justified his contention on thoroughly mercantilist grounds, since New England had always been a source of competition for the mother country. At any rate, Britain would have little difficulty in keeping an economic upper hand over New England, who would always buy British goods as long as they were cheap. Jenkinson's ideas had developed along an amazing path since the conversations with North in 1777. He had decided that tobacco, linens, and silks were the only articles worth monopolizing: "I bow with reverence to the Act of Navigation, but I pay very little respect to the Acts of Trade."

ceased to be a party manager was the road toward a commonwealth of nations discernible. Such a retreat would be forced upon George III by a cruel necessity, loss of his sanity. The full development of the modern British party system, begun in his reign, would prevent his successors from achieving the commanding position in politics which he had gained.

The federal principle would not be accepted by British empire builders for well on half a century, and its need would have to be underlined by another colonial revolt, this time in Canada. The day would come, however, when Great Britain, possessed of her modern party system, freed by the Industrial Revolution from the fear of an empire of competitors, and remembering her agony in the American Revolution, would turn to that idea. She would accept it as the only means whereby she, as a free nation, could build and keep an empire. When that day came she would find in her monarch no party manager but a beloved symbol of her imperial unity. It was the American experience which had first pointed the way to that solution.

NOTES ON SOURCES

CHAPTER I: *The American Problem and the Grenville Ministry*. Of primary importance are the Liverpool Papers, British Museum Additional Manuscripts (hereafter referred to as "Add. MSS") 38197–38470. The papers of Charles Jenkinson, later first Earl of Liverpool, constitute a rich collection little utilized by American or British historians. Successively political agent, associate of Lord Bute, secretary to the Treasury for Grenville, and member of the Treasury and Admiralty Boards, Jenkinson, the archetypal King's Friend, was in an excellent position to know the internal workings of the government. Of special value is the mass of "routine" material demonstrating the formation of the Grenville Ministry's plan to derive a revenue from America. Miss Nanette Jucker's excellent volume *The Jenkinson Papers* (London, 1949), while limited in scope, is a convenient introduction to the collection.

The Hardwicke Papers, Add. MSS 35360–35429, 35910–11, 36226, contain extremely valuable material relating to the drafting of the Stamp Act. As attorney general, Charles Yorke was constantly consulted on legal questions relating to the act.

The Hinchingbrooke (Sandwich) Papers are of minor importance, but serve to throw light on a veteran politician striving for office.

Grenville's papers in the Stowe Collection, now deposited in the Huntington Library, are generally disappointing.

Of the published sources, the most important is, of course, the *Grenville Papers* (ed. by W. J. Smith, 4 vols., London, 1852–53).

Manuscript sources were followed throughout this book whenever discrepancies between manuscripts and the published version of documents were found.

CHAPTER II: *The Year of the Old Whigs.* The papers of the Marquis of Rockingham and Edmund Burke, comprising the Wentworth-Woodhouse collection at the Public Library, Sheffield, have only recently been made available to the scholarly world. They are indispensable for a study of the two Old Whig ministries, and throw much light on the policy and tactics of the Opposition during the American war. Both the *Rockingham Memoirs* (ed. by Earl of Albemarle, 2 vols., London, 1852) and *Burke's Correspondence* (ed. by C. William, Earl Fitzwilliam, and Sir Richard Bourke, 4 vols., London, 1844) contain many inaccuracies, deletions and suppressions, and must be used with caution. The attempts of the editors to place their heroes in as favorable a light as possible are obvious.

Similarly, the *Chatham Correspondence* (ed. by W. S. Taylor and J. H. Pringle, 4 vols., London, 1838–40), while less open to such criticism, must be checked against the Chatham Papers, Public Record Office 30/8. Several unpublished letters to Pitt demonstrate the development of the American controversy. See, for instance, Chatham Papers, 97, for a letter from John Dickinson to Pitt; bundle 55 contains Pitt's correspondence with Stephen Sayre.

The Hardwicke Papers portray the stresses and strains, both internal and external, under which the Rockingham Ministry labored. The Liverpool Papers and the Hinchingbrooke Papers provide sources for a study of Opposition activities during the Old Whig Ministry. The published sources are voluminous. In addition to those mentioned above, *The Correspondence of George III* (ed. by Sir John Fortescue, 6 vols., Lon-

lon, 1927–28) is of great use, but it must be corrected by L. B. Namier, *Additions and Corrections* (Manchester, 1937).

CHAPTER III: *Chatham, Faction, and America.* The hundred volumes of Chatham Papers in the Public Record Office furnish the major source. The collection has yielded several "nuggets." Shelburne's plan for the disobedient assembly of New York, which he included in a letter to Chatham, has been suppressed both in the *Chatham Correspondence* and in Fitzmaurice's *Life of Shelburne* (2 vols., London, 1912). Of considerable interest, too, is Chatham's sketch for a new ministry which he composed during the formation of his government. The outline lists Chatham as holding a new office, the secretaryship of state for America. Although the scheme was dropped, the document underscores Chatham's determination to solve the American problem.

The Liverpool Papers are valuable in portraying the emergence of the King's Friends as a well-defined "party" grouping. (See particularly Add. MSS 38339, ff. 307–10; printed by Jucker.) Here, too, is graphic evidence of Chatham's failure to extirpate faction.

Accounts of his stormy relations with the Old Whigs are to be found in the Hardwicke Papers (particularly in Add. MSS 35430), and in the Wentworth-Woodhouse collection. Published sources, the *Grenville Papers* and the *Bedford Correspondence* (ed. by Lord John Russell, 3 vols., London, 1842–46) give good accounts of the remainder of the Opposition. The latter contains portions of Bedford's private journal which is of great use in tracing the growth of the Grenville-Bedford alienation. The Hinchingbrooke Papers indicate Bedfordite eagerness to win office under the Chatham Ministry even at the expense of the Grenville alliance.

CHAPTER IV. *The Fall of the Chatham System.* Evidence of Old Whig leadership of the successful move to reduce the land tax is to be found in the Wentworth-Woodhouse Papers. The vast number of Treasury Board minutes and the reports from the American Commissioners of the Customs in the Liverpool Papers show the growth of American resistance to the Townshend taxes, and the Grafton Ministry's confusion.

The correspondence of John Wilkes with committees of the American Sons of Liberty is to be found in the Wilkes Papers, Add. MSS 30865–30887. Evidence of the hardening conservative reaction to American resistance is seen not only in the Liverpool Papers but also in the Wentworth-Woodhouse Papers and the Hardwicke Papers. A growing acceptance of Grenville's idea that requisitions were unconstitutional means of raising revenue is to be seen in this latter collection.

The petitioning movement for the dissolution of a Parliament corrupted by the expulsion of Wilkes—and the failure of that movement to touch the American problem—is to be traced in the Wentworth-Woodhouse Papers, the *Grenville Papers*, and the *Burke Correspondence*.

CHAPTER V: *Prelude to Civil War*. The development of the American crisis and Dartmouth's futile attempts to solve it are best seen in the Liverpool Papers and in the *Royal Historical Manuscripts Commission Reports, Dartmouth Papers* (3 vols., London, 1887, 1895, 1896). North's unhappy position in his cabinet emerges from the Auckland Papers, Add. MSS 34412–34417, and Fortescue's *Correspondence of George III*. His plan to decrease the navy as a means of paring expenses, his refusal to allow an increase in British naval strength, and Sandwich's violent opposition to North's false sense of economy are to be found in the Hinchingbrooke Papers.

The Wilkes Papers portray the internal quarrels of the London Radicals; while Opposition affairs, the increasing gulf between Opposition and public, and the growing conservative reaction to American radicalism are best studied in the Hardwicke Papers, the Chatham Papers, and the Wentworth-Woodhouse Papers.

Burke's Letterbook in the Wentworth-Woodhouse collection includes his inflammatory letters to the New York Assembly and to politicians of that province.

CHAPTER VI: *Civil War*. The government's reaction to the outbreak of hostilities and the formation of its plans for crushing the rebellion are to be found in the Auckland Papers, the Liverpool Papers, the *Sandwich Papers*, and the Hardwicke Papers. Facsimiles of many important documents in the Auckland Papers are to be found in B. F. Stevens, *Facsimiles* (25 vols., London, 1889–98). Dartmouth's desperate attempts to arrive at a peaceable settlement of the dispute are seen in the *Dartmouth Papers*. The sources for the Howe Peace Commission—its formation and the bitter cabinet controversy concerning it—are the Auckland Papers, the *Dartmouth Papers*, the Royal Historical Manuscripts Commission Reports on the *Stopford-Sackville Papers* (2 vols., London, 1904, and Hereford, 1910), and the *Knox Papers, Various Collections*, VI (Dublin, 1909).

Sandwich's insistence on a naval build-up to counter French preparations, and North's and the King's refusal to allow such measures are seen in the Hinchingbrooke Papers and in Fortescue's *Correspondence of George III*, with some correspondence relating to this subject printed in the Navy Record Society publication, the *Sandwich Papers* (4 vols., London, 1932). Evidence of North's growing melancholy and the King's increasing dependence upon John Robinson to keep North in good spirits are to be found in the correspondence of John Robinson with George III, Add. MSS 37833–37835. The story of the collapse of Opposition's efforts to counter the ministerial American policy and of their hopes for the defeat of British arms is told in the Wentworth-Woodhouse Papers.

CHAPTER VII: *Agony and Revelation*. The most important source for reaction to Burgoyne's surrender and the formation of the Carlisle Peace Commission is the Auckland Papers. It is a measure of Eden's great influence with North that this source is also of primary importance in following the spate of "unofficial" British negotiations with the American commissioners in Paris. Sidelights on these interesting but futile attempts to stop the war are found in the *Stopford-Sackville Papers* and in *Franklin's Works* (ed. by J. Sparks, 10 vols., Chicago, 1882). North's pathetic struggle to be allowed to resign emerges from Fortescue's *Correspondence of George III*.

The gradual acceptance of the idea of at least a partial loss of the American Colonies is to be found in the Liverpool Papers. The two great sources for the functioning of the Carlisle Peace Commission are the Auckland Papers and the *Royal Historical Manuscripts Commission Reports, The Carlisle Papers* (London, 1897).

The account of the split between the Chathamites and the Old Whigs on the point of American independence is based on the Chatham Papers (especially bundles 54 and 56), the *Chatham Correspondence*, and the Wentworth-Woodhouse Papers.

BIBLIOGRAPHY

MANUSCRIPT SOURCES

Auckland Papers. British Museum Additional Manuscripts 29475, 34412–34417. Papers and correspondence of William Eden, first Lord Auckland, undersecretary of state and peace commissioner to America. They are especially valuable for the formation and functioning of the Howe and Carlisle Peace Commissions.

Chatham Papers. Public Record Office, 30/8. Bundles 1–100. The first four volumes are arranged more or less in accordance with the printed edition of the *Chatham Correspondence (q. v.)*. In footnote references, the Arabic numeral refers to the bundle number in this collection.

Hardwicke Papers. British Museum Additional Manuscripts 35360–35430, 35511, 35910–11, 36226. The papers of Charles Yorke, attorney general, have yielded hitherto unsuspected information concerning the Stamp Act. The correspondence of the second Earl with his brother John and with Thomas Hutchinson portrays the growing conservative reaction to American radicalism.

Hinchingbrooke (Sandwich) Papers. The papers and correspondence of John, fourth Earl of Sandwich, preserved at his country seat, Hinchingbrooke, Huntingdonshire.

Liverpool Papers. British Museum Additional Manuscripts 38191, 38197–38470, 38577. The papers and correspondence of the Earls of Liverpool. The author has used only those belonging to Charles Jenkinson, later first Earl of Liverpool.

Newcastle Papers. British Museum Additional Manuscripts 32709, 32731, 32862, 32973, for an identification of Henry Mc-Culloh and his connection with the Stamp Act.

Robinson, John; his correspondence with George III. British Museum Additional Manuscripts 37833–37835.

Stowe Collection, Huntington Library, San Marino, California.

Wentworth-Woodhouse Papers. Public Library, Sheffield. The papers and correspondence of the Marquis of Rockingham and of Edmund Burke. The collection throws much light on the Old Whigs and their American views. Unfortunately, the papers are in great confusion and have not been adequately catalogued. It has been, therefore, impossible to make references to volumes and folio numbers. Many of the letters published in the *Rockingham Memoirs (q. v.)* are to be found in these papers.

Wilkes Papers. British Museum Additional Manuscripts 30865–30887. The papers and correspondence of John Wilkes. Valuable for ascertaining the connection between British and American radicalism.

FACSIMILIES

Stevens, B. F. *Facsimilies of MSS. in European Archives Relating to America, 1773–1783.* London. 1889–98. 25 vols. Stevens has drawn largely upon the Auckland Papers and the RHMCR. *Carlisle Papers (q. v.).* A limited edition of 200 copies of this monumental work was published and the photographic plates destroyed.

PERIODICALS

American Historical Review:

Andrews, C. M. "The American Revolution: An Interpretation." Vol. XXXI, No. 2 (January, 1926), 219–32.

———. "Anglo-French Commercial Rivalry." Vol. XX, No. 4 (July, 1915), 761–80.

———. "Colonial Commerce." Vol. XX, No. 1 (October, 1914), 43–63.

Basye, A. H. "The Secretary for the Colonies, 1768–1782." Vol. XXVIII, No. 1 (October, 1922), 13–23.

Becker, C. B. "Election of Delegates from New York to the Second Continental Congress." Vol. IX, No. 1 (October, 1903), 66–85.

———. "Growth of Revolutionary Parties and Methods in New York Province, 1765–1774." Vol. VII, No. 1 (October, 1901), 56–76.

———. "Horace Walpole's Memoirs of the Reign of George III." Parts I and II. Vol. XVI, No. 2 (January, 1911), 255–72.

Carter, C. E. "Observations of Superintendent John Stuart and Governor James Grant of East Florida on the Proposed Plan of 1764 for the Future Management of Indian Affairs." Vol. XX, No. 4 (July, 1915), 815–31.

———. "The Significance of the Military Office in America, 1763–1775." Vol. XXVIII, No. 3 (April, 1923), 475–88.

Clark, J. "Responsibility for the Failure of the Burgoyne Campaign." Vol. XXXV, No. 3 (April, 1930), 542–59.

Clarke, M. D. "The Board of Trade at Work." Vol. XVII, No. 1 (October, 1911), 17–43.

Corwin, E. S. "The French Objective in the American Revolution." Vol. XXI, No. 1 (October, 1915), 33–61.

———. "The Progress of Constitutional Theory Between the Declaration of Independence and the Meeting of the Philadelphia Convention." Vol. XXX, No. 3 (April, 1925), 511–36.

Davidson, P. G. "Whig Propagandists of the American Revolution." Vol. XXXIX, No. 3 (April, 1934), 442–53.

Doysié, A. "Journal of a French Traveler in the Colonies, 1765." Part I. Vol. XXVI, No. 4 (July, 1921), 726–47. The anonymous traveler heard Patrick Henry's famous speech and recorded the reaction of the people in Virginia to the Stamp Act: "Some of them mutter betwixt their teeth, let the worst Come to the worst we'l Call the french to Our succour." (p. 747.) Part II. Vol. XXVII, No. 1 (October, 1921), 70–89.

Farrand, M. "The Taxation on Tea, 1767–1773." Vol. III (1898), 266.

Gipson, L. H. "Connecticut Taxation and Parliamentary Aid Preceding the Revolutionary War." Vol. XXXVI, No. 4 (July, 1931), 721–39.

Guttridge, G. H. "Adam Smith on the American Revolution: An Unpublished Memorial." Vol. XXXVIII, No. 4 (July, 1933), 714–20.

————. "Lord George Germain in Office." Vol. XXXIII, No. 1 (October, 1927), 23–43.

Laprade, W. T. "The Stamp Act in British Politics." Vol. XXXV, No. 4 (July, 1930), 735–57.

Ogden, H. V. S. "The State of Nature and the Decline of Lockian Political Theory in England, 1760–1800." Vol. XLVI, No. 1 (October, 1940), 21–44.

Ritcheson, C. R. "The Elder Pitt and an American Department." Vol. LVII, No. 2 (January, 1952), 376–83.

Van Tyne, C. H. "Influence of the Clergy, and of Religious and Sectarian Forces, on the American Revolution." Vol. XIX, No. 1 (October, 1913), 44–64.

————. "Influences which Determined the French Government to make the Treaty with America, 1778." Vol. XXI, No. 3 (October, 1916), 528–41.

English Historical Review:

Carter, C. E. "The British Policy Toward the American Indians in the South." Vol. XXXIII, No. 129 (January, 1918), 37–56.

Davis, A. Mc. "The Employment of Indian Auxiliaries in the American War." Vol. II (1887), 709–28.

Egerton, H. E. "Lord George Germain and Sir William Howe." Vol. XXV (1910), 315–16.

Garth, Charles. Vol. LIV (1939), 646–49.

Hughes, E. "The English Stamp Duties, 1664–1764." Vol. LVI, No. CCXXII (April, 1941), 234–64.

Humphreys, R. A. "Lord Shelburne and British Colonial Policy, 1766–1768." Vol. L, No. CXCVIII (April, 1935), 257–77.

————. "Lord Shelburne and the Proclamation of 1763." Vol. XLIX, No. CXCIV (April, 1934), 241–64.

Imlach, G. M. "Earl Temple and the Ministry of 1765." Vol. XXX (1915), 317–21.

Namier, L. B. "Charles Garth and His Connexions." Part I. Vol. LIV, No. CCXV (July, 1939), 443–70; Part II. Vol. LIV, No. CCXVI (October, 1939) 632–52.

Sutherland, L. Stuart. "Edmund Burke and the First Rockingham Ministry." Vol. XLVII, No. CLXXXV (January, 1932), 46–72.

————. "Lord Shelburne and East India Company Politics, 1766–1769." Vol. XLIX, No. CXCV (July, 1934), 450–86.

Williams, B. "Chatham and the Representation of the Colonies in the Imperial Parliament." Vol. XXII (1907), 756–58.

Winstanley, D. A. "George III and his First Cabinet." Vol. XVII (1902), 678–91.

Parliamentary Affairs, the Journal of the Hansard Society:

Ritcheson, C. R. "The American Revolution: Its Influence on the Development of the British Empire." Vol. IV, No. 2 (Spring, 1951), 245–60.

William and Mary Quarterly:

Morgan, E. S. "The Postponement of the Stamp Act." Third Series, Vol. VII (1950), 353–92.

Ritcheson, C. R. "The Preparation of the Stamp Act." Third Series, Vol. X (1953), 543–59.

Sellers, Charles G., Jr. "Private Profits and British Colonial Policy: The Speculations of Henry McCulloh." Third Series, Vol. VIII (1951), 535–51.

PRINTED SOURCES AND CONTEMPORARY WORKS

Acts of the Privy Council (Colonial), George III, 1613–1783. Ed. by W. L. Grant and J. Munro. London, 1908–12. 6 vols.

Adams, John. *Works.* Boston, 1856. 10 vols.

Annual Register. London, 1760, etc.

Auckland Journal and Correspondence. By Eden's son, the Bishop of Bath and Wells. Ed. by G. Hogge. London, 1861–62. 4 vols. These volumes deal chiefly with a period later than that here treated, but are a convenient introduction to the study of the Auckland Papers.

Bedford Correspondence. Ed. by Lord John Russell. London, 1842–46. 3 vols.

Beloff, M. *The Debate on the American Revolution.* London, 1949. A collection of pamphlets, speeches, etc., in extract and with notes.

Bolingbroke's Miscellaneous Works. Edinburgh, 1768. 4 vols.

Burke's Correspondence. Ed. by C. William, Earl Fitzwilliam, and Sir Richard Bourke. London, 1844. 4 vols. Examination of the Wentworth-Woodhouse Papers has revealed many errors and unmarked deletions.

Burke's Works. London, 1826. 16 vols.

Calendar of New York Historical Manuscripts, (English). Ed. by E. B. O'Callaghan. Part II, 1664–1776. Albany (New York), 1866.

Cavendish, Henry. *Debates of the House of Commons, 1768–1771.* London, 1841–43. 2 vols.

———. *Debate on the Second Reading of the Quebec Act.* London, 1839.

Channing, E. and A. C. Coolidge (eds.). *Barrington-Bernard Correspondence, 1760–1770.* Cambridge (Mass.) and London, 1912.

Chatham Correspondence. Ed. by W. S. Taylor and J. H. Pringle. London, 1838–40. 4 vols. Examination of the Chatham Papers in the Public Record Office has revealed many errors and important and unmarked deletions, especially in the letters from Shelburne to Chatham at the time of the crisis occasioned by the disobedience of the assembly of New York.

Colonial History of New York, Documents. Albany (New York), 1856. 8 vols.

Documentary History of New York. Vol. III. Albany (New York), 1850. 4 vols.

Fitzmaurice, Lord. *Life of William Earl of Shelburne.* London, 1912. 2 vols.

Force, P. *American Archives, Fourth Series.* Ed. by M. St. C. Clarke. Washington, 1837–51. 6 vols.

Fortescue, Sir John. *Correspondence of George III.* London, 1927–28. 6 vols.

Franklin's Works. Ed. by J. Sparks. Chicago, 1882. 10 vols.

Grafton, Third Duke of. *Autobiography and Political Correspondence.* Ed. by Sir William Anson. London, 1898.

Grenville Papers. Ed. by W. J. Smith. London, 1852–53. 4 vols.

Guttridge, G. H. (ed.). *The American Correspondence of a Bristol Merchant, 1766–1776.* Berkeley, 1934.

Hutchinson, Thomas. *Diary and Letters.* Ed. by P. O. Hutchinson. London, 1883–86. 2 vols.

Jesse, J. H. *George Selwyn and His Contemporaries.* London, 1843–44. 4 vols.

——. *Memoirs of the Reign of George III.* London, 1867. 3 vols.

Jucker, N. S. *The Jenkinson Papers, 1760–1766.* London, 1949. Based on a study of the Liverpool Papers in the British Museum.

Knox, William. *Extra Official State Papers.* London, 1789.

Locke, J. *Of Civil Government and Toleration.* Ed. by Henry Morley. London, 1884.

Mahon, Viscount. *History of England from the Peace of Utrecht to the Peace of Versailles.* London, 1836–54. 7 vols.

Morison, S. E. *Sources and Documents Illustrating the American Revolution, 1764–1788.* Oxford, 1923. A convenient collection of contemporary documents, pamphlets, etc., printed in extract and with notes and an excellent introductory essay.

Parliamentary History. Ed. by Wm. Cobbett and J. Wright. Vols. XV–XXI. London, 1813–14. 36 vols.

Pickering, D. *Statutes at Large from the Magna Charta to . . . 1806.* Vols. XXV–XXXIII. Cambridge, 1763–1807. 46 vols.

Pownall, T. *The Administration of the Colonies.* Part I. London, 1764. 2nd ed. 1765. Part II. London, 1774.

Rockingham Memoirs. Ed. by the Earl of Albemarle. London, 1852. 2 vols.

Royal Historical Manuscripts Commission Reports:

Abergavenny Papers. Report X. Appendix, Part VI. London, 1885. The political correspondence of John Robinson.

American MSS. in the Royal Institution of Great Britain. Vol. I. London, 1904. Vol. II. Dublin, 1906. Military affairs.

Bathurst Papers. London, 1923. A few letters to and from North's Lord Chancellor, pp. 11–19.

Carlisle Papers. Report XV. Appendix, Part VI. London, 1897. Indispensable for a study of the Peace Commission of 1778.

Dartmouth Papers. Vol. I. Report XI. Appendix, Part V. London, 1887. The letters from Hutchinson and Joseph Reed are especially interesting.

———. Vol. II. Report XIV. Appendix, Part X. London, 1895. American papers. Indispensable.

———. Vol. III. Report XV. Appendix, Part I. London, 1896.

Denbigh Papers. Part V. London, 1911. Some letters of general interest during the early years of the reign of George III.

Gray (Charles) Papers. The Round MSS. Report XIV. Appendix, Part IX, London, 1895.

Knox Papers. Various Collections, VI. Dublin, 1909.

Lindley Wood Papers. Various Collections, VIII. Hereford, 1913.

Lothian Papers. London, 1905. Includes the papers of George Grenville's friend, the second Earl of Buckinghamshire.

Savile-Foljambe Papers. Report XV. Appendix, Part V. London, 1897. Letters of Sir George Savile are calendared, pp. 141–60.

Stopford-Sackville Papers. Vol. I. London, 1904. The papers of Lord George Germain.

———. Vol. II. Hereford, 1910.

Townshend Papers. Report XI. Appendix, Part IV. London, 1887. Includes many of Charles Townshend's letters.

Weston Papers. MSS of C. F. Weston Underwood. Calendared in the report on the MSS of the Earl of Eglinton and others. London, 1885. The *Weston Papers* are those of Edward Weston, long-time undersecretary of state under George II and George III.

Sandwich Papers. Publication of the Navy Record Society. Vol. LXIX. London, 1932. 4 vols. Based on the Hinchingbrooke Papers, but chiefly confined to Admiralty affairs and naval operations.

Sedgwick, Romney. *Letters from George III to Lord Bute, 1756–1766*. London, 1939. With a brilliant introductory essay.

Smith, Adam. *Wealth of Nations*. Ed. by E. Cannan. London, 1904. 2 vols.

Tucker, J. *The Humble Address and Earnest Appeal to those ... fittest to decide whether a connection with, or a separation from the Colonies of America be most for the National Advantage*. London, 1775.

Van Doren, C. *Benjamin Franklin's Autobiographical Writings*. London, 1946.

Walpole, H. *Memoirs of the Reign of George III*. London, 1845. 4 vols.

———. *Correspondence wih George Montagu*. Ed. by W. S. Lewis and R. S. Brown. The Yale Edition of *Walpole's Correspondence*. Vol. X. New Haven, 1941. 16 vols.

Woodfall, H. S. *Junius*. London, 1772. 2 vols.

Wraxall, Sir N. W. *Memoirs*. London, 1884. 5 vols.

Yorke, P. C. *Life and Correspondence of Philip Yorke, Earl of Hardwicke*. Cambridge, 1913. 3 vols.

LATER WORKS

Albion, R. G. *Forests and Sea Power*. Cambridge (Mass.), 1926.

Alvord, C. W. *The Mississippi Valley in British Politics*. Cleveland, 1917. 2 vols. A definitive study of the colonial west.

Andrews, C. M. *The Colonial Background of the American Revolution*. New Haven, 1924.

Barrington, Shute. *Political Life of W. W. Viscount Barrington*. London, 1814.

Bayne-Powell, R. *Eighteenth Century London Life*. London, 1937.

Beer, G. L. *British Colonial Policy, 1754–1765*. New York, 1907. Reprinted, 1933.

————. *The Old Colonial System*. New York, 1933. 2 vols.

Bemis, S. F. *Diplomatic History of the United States*. 3rd ed. New York, 1950.

Butterfield, H. *George III, Lord North, and the People, 1779–1780*. London, 1949.

Cambridge History of the British Empire. Ed. by J. H. Rose, A. P. Newton, and E. A. Benians. Vol. I. *The Old Empire*. Cambridge, 1929. 8 vols.

Channing, E. *History of the United States*. Vol. III. New York, 1927. 6 vols.

Clark, D. M. *British Opinion and the American Revolution*. New Haven, 1930.

Coupland, R. *The Quebec Act*. Oxford, 1925.

————. *The American Revolution and the British Empire*. London, 1930.

Dictionary of National Biography. Ed. by Leslie Stephen and Sidney Lee. London, 1885–1901.

Egerton, H. E. *A Short History of British Colonial Policy, 1606–1909*. 12th ed. Revised by A. P. Newton. London, 1950.

Eyck, Erick. *Die Pitts und Die Fox*. Erlenbach-Zurich, 1946.

Feiling, K. G. *A History of the Tory Party, 1640–1715*. Oxford, 1924.

————. *A History of England*. London, 1950.

————. *The Second Tory Party, 1714–1832*. London, 1938.

Fitzgerald, P. *The Life and Times of John Wilkes*. London, 1888. 2 vols.

Greene, E. B. *The Provincial Governor*. Cambridge (Mass.), 1898.

Guttridge, G. H. *David Hartley, M. P., An Advocate of Conciliation, 1774–1783*. Berkeley, 1926.

Hotblack, K. *Chatham's Colonial Policy*. London, 1917.

Jones, T. *History of New York during the Revolutionary War*. Ed. by E. F. de Lancey. New York, 1879. 2 vols.

Keith, A. B. *Constitutional History of the First British Empire*. Oxford, 1930.

Labaree, L. W. *Royal Government in America.* New Haven, (Conn.), 1930.

———. *Royal Instructions to British Colonial Governors.* New York and London, 1935. 2 vols.

Macaulay, T. B. *Critical and Historical Essays.* Vol. II. 2nd ed. London, 1843. 3 vols.

McIlwain, C. A. *The American Revolution.* New York, 1923.

Magnus, Sir P. *Edmund Burke.* London, 1939.

Mantoux, P. *The Industrial Revolution in the Eighteenth Century.* 2nd ed. Revised and translated by M. Vernon. London, 1948.

Morgan, E. S. and H. M. *The Stamp Act Crisis.* Williamsburg, 1953. See the author's review in *William and Mary Quarterly,* Vol. X, Third Series (October, 1953), 633–35.

Namier, L. B. *Additions and Corrections to Sir John Fortescue's Edition of the Correspondence of George III.* Manchester, 1937.

———. *England in the Age of the American Revolution.* London, 1930.

———. *The Structure of Politics at the Accession of George III.* London, 1929. 2 vols.

Newman, B. *Edmund Burke.* London, 1927.

Osgood, H. L. *The American Colonies in the Eighteenth Century.* New York, 1924. 4 vols.

Petrie, Sir Charles. *The Four Georges.* 2nd ed. London, 1946.

Roseberry, Lord. *Chatham, His Early Life and Connections.* London, 1910.

Ruville, A. von. *William Pitt, Earl of Chatham.* Translated by H. G. Chaytor and Mary Morison. London and New York, 1931. 3 vols.

Schuyler, R. L. *Josiah Tucker.* New York, 1931.

———. *Parliament and the British Empire.* New York, 1929.

Stephans, A. *Memoirs of John Horne Tooke.* London, 1813. 2 vols.

Trevelyan, Sir G. O. *The American Revolution.* Part I. 2nd ed. London, 1899. Part II. Vol. II. London, 1903. Part III. London, 1907. 3 vols.

———. *George III and Charles Fox.* London, 1912 and 1914. 2 vols.

Tunstall, B. *William Pitt, Earl of Chatham.* London, 1938.

Van Tyne, C. H. *The Causes of the War of Independence.* Boston and New York, 1922.

──────. *The Loyalists in the American Revolution.* New York, 1902.

Williams, B. *The Life of William Pitt, Earl of Chatham.* London, 1914. 2 vols.

──────. *The Whig Supremacy, 1714–1760.* Oxford, 1939. Reprinted with corrections, 1949.

Winstanley, D. A. *Lord Chatham and the Whig Opposition.* Cambridge, 1912.

──────. *Personal and Party Government.* Cambridge, 1910.

INDEX

3 3226 00303227 5